Neuroeconomics of Prosocial Behavior

Neuroeconomics of Prosocial Behavior

The Compassionate Egoist

Carolyn Declerck

Christophe Boone

ELSEVIER

AMSTERDAM • BOSTON • HEIDELBERG • LONDON
NEW YORK • OXFORD • PARIS • SAN DIEGO
SAN FRANCISCO • SINGAPORE • SYDNEY • TOKYO

Academic Press is an imprint of Elsevier

Academic Press is an imprint of Elsevier
125, London Wall, EC2Y 5AS.
525 B Street, Suite 1800, San Diego, CA 92101-4495, USA
225 Wyman Street, Waltham, MA 02451, USA
The Boulevard, Langford Lane, Kidlington, Oxford OX5 1GB, UK

Notices
Knowledge and best practice in this field are constantly changing. As new research and experience broaden our understanding, changes in research methods or professional practices, may become necessary.

Practitioners and researchers must always rely on their own experience and knowledge in evaluating and using any information or methods described herein. In using such information or methods they should be mindful of their own safety and the safety of others, including parties for whom they have a professional responsibility.

To the fullest extent of the law, neither the Publisher nor the authors, contributors, or editors, assume any liability for any injury and/or damage to persons or property as a matter of products liability, negligence or otherwise, or from any use or operation of any methods, products, instructions, or ideas contained in the material herein.

ISBN: 978-0-12-801303-8

Library of Congress Cataloging-in-Publication Data
A catalog record for this book is available from the Library of Congress

British Library Cataloguing-in-Publication Data
A catalogue record for this book is available from the British Library

For Information on all Academic Press publications
visit our website at http://store.elsevier.com/

CONTENTS

PREFACE

How do we explain the ubiquity of prosocial behavior among humans, when nature is "red in tooth and claw?" How come a person can be sometimes generous, helpful, and cooperative, yet other times self-absorbed, rude, or even abusive? This puzzle, of enduring interest in both the social and the biological sciences, has elicited much scientific collaboration along with heated discussion and conflicting opinions. The discord exists in part because prosocial behavior can be studied at different levels of analysis. On the one hand, ultimate causes of prosociality focus on the selection pressures that have shaped human behavior to respond adaptively in social interactions. On the other hand, proximate explanations try to interpret the human psychology and address the mix of motivations that drive individuals to make decisions according to *hic et nunc* conditions.

The new and growing field of neuroeconomics has much to offer with respect to solving the prosociality paradox by creating a bridge between these two levels of analysis: at the proximate level, the (un)cooperative choices people make are driven by neural activation corresponding with the leading motivation at that time. But ultimately, the pattern of neural activation underlying any behavior is generated by a brain and evolutionary conserved neuropeptide systems that have been continuously molded over many generations to match different environmental pressures. In addition, brain plasticity allows for socialization and learning, fine-tuning decision making in accordance with local conditions. The result is a brain that is wired to accommodate multiple sets of information at the same time, filtering out those behaviors that prove to yield—on average—the highest fitness gain.

This book summarizes the existing evidence for the hypothesis that, at the proximate level, prosocial decisions are driven by the anticipation of reward, which can be economically lucrative or emotionally pleasing. The value attached to cooperation is established in the brain's reward system, which receives input from a cognitive control system computing the benefits to the self, and a social cognition system ("the social brain"), which is sensitive to subtle social information regarding the cooperative intentions of others. Which of the two systems will prevail in the decision-making process will depend on the local conditions (the presence or absence of incentives and the perception of trustworthiness of others) and any preexisting tendencies (or preferences) to behave either prosocially or selfishly. Ultimately, evolution created neither a cooperative nor a selfish default, but a brain that steers decision making toward the most *valued* outcome. These values are subject to change, giving each one of us the potential to hover between compassion and egoism.

Our study adds a new angle to the century-old debate regarding human nature and the processes that govern human reasoning. The propositions in this book suggest that the concept of "rationality," when it comes to cooperative behavior, should not be interpreted without considering an individual's intrinsic values. Rational behavior is relative. In repeated social interactions, the benefits of cooperation, whether through synergy, accumulating profits, or through (in)direct reciprocity, can be established, making prosocial behavior economically rational. But in the absence of such benefits, prosocial behavior should not necessarily be considered an "irrational" by-product of behavior in repeat interactions. Humans do not willingly forsake their own well-being. They never intend to lose, and therefore avoid exploitation as much as possible by constantly and intuitively gauging the social environment for potential traitors. Within the boundaries of one's intimate group, the "warm glow of giving" and the "need to belong" can make cooperation socially rational. But individuals who are intrinsically motivated to act prosocially and consequently enjoy the emotional as well as collective benefits of mutual collaboration are also able to reverse this behavior when they sense it is no longer adaptive.

The neuroeconomic framework is what differentiates this book from other works on this topic. By combining the experimental paradigms from game theory with neuroimaging techniques, it has become possible to open the "black box" of human decision making. Through a joint effort of psychologists, neuroscientists, and behavioral economists, the latent drivers of choice behavior have been revealed experimentally, corroborating the interplay of both affective and cognitive processes that influence conscious deliberation as well as heuristic decision making. With this approach, we hope to fine-tune the "rational choice" behind cooperation and we put forth the proposition that prosocial decision making balances both economically and socially rational motives.

The book is divided into five parts. In Chapter 1, "Two Routes to Cooperation," we define various types of prosocial behaviors and point to their origins and universality. We summarize the generalizations that have emerged from field studies and laboratory experiments in behavioral economics and social psychology. We note that the extant literature comprises two, mostly independent, streams of research that have revealed two fundamentally different logics behind cooperation, one claiming that cooperation is economically rational, the other that it is socially rational. These two logics are the result of distinct motives that are present within each individual. Following the economically rational route to cooperation, people are motivated to pursue self-interest, but cooperate readily when self-interest coincides with collective interest. This research stresses the importance of extrinsic incentives, such as pay-offs, synergy, accumulating benefits, reciprocity, and reputation benefits. Following the socially rational route, people strive for group inclusion, and cooperation is an effective way to strengthen belonging, build social networks, and avoid ostracism. Social norm internalization and trust are especially important here.

In Chapter 2, "The Neuroanatomy of Prosocial Decision Making," we draw on research in neuroeconomics to substantiate that the brain is wired for both an economic and a social rationality. We summarize the results of a number of experiments showing that economically and socially rational choices are rooted in different neural networks that operate in concert and independently modulate decision making. Prosocial decisions can be explained as motivated choices that yield either economically or socially valuable rewards. These choices are contingent on the presence of extrinsic rewards that align self-interest with collective interest and/or trust signals that minimize the chance of exploitation. We identify three brain systems that are consistently recruited when people face ambiguous situations that call for cooperation. These are the neural networks dedicated to reward processing, cognitive control, and social cognition. We propose that these three brain systems are linked together in such a way that an (un)cooperative decision is the result of the modulatory influences of cognitive control and social cognition on the reward-processing system of the brain.

In Chapter 3, "The Neurochemistry of Prosocial Decision Making," we elaborate on the neural networks that are responsible for generating (un)cooperative decisions, and devote this chapter to the contribution of neurotransmitters. Recently, much attention has been given to the role of the neuropeptide oxytocin in regulating social interaction. Oxytocin is likely to facilitate socially rational prosocial decision making by reducing social anxiety, increasing empathy, and by linking it to the capacity to experience reward from social interaction. In addition, oxytocin is likely to promote behaviors that benefit the group. The monoamines dopamine and serotonin also have documented roles in decision making, especially with respect to reward processing. These neurotransmitters are also crucial in sustaining cognitive control. However, in the domain of *social* decision making, especially serotonin, more than dopamine, is likely to contribute to economic rationality.

In Chapter 4, "Individual Differences in Prosocial Decision Making," we address the extensive heterogeneity in social values that suggest that social and economic rationality do not have to be expressed equally in all individuals. Temperamental dispositions combined with experience-based differences in social learning may lead to stable differences in values that are tracked by idiosyncratic activation patterns of the brain's reward system. Values are a compass that help people navigate through the social world: they determine which environmental information people will more likely attend to, influencing the degree to which networks dedicated to cognitive control or social cognition will be recruited in the decision-making process. The end result is that each individual develops his or her own neural signature that facilitates or hampers cooperation.

To conclude, in Chapter 5, "Beyond Parochialism: Cooperation across the Globe," we address a darker side of prosocial behavior. Cooperation heuristics that are economically or socially rational within the boundaries of a particular social group tend to bias decision making in favor of same-group members. When the group is threatened, such parochial behavior may turn into more extreme forms, including ethnocentrism, racial discrimination, political feuds, and religious wars. Ironically, overcoming the negative side-effects of prosociality relies on the neural network of cognitive control that we earlier associated with economically rational decision making. To extend human cooperation to a more global level, prosocial values, cultivated by parents and social institutions to promote group-appropriate behaviors, are best balanced with a healthy dose of reasoning.

These five chapters, united under one title, would not have been accomplished without cooperation. We (Carolyn and Christophe) have been collaborating on projects for more than a decade, this book being one of them. There already is a vast, interdisciplinary literature on the topic of prosocial decision making, so it was our aim to integrate information and points of view coming from different angles and research programs. By focusing on the evidence from actual neuroscience experiments (rather than its potential), we hope to have demonstrated the usefulness for interdisciplinary work, also on a holistic topic such as cooperation.

Perhaps it was an ambitious project to rely on the new field of neuroeconomics to find a common thread in the study of prosocial behavior carried out in behavioral economics, social psychology, and evolutionary biology. Surely, neuroeconomics is a blooming and fast-growing field, and therefore an enticing eye-catcher. Simply typing "neuroeconomics" into the search engine of the Web of Science yields 0 hits in the year 2000, only 7 have accumulated by 2003, 46 by 2005, and by 2015 there are 63 *pages* of references! Much of its success has arguably to do with the progress in neuroimaging techniques and the development of fMRI in the 1990's. The first economist to use this technique to study social decision making in 2001 was Vernon Smith at the University of Arizona (his experiment is reported in Chapter 4). But as with any success story, fMRI studies are also experiencing growing pains. Its poor temporal resolution and complex inferential statistics make it difficult to interpret the data, leaving much room for speculation and "reverse inferencing." Despite these difficulties, the field is making great strides by encouraging replications and putting rigorous constraints on methodologies (including statistical analyses). Already meta-analyses on over 200 studies investigating similar phenomena are being conducted to find patterns in the data that have now been accumulating for nearly two decades.

This said, we want to acknowledge that much of the theorizing in this book is based on generalization and personal interpretation of the available evidence that is still relatively scarce and sometimes debatable. Our propositions are scientific, in the sense that they are based on logical inference of the current state of the art. We believe that generalizations, such as the ones offered by the models in Chapters 2 and 4, can be fruitful because they are a great way to stimulate hypothesis building, which can then be tested empirically. The results of theory-driven experimentation give us temporary insights into the workings of very complex phenomena which would not have been possible if these models had not been available. But only time will prove if our insights are correct. As scientists in many fields become increasingly interested in studying human nature from the *bottom up*, more data will accumulate, increasing the power of scientific falsification. It is our hope that, with additional research, the templates we provide in these next chapters can be refined or revised to eventually find consilience in a now fragmented field.

In one way or another, everyone is interested in understanding human nature. As an economist and an ecologist, we want to know why we decide the way we do and how this is influenced by life experiences, culture, and the subtleties of the environment that frame how we view things. Ironically, living with the consequences of our decisions often proves to be much more challenging than deciding in the first place. Hence we are eager to shed light on the gray box that makes our mind tick.

Of course, we have also benefitted from ideas and comments of many colleagues and experts in the fields. We are especially grateful to Lesley Newson and Fred Previc for the care and attention they devoted to reading an earlier version of the manuscript. Their insights were particularly constructive and have helped us to continuously improve our work. We thank our coworkers and graduate students – current and past- for sharing our interest in this topic: Sandy Bogaert, Griet Emonds, Toko Kiyonari, Bruno Lambert, Paul Parizel, Loren Pauwels, Ruth Seurinck, Sigrid Suetens, Anne Van Der Planken, Everhard Vandervliet, Wim Van Hecke, Anja Waegeman. They all contributed to make this work possible, and the long conversations we had with some of them were productive in shaping our thoughts. We also extend our thanks to publisher Nikki Levy and production manager Anusha Sambamoorthy at Elsevier for taking us through the production process.

Finally, we dedicate this book to Bert De Brabander for demonstrating the way to blur the artificial boundaries between scientific disciplines.

CHAPTER 1

Two Routes to Cooperation

Large-scale cooperation may well be the thumbprint of our species, but explaining why and how people work together is not at all straightforward. Unlike the eusocial insects, for whom successful cooperation typically depends on a sterile worker caste (Wilson, 1971), prosociality in primates seems to revolve around a number of moralistic traits such as attachment and bonding, sharing and caring, trust and loyalty, and feelings of sympathy and empathy. Yet despite these sentiments for prosocial behavior, a view inspired by David Hume, and later also by Darwin, human history has not painted a rosy picture: political wars and genocides, terrorist attacks, bigotry, the atomic bomb, arms races, and economic scandals are the testimony that torture, callousness, and deception are also a part of human nature. Certainly the gap between the poorest and the richest on earth attests to the fact that goodwill and concern for the welfare of others cannot be the sole or single most important motivating factor for societal well-being. Neither will an "invisible hand" guarantee global prosperity when resources are scarce and competition unrestrained (Frank, 2012). Considering the prevalence of greed and self-indulgence, it is surprising that our species has not succumbed to the Hobbesian "war of all against all."

One of the major reasons we do not live the Hobbesian war is that, as individuals, we value cooperation and we are aware of the benefits of teamwork and mutual support. We comprehend that we can accomplish more when we collaborate as a group, and that this also increases our individual success. However, group living is not an easy task for a cognitively gifted species: lacking assurance of the good intentions of others with whom we interact, we must constantly be vigilant that the fruits of cooperation are not lost to corruption. This idea of balancing the costs and benefits of cooperation could potentially be captured by economic models of expected utility-like functions whereby a cooperative decision would be a function of what cooperation is worth to a person multiplied by the probability that cooperation will not be betrayed (Pruitt & Kimmel, 1977). The precise value of cooperation is, however, harder to

Neuroeconomics of Prosocial Behavior. DOI: http://dx.doi.org/10.1016/B978-0-12-801303-8.00001-X

pinpoint. Its value would be rather low in comparison to selfishness if we adhere to the long tradition in economics that considers human nature to be the personification of *Homo economicus*, a "rational" self-interested agent driven to maximize personal gains. This term, much used in the late nineteenth century in response to the utilitarian views of John Stuart Mill (Persky, 1995), was, however, rebutted by introducing the *Homo reciprocans*, driven by principles of justice and cooperativeness, and the *Homo sociologicus* (Dahrendorf, 1973), who does not act to pursue self-interest but to fulfill social roles imposed by culture and society, with many of these roles being prosocial and serving the greater community.

Yet, the ubiquity of prosocial behaviors among humans continues to puzzle many scholars because, from both an economic and an evolutionary point of view, it remains difficult to reconcile self- and collective interest and resolve the mixed motives behind any prosocial act. How can we value the greater collective above self-interest if the latter appears to be more profitable and/or less risky than the former? The common denominator of behaviors such as parent care, trusting strangers, tipping a waiter, or heroic deeds such as entering a burning house to save someone else's child, is that they provide benefits to others at a cost to oneself. This question raises the puzzle to a new level: how can prosocial behavior increase fitness and evolve by natural selection? Typically the problem is stated as follows: even if providing benefits to others enhances the welfare of the *group*, how can such a trait spread if selfishness (the antipode) confers an advantage to each *individual*? How come a group of altruists is not invaded by egoists?

This "altruism paradox" has elicited decades of discourse among researchers in different fields, including evolutionary biology, psychology, moral philosophy, anthropology, and behavioral economics, without settling on a unifying theory. Their different approaches have clouded the field with two notable sources of confusion. First, prosociality can be elucidated at different levels of explanation: ultimate reasons focus on how prosocial behavior was shaped by natural selection, while proximate explanations try to identify how *hic et nunc* prosocial decisions are made. These two sorts of explanations are not mutually exclusive; on the contrary, they are both essential to fully understand a behavioral phenomenon (e.g., Barclay, 2012; Tinbergen, 1968). The former seeks to illustrate the "raison d'être" of a particular behavior (or why it was favored by selection), while the latter attempts to unfold the psychological mechanism that makes that behavior possible. Because people are not consciously trying to increase their fitness, ultimate and proximate reasons may be decoupled. Or, to paraphrase Dawkins (1976): the genes are selfish, but that does not mean the person is.

A second source of confusion is that prosociality is studied at different levels of biological organization, such as the gene, organism, or population, and the outcome of evolution at these different levels does not have to be the same. Any biological entity that has variation, reproduction, and heritability can evolve by natural selection, so that the evolutionary accrual of (for example) genes promoting "benefits to others" may occur independently of fitness changes at other levels of selection (Lewontin, 1970). Accordingly, prosocial behavior may be the result of different selection pressures acting in concert but at different levels (i.e., multilevel selection). First proposed by Darwin,[1] the concept of multilevel selection further implies that the fitness (dis) advantages of prosociality at the level of the individual do not have to coincide with those at the level of the group, and that tensions may arise due to behaviors that were selected for different purposes.[2] Given the medley of different interests among researches and their different focal points on units of selection and levels of explanation, it appears that the scholars have been more in conflict than their theories.

[1]Darwin's notion of natural selection was compatible with what is called today multilevel selection. In *The Descent of Man*, Darwin wrote: "A tribe including many members who, from possessing in a high degree the spirit of patriotism, fidelity, obedience, courage, and sympathy, were always ready to aid one another, and to sacrifice themselves for the common good, would be victorious over most other tribes; and this would be natural selection." (Darwin, 1871/2007, p. 207). Darwin, of course, never implied that the natural selection of groups, as just described, had a genetic basis. Today, many authors challenge that group selection could have been a powerful force with regards to the evolution of human behavior, as it is difficult to obtain groups that are sufficiently genetically differentiated from each other for gene-based selection to have occurred (e.g., Cronk & Leech, 2013; Pinker, 2012). Nevertheless, sufficient other authors have theorized on how different levels of selection can be reconciled by showing the importance of cultural group selection and the existence of gene-culture coevolution for many behavioral traits, which is the view we adhere to in this book (e.g., Bowles & Gintis, 2011; Fehr & Fishbacher, 2003; Haidt, 2012; Richerson et al., 2015). Hence when we write about "natural selection" we imply that it can occur at multiple levels, including gene-, kin-, and (cultural) group-selection.
[2]A successful hunter who does not share his prey but keeps it all to himself acquires more calories compared to other tribe members, which may give him, as an individual, a fitness advantage. This strategy, however, puts the selfish member at risk for social exclusion because his selfish act goes against the interest of the entire tribe, which is to distribute the calories and ensure the health (and strength) of all clan members, giving it a competitive advantage and an increased survival chance relative to other tribes.

The debate on the origins of prosociality has given rise to yet another scholarly dispute regarding human nature. Are we *innately* prosocial or are we born selfish? Under the influence of rational choice theory, the dominant view in neoclassical economics has long been the latter, namely to view humans as utility-maximizing agents who deep down care little about how their actions might affect others. A similar view has reigned in biology ever since the publication of "*Adaptation and Natural Selection*" (Williams, 1966), a book that undermined group selection as an evolutionary force and drew attention to the gene-centered view of evolution whereby adaptations are designed to maximize the survival chances of the individual – a view that would later be reiterated in Dawkins' *The Selfish Gene* (1976). Accordingly, the idea that all human prosocial behavior was so-called "self-interest in disguise" became widespread and fit well with economists' findings that the incentive to free-ride is pervasive in all social groups and a major obstacle in achieving large-scale cooperation (Olson, 1971/1965). This last decade, however, the tide is turning, and there are an increasing number of researchers who attribute our extensive and unique capacity for altruistic behaviors to innate cognitive skills. Tomasello (2009) points out that human children are intrinsically helpful and understand others' needs, whereas other primates, like chimpanzees, are not. Finally, Nowak and Highfield (2011) refer to humans as "super cooperators" because we rely on multiple mechanisms (including gene-, kin-, and group selection) and indirect reciprocity ("I help you, and someone else helps me") to achieve large-scale cooperation. They argue that language, cognition, and morality are evolutionary spinoffs of a fundamental need to cooperate, and that successfully doing so relies on being generous, helpful, and forgiving.

The position that will be argued in this chapter, and elaborated on in the rest of this book, is that there is no selfish or altruistic default that surfaced as the product of evolution. What we inherited from our ancestors is a brain that remained sufficiently plastic in order to solve *ad hoc* the tension that arises from two core motives which may, at times, conflict: we are driven by self-interest, but at the same time we have a compulsory need to belong and be part of the group. In order to satisfy these two motives, the process by which we arrive at *hic et nunc* decisions is malleable and subject to experience, cultural learning, framing effects, and individual values. It is the plasticity built into the wiring of our brain, making continuous small-grained adaptations possible, that best explains our paradoxical nature, including the many inconsistencies in our social behaviors.

In this chapter we will begin by elaborating briefly on the evolutionary origins of the different psychological motives that underlie our propensity for being both prosocial and antisocial. Then we start with the main objective of this book, to summarize the evidence that brain processes are flexible enough to solve conflicts that arise when motives compete, and to identify those conditions that determine which motive will dominate at any particular time, tipping *hic et nunc* decisions in one or the other direction.

1.1 THE EVOLUTIONARY ORIGINS OF PROSOCIAL BEHAVIOR

It is not an easy task to disentangle environmental and evolutionary explanations for human behavior (e.g., Newson & Richerson, 2009). Environmental accounts of prosociality emphasize the fact that individuals are presently responding to contemporaneous changes in the social environment. For example, changes in the economic structure, new technology and communication channels, globalization, and improved health care are all factors which are known to significantly influence current and future prosocial behaviors. But inasmuch as behavior can be traced back to replicating genes, antecedents of the traits we observe today were likely set in motion in the distant past. Identifying the evolutionary origin of these traits is, however, unduly complex and complicated by many issues.

First, many evolutionary processes are operating in concert. Natural selection is a well-known, and classic evolutionary force which can account for both gradual and sudden changes in form and function, but it is not the only one. Evolutionary changes can accrue due to chance fluctuations of gene frequencies in small populations (genetic drift), or the arrival of new migrants into the population (gene flow), or sudden environmental calamities that randomly wipe out a substantial portion of the genepool. Evolution is also path dependent, meaning that it does not "create" novel adaptations, but that it has to mold already existing phenotypes. This makes evolution a tinkerer rather than an engineer (Jacob, 1977). Therefore, any model trying to capture evolutionary processes (including the one we will present in this chapter) is bound to be highly simplified, capturing only a few features to which we pay attention, perhaps disproportionately so.

Second, natural selection itself is not a unitary force but, as mentioned earlier, operates at multiple levels (see footnote 1). A gene that promotes a particular behavior (e.g., an empathic response)[3] will be naturally selected if this behavior confers a fitness advantage to the individual, or to any of its relatives that carry the same copy of that gene. (i.e., kin selection). Culture too can impose selection pressures on groups (i.e., cultural group selection), altering their genetic composition when groups differentiate, leading to gene-culture co-evolutionary processes (Richerson et al., 2015).

The third complicating issue in deciphering the evolutionary origins of traits is that we may have inadvertently overestimated the number of so-called human "universals." In a *Behavioral and Brain Sciences* article with the savvy title, The WEIRDEST[4] people in the world (Henrich, Heine, & Norenzayan, 2010), we are confronted with the imbalance between the vast number of studies conducted on Western subjects, and the scant anthropological data. The latter reveal that behavioral heterogeneity across the globe may be more substantial than we make it out to be in the West. The authors conclude that we have no *a priori* grounds to claim that certain psychological processes are "universals" or "fundamental" in the sense that they are the result of uniform evolutionary pressures in the past. Such predictions would depend on knowing the ancestral environment, which is difficult to reconstruct and always debatable. From paleogeography we now know that the Pleistocene (2.5 million years to 11,700 years ago) was a very unstable environment with extreme climate changes and repeated glaciation periods that occurred over very short time spans (Richerson, Boyd, & Bettinger, 2001). This epoch, which could probably not support large populations of humans (who were more likely the hunted than the hunters), may still have been the nurturing ground for prosocial behavior, as harsh environments do encourage cooperation (Bowles & Gintis, 2011; Smaldino, Newson, Schank, & Richerson, 2013).[5] This does not mean that cooperation became a hard-wired strategy. Genes would not have had the time to adapt to the recurrent and rapid climate changes.

[3]There are many indications that individual variation in empathy and other prosocial behaviors are related to polymorphisms of the oxytocin receptor gene. We elaborate on this in chapter 4.
[4]The acronym WEIRD refers to Western, educated, industrial, rich, and democratic individuals, which make up the bulk of participants in psychological experiments.
[5]An alternative hypothesis for the origin of prosociality is that it emerged more than 1.8 million years ago when humans became cooperative breeders, perhaps as a response to moving into savannah habitats were foraging success was severely impaired for youngsters. Mothers on their own could not provide sufficient food to their infants to allow their brains to grow to full capacity, so the infants depended on allomaternal care to survive (Burkart et al., 2014; Hrdy, 2009).

More likely, it is the ability to learn and pass on information to the next generation (cultural transmission) that would have been very valuable during hard times, so that the younger generations could have benefited from the acquired knowledge of the older generation.

If it is the capacity for learning and flexibility that was naturally selected, then the conventional dichotomy between associating human "universals" with evolutionary processes, while ascribing individual differences to environmental processes, is bound to be wrong. Evolution itself has kept sufficient heterogeneity in the running so that individuals can diversify and become locally adapted to environments by non-genetic processes. In this sense *learning* is the universal process by which evolution has endowed humans with the capacity to diversify. Through developmental plasticity and learning, each individual is capable of a range of adaptive phenotypes, contingent on certain conditions. For example, bicultural individuals today may be fully capable of identifying both with collectivist and individualist values, but their actual behavior will be dictated by the country they reside in.

Knowing that adaptive behaviors are linked to developmental plasticity and the capacity to learn, we should be able to trace these features back to the brain, the organ through which all behavior is enacted, and which itself is a product of natural selection. While humans share with other mammals a number of very basic emotional and motivational systems laid down in evolutionary old subcortical systems, the more specialized and flexible abilities (such as learning when and where to cooperate) may only emerge as a result of specific types of life experiences and furthermore depend on interactions with more recently evolved neocortical brain systems (Panksepp & Panksepp, 2000). Building on this perspective, we propose that the evolutionary old subcortical system endowed us (through multilevel selection) with two core psychological motives that are relevant when it comes to prosocial decision-making: self-enhancement and group inclusion (see also Fiske, 2004). As long as self-interest coincides with group-interest, the two core motives do not conflict, and they will elicit similar prosocial behaviors. However, pursuing self-interest often undermines group-interest, in which case social inclusion may become jeopardized. And vice versa, some people want to belong so much they hurt themselves in the process. To solve this recurrent dilemma that emerges when motives compete, two simple decision rules (heuristics) supported by neocortical brain systems facilitate

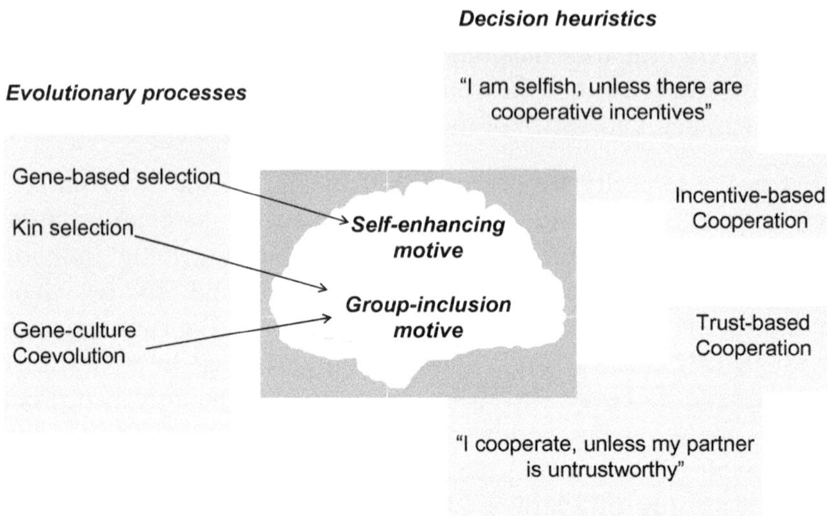

Figure 1.1 Two routes to prosocial decision-making. Legend: multilevel selection shaped the brain to drive behaviors that fullfil two core motives: self-enhancement and group inclusion. When motives conflict, two heuristics supported by more recently evolved brain regions facilitate either incentive-based or trust-based cooperation taking into account relevant environmental features.

adaptive decision-making, taking into account developmental experiences and very specific *hic et nunc* features of the environment.

In Figure 1.1 we delineate the evolutionary processes we believe preceded two alternative routes to extant prosocial decision-making. The first route is made possible by gene-based selection which shaped the brain to motivate behaviors to attend to self-interest. It is supported by the heuristic "I am selfish UNLESS there are incentives to cooperate," and it confers a fitness advantage to the individual. This rule is compatible with the view inspired by classical economics that most forms of helping are self-interest in disguise, operating with a long time horizon (Bowles & Gintis, 2011). Theories of reciprocal altruism (Axelrod & Hamilton, 1981; Trivers, 1971), indirect reciprocity (Nowak & Sigmund, 1998), reputation formation and costly signaling (Zahavi, 1975) are all consistent with the existence of such a decision rule. If none of these incentives are present, the "selfish" rule of thumb should drive an individual to defect. Therefore, we refer to this heuristic process as "incentive-based" cooperation.

The second route to cooperation is the result of kin-selection and gene-culture coevolution that shaped behavior to maintain affiliative bonds and to focus primarily on group inclusion. There is a vast literature indicating that people value group belonging and that they derive pleasure from being in a group (Baumeister & Leary, 1995). Showing one's intrinsic willingness to cooperate with the ingroup is thereby an effective way to strengthen belonging, build social networks, and avoid exclusion (Caporael, Dawes, Orbell, & Vandekragt, 1989). Voluntary efforts to maintain group ties will also make it more likely that the group will succeed, whereby each member can potentially profit from the victory. But people do not have to be consciously aware of these advantages conferred by group success. It is the social reward of group belonging that motivates people to serve the group, rather than the survival advantages. A major pitfall, however, is that the cooperative efforts of individuals who are group-minded are always at risk of being undermined by selfish others, hence the heuristic supporting this route to cooperation needs to be contingent on signals that diminish the chance of exploitation. Therefore the second decision rule, "I cooperate UNLESS my partners are not trustworthy," is probably closely knit to other evolved mechanisms which facilitate trust, the recognition of kin and other group members, and the capacity to maintain group boundaries with formal rules of conduct which can be passed on to future generations through cultural inheritance (Bowles & Gintis, 2011; Richerson et al., 2015; Sober & Wilson, 1998). We briefly elaborate on these mechanisms next.

The evolutionary origins of cooperation in the absence of incentives (i.e., the trust-based route to cooperation) has been heavily contested because it hinges on selection other than genes (see also footnote 1). Trust-based cooperation is rooted in the concept of inclusive fitness, meaning that the evolutionary success of this route relies in part on a group structure where individuals are likely to interact with other individuals that use the same rule, i.e., there has to be a sufficient number of trustworthy (and hence cooperative) people in the group for prosociality to pay off. Group selection can explain how prosocial behavior in the absence of clear incentives can be evolutionarily sustained in such close groups of like-minded people. First, group living is essential for humans to survive. Second, groups differ in their evolutionary success (some groups are expanding and proliferating, while other groups succumb to environmental crises or warfare). Third, groups in which individuals have more selfless tendencies tend to cooperate more, giving them an advantage over other groups that lack cooperators and with whom they compete (Bowles & Gintis, 2011).

Skeptics of group selection, however, point out that altruistic traits without individual benefits could only evolve on theoretical grounds, or, at best, in unduly small and isolated populations with virtually no migration. And even so, the individual selection against altruistic traits within groups would be so strong that it would easily override the forces of between-group selection. Therefore, by itself, group selection is unlikely to account for the empirical finding that a significant proportion of humans are unconditional altruists who help others without the intent of ever being paid back with material rewards. The capacity for social learning and cultural transmission are likely to have additionally impacted the evolution of human prosociality (e.g., Bowles & Gintis, 2003; Fehr & Fischbacher, 2003; Gintis, Bowles, Boyd, & Fehr, 2003; Richerson et al., 2015). The reason is that social norms, together with cultural institutions that punish norm violators, would significantly weaken the individual selection against altruistic traits. Avoiding punishment and imitating the successful cooperative behavior of others (i.e., social learning), furthermore prevent the erosion of group differences (in terms of the relative frequency of cooperative members in each group, see Fehr & Fischbacher, 2003). This in turn strengthens group boundaries and facilitates gene-culture co-evolutionary processes from which group-beneficial behaviors can emerge.

Social learning and the subsequent cultural transmission of norms from one generation to the next allow humans to more rapidly adapt to changing environments by modifying the individual fitness-maximizing selection pressures when they are not beneficial on average to the members of the group (Boyd & Richerson, 2000). Especially when resources are scarce and between-group competition is fierce, the quick proliferation of prosocial norms might make the difference between group survival or group extinction. Gene-culture interactions may lie at the root of social norms, but once in existence, these internalized prosocial norms that result from social learning and induce people to conform to leading group principles (including cooperating for the sake of the group) are in fact the motivational drivers and hence the proximate reasons for this trust-based route to cooperation (Bowles & Gintis, 2011).

In summary, evolution endowed each and every-one of us with two core motives, fulfilling self-interest and safeguarding group inclusion, and a brain that supports two heuristics to bias decision-making towards or away from cooperation. The motivational system of the brain is itself neutral with respect to the outcome of decision-making, as it was not necessarily "selected" to make us pro- or antisocial. If a system works properly to fulfill a certain function, it does not imply that it was necessarily designed for that function. As all i-Phone users know, a paperclip is the ideal tool to open the phone's battery container, yet no-one will confuse that one bizarre function of the paperclip with its reason of existence. Similarly, heuristics were not designed to make us cooperate. Instead, they match the possible decision outcomes to the presence or absence of cooperative incentives and/or trust signals in the environment. Before elaborating in more detail on these two logics for cooperation, we first diverge on the different types of commonly encountered (pro)social behaviors and on the dilemma-type situations where prosociality is more difficult to achieve.

1.2 WHAT DO WE MEAN BY PROSOCIALITY?

1.2.1 Different Types of Prosocial Behaviors

"Prosocial" may refer to different types of behaviors, including cooperating, sharing, helping, giving, and trusting. On the antisocial side, behaviors include (but are not limited to) betraying, defecting, harming, and stealing. Which decision will be made depends on the expected outcome, which, in turn, will be a function of the expected benefits, given a particular social context. Following the tradition in ecology, decisions that are made in social interactions can yield four different classes of outcomes: (1) mutualism (+/+), where all parties benefit, (2) altruism (−/+), where ego sacrifices itself to the benefit of others, (3) selfishness (+/−), where one party benefits to the detriment of the others, and (4) spite (−/−), where both parties are hurt.

The defining feature of mutualism (+/+) is that the interaction provides synergy. However, there is substantial variation in the processes by which mutualism can be achieved in nature, ranging from *simple coordination* to *costly cooperation.* At the simplest level, mutualistic interactions between species emerge from mimicking behavior and simple operant conditioning whereby each animal is rewarded for synchronizing its behavior with another animal (Brosnan & Bshary, 2010; Bshary, Hohner, Ait-El-Djoudi, & Fricke, 2006). This is likely how mutualistic relations between plants and bacteria, or coordinated actions of coral reef fish in pursuit of prey, become established. In human societies, market exchanges between buyers and sellers are a good example, as these sorts of interactions are likely to confer net benefits to both parties.

In comparison to coordination, cooperation is cognitively much more complex for at least two reasons. First, collaborative efforts (e.g., during cooperative hunting of social mammals) require complementarity (keeping track of each other's actions) and working memory to keep track of who is reciprocating who. Second, subsequent sharing the common good (e.g., the prey) may set the stage for cheating or free riding, challenging the accrual of benefits for those who are not tempted by greed and are playing it straight. Thus, while cooperation is a process intended to yield a mutually beneficial outcome, it can turn out to be costly when betrayal becomes possible. When two students collaborate on a task and deliver homework that is better than either one of them could have accomplished alone, their mutual cooperation has created synergy, but each of them took the risk that the other one could have been a poor collaborator or disloyal at the end.

Because it can be costly, and in contrast to other eusocial species where cooperation evolved to be a genetically preprogrammed part of behavior, large-scale cooperation in humans relies much on cognition. Costly cooperation, as we know it, is rare in the animal kingdom in part because of the limited cognitive skills of most animals. Ironically, the cognitive skills that gave humans strategizing skills and the ability to be manipulative are the same skills that allow us to reflect *hic et nunc* about the potential benefits of joining efforts and to suppress selfish urges to realize the long-term benefits of cooperating with others. Reciprocity (I'll scratch your back if you scratch mine) is one of these forms of cooperation whereby profits accumulate as long as two parties remain loyal to each other.

In contrast to the synergy obtained from mutualistic interactions, altruistic acts (−/+) occur without the intention of being paid back. A classic example is donating anonymously to charity. Altruistic acts are common in our species, especially among families and close groups of friends with whom we interact frequently. The more we identify with the beneficiaries, the more compassion we feel for the fate of others, the more we are inclined to be altruistic (Tomasello, 2009). In these cases, human altruism goes far beyond reciprocity. Behavioral economists have given the term "strong reciprocity" to the individual propensity to bear the cost to reward cooperators who are not genetically related, and to punish defectors who violate group norms, solely for the satisfaction of doing so. But despite their good nature and the fact that they do not intend to gain whatsoever from their altruistic acts, strong reciprocators are not immune to free riders. The possibility that they succumb to defection as well if they encounter too much abuse is real. This possibility, of course, becomes more prominent as groups grow in size and become more anonymous.

Therefore, in all groups, trust becomes an essential part of prosocial interactions such as costly cooperation or strong reciprocity. Indeed, trust has been described as a social lubricant with positive externality because it reduces uncertainty and transaction costs in economic exchanges (Arrow, 1974). Unlike gullibility, which implies being insensitive to information regarding others' trustworthiness, trust means having default expectations of reciprocity (Rotter, 1980; Yamagishi, 2011). Trust also differs from assurance which is not socially constructed and has no emotional connotation (Yamagishi & Yamagishi, 1994). For example, one can be assured a fair treatment by the law and judicial system without the need to trust. In contrast to assurance, trust can be considered a "behavioral primitive" that reduces selfishness and intuitively guides social interaction (Berg, Dickhaut, & McCabe, 1995). From trust and reciprocity emerge stable, long-term, and mutually beneficial relationships.

Opposite to mutualism and altruism are the social interactions with negative externalities: selfishness (+/−) and spite (−/−). Selfishness surfaces when an individual takes on a competitive rather than a cooperative stance in social interaction, or when a defector betrays another's trust. Spite refers to retaliating on a harmful act. What factors determine whether someone will trust and cooperate, betray, or retaliate? Much of what we know regarding these social interactions comes from research on social dilemmas.

1.2.2 Social Dilemmas

In social exchanges, valuable goods or services are often allocated in such a way that the gains of one party do not equal the losses of the other party. Many social situations can be modeled as "non-zero-sum" games, meaning that all participants can benefit from the interaction, or they can all suffer collectively. When, in such a situation, people face the choice of serving the greater collective versus serving self-interest, they are stuck in a social dilemma. The economically rational choice is to favor self-interest. But in a social dilemma this choice is suboptimal from the collective point of view. And if too many people choose the self-interest option, everyone loses in the end.

The essence of a social dilemma was described by Hardin (1968) in a well-known *Science* article with the title "The tragedy of the commons." As a consequence of the pressing problem of an exponential increase in population growth (already obvious in the 1960s), Hardin portrays how the freedom of individual choices would eventually lead to a depletion of public goods ("the commons"). The article is meant to be a rebuttal to Adam Smith's popularized view that "an individual who intends only his own gain is, as it were, led by an invisible hand... to promote the public interest." Adam Smith never meant this statement to be invariably true (and neither did many of his followers), so Hardin borrows the following metaphor from a mathematics amateur named William Forster to illustrate the tragedy that would follow if one assumes that self-interested decisions are in fact the best for an entire society: consider a public pasture open to all. If every herdsman in town decides in his best interest to keep as many cattle as possible, the proceeds from the cattle for each herdsman will be positive at the start. But with each additional cow, overgrazing becomes a reality, until finally, the herdsmen all together face the loss of the pasture (Hardin, p. 62).

The reality of social dilemmas today is especially noted in sustainable resource management, such as obeying fish quotas to not deplete the world's oceans, voluntary restraints on water usage, employing renewable sources of energy, or recycling and carpooling to control waste and air pollution. Examples of social dilemmas also emerge in politics and legislation (as in bilateral disarmament agreements, showing up to vote during elections, not evading taxes), and in all aspects of daily life that yield the opportunity to free ride on the efforts of others.

Social dilemma research in economics and psychology has typically relied on experimental games in which players are interdependent and the choices offered in the game are made to vary with respect to the benefits they provide to self and other. The actual choices made by the players are then compared to the game-theoretic expectations based on the assumption that each player would be a "rational" agent (in the classical economic sense) maximizing narrow self-interest.

A prototypical example of an experimental game is the two-player prisoner's dilemma, named after a hypothetical scenario in which two friends are convicted for misdemeanor. Evidence for sentencing them to prison is sparse, so a judge decides to interrogate the two friends separately. If both friends remain loyal and don't tell on each other (the cooperative thing to do), they will be sentenced on a lesser charge, and each one will spend two months in prison. If, however, one testifies against the other, he or she goes free, leaving the friend with a two-year sentence. If both tell on each other, they will both go to prison for one year. In this scenario, it is tempting to betray the friend, because this option is more rewarding than staying loyal (going free versus a two-month prison term). Furthermore, someone who does not betray is at risk for the "sucker payoff" (two-year prison term), which is worse than sharing the sentence when both parties betray (one year in prison). In games such as the prisoner's dilemma, defecting (or betraying the friend) is the dominant response, because neither player can improve his or her situation (relative to the other player) by choosing to be cooperative (or loyal) when the other defects.

Changing the time horizon of the prisoner's dilemma holds a more optimistic prospective. In the iterative version, when interactions are endlessly repeated, each partner has an incentive to avoid the pitfalls of mutual defection and to pay the initial cost of cooperation to establish a long-term mutually cooperative relationship during which benefits can accrue. The two friends who are interrogated on the account of misdemeanor in this example are better off remaining loyal to each other if it is in their best interest to continue their friendship in the future. Similarly, a "tit for tat" strategy, whereby a person in a dyadic, repetitive interaction starts out cooperating and thereafter reciprocates all responses of the partner, has been shown to outcompete all other strategies (Rapoport & Chammah, 1965). Because greedy strategies tend to do worse over time, "tit for tat" cooperation can be evolutionary stable (Axelrod & Hamilton, 1981).

Repeated interactions are, however, not usually effective in boosting cooperation in large, anonymous groups. This can be illustrated using *n*-player social dilemma games, of which the public goods game is probably the best known: here, participants have the choice to contribute a portion or all of their initial endowment to a common fund (the public good). The fund then becomes multiplied by a factor and shared equally among all the participants in the game. Thus, each player has the incentive to keep as much of the endowment to him or herself, while benefitting at the end from the contributions made by others. When the game is repeated with the same players, contributions typically decline. A possible reason for this is inequity aversion (Fehr & Schmidt, 1999). As the high contributors learn throughout the game that there are free riders in the group, they will adjust their own contributions to the lower group mean. Eventually, cooperation dwindles to zero. This happened in Stephen King's experiment when he intended to publish a book in installments on the internet. He asked all his readers to pay—based on an honor system—$1 for each installment they downloaded, and he would continue to post subsequent installments on the internet if 75% of the readers paid for the downloads. King obtained this desired fraction for the first installment. After six installments, the fraction dropped to 46%.[6] The book is yet unfinished.

Yet large-scale cooperation has not yet collapsed and lies at the source of success in most societies (see books by Bowles & Gintis, 2011; Diamond, 2013). In the next subsection we examine some of the common proximate reasons why individuals *do* decide to cooperate, emphasizing the point that there are multiple motives behind cooperative decision making. In line with the two decision heuristics proposed in Section 1.1, we have delineated two logics behind cooperation: one whereby cooperation is self-enhancing and yields tangible, individual rewards (incentive-based cooperation), and another without tangible rewards but that is sensible from a social point of view because it promotes group functions and secures social inclusion, provided others in the group are trustworthy (trust-based cooperation).

1.3 *HIC ET NUNC* REASONS FOR PROSOCIAL BEHAVIOR: TWO ROUTES TO COOPERATION

At the proximate level, which of the two routes to cooperation predominates at any particular time will depend on the decision context as well as on the individual's learned and idiosyncratic value attached to the outcome.[7] Put differently, the motivational system in the brain that drives human decision making can be slanted at any time depending

[6] *Wired*, "Stephen King's *The Plant* Uprooted," 28 November, 2000.
[7] Individual differences will be addressed in detail in Chapter 4.

on (1) how much the outcome of a particular prosocial decision enhances self-interest (following decision- heuristic one) and on (2) how much value and trust is placed on the relationship with the group (following decision- heuristic two, see Figure 1.1). How the subjective value of a prosocial decision is computed[8] will be the subject of the next chapter. In the remainder of this chapter we summarize the evidence that *hic et nunc* prosocial decisions can be ecologically sound on two accounts: when they provide benefits to the self (and thereby curb selfishness) and when they promote group survival (while safeguarding the self against possible defectors).

1.3.1 Incentive Based Cooperation

Much of social dilemma research in behavioral and experimental economics revolves around finding strategic solutions to incentivize players to cooperate (e.g., Bornstein, 2003). By incorporating extrinsic cooperative incentives that are ecologically relevant into payoff structures of social dilemmas, self-interest and collective interest become aligned. This removes the temptation to free ride and motivates prosocial behavior, even among those who are not naturally inclined to cooperate. Extrinsic cooperative incentives objectively transform the payoff structure of a social dilemma so that cooperation becomes a rational choice with tangible rewards (Boone, Declerck, & Kiyonari, 2010; Declerck, Boone, & Emonds, 2013).

Repeated interactions in dyadic exchanges are one example of an extrinsic incentive to cooperate, because a long-term mutually cooperative relationship is usually more lucrative that the payoff for a single instance of unilateral defection. The accrual of benefits generate incentives that turn the temptation to free ride into a game of eliciting reciprocity. Other examples of extrinsic cooperative incentives are creating synergy, imposing sanctions to deter noncooperation, and providing reputation benefits that set the stage for indirect reciprocity.

When interactions lead to synergy, the conflict between self- and collective interest is eliminated, the temptation to defect is removed,

[8]"Computation" in this sense does not equal "conscious deliberation." We use the term in a broader sense, implying that computation can also be performed by the brain outside of consciousness based on heuristic processes that were shaped by natural selection, individual experiences, and learning processes to efficiently attain an ecologically sound outcome given the cognitive limitations of the human nervous system. We return to this point at the end of this chapter and in Chapter 2.

and cooperation becomes much easier. This is, for example, the case in team tasks, where members possess complementary skills, or in public goods games where payoff structures are in the form of complements rather than substitutes (Boone, Declerck, & Suetens, 2008; Potters & Suetens, 2006). It becomes in each player's best interest to imitate the cooperative effort of other players. Everyone gains when efforts are pooled. Similarly, a prisoner's dilemma can be transformed to a coordination game by lowering the payoff for unilateral defection to the level below or at the payoff for cooperation.[9] This structural change generates a strong incentive to cooperate, because now the best choice for an individual is also the best choice from the collective point of view. In economic terms, in a coordination game, the cooperative Nash equilibrium is also pareto-optimal. But mutual cooperation in a coordination game still does not follow automatically, because decisions are made in conditions of uncertainty, with no guarantee that partners will in fact be cooperative. A labor strike is a good example: the outcome may well be in each worker's best interest, but only so if *all* other workers are joining the strike. The outcome may be worse for all if too many workers bail.

Another category of solutions for social dilemmas is to incorporate sanctions. When they substantially increase the cost of noncooperation, sanctions can be a powerful class of negative incentives that boost cooperative behavior. Numerous laboratory and field studies have shown that monetary fines, verbal criticism, and the threat of social exclusion are all effective at reducing free riding. A classic experiment by Fehr and Gachter (2002) showed that, in public goods games (described earlier), the decline in cooperation with increasing rounds can be prevented when game players have the opportunity to impose a monetary fine on noncontributors. A subsequent experiment indicates that players prefer to participate in games where sanctioning is possible than in games with no sanctions (Fehr & Rockenbach, 2004). Apart from economic games, people also support sanctioning institutions in

[9]This type of coordination game is also known as the *stag hunt*. It is named after a fictitious scenario where two individuals go out hunting. If they are hunting by themselves, they can only pursue small prey, such as rabbits. But if they join their efforts, they can go after large game, such as stag. The shared stag provides them each with more meat then they would obtain from the individual catch of rabbits. However, the two hunts cannot be reconciled, and the hunters become mutually dependent on each other. If one of the hunters bails and does not cooperate, the stag is lost to both, and the other one can no longer get the rabbits. But if they each trust that the other will join in the stag hunt, there is no incentive to defect.

real life, and social institutions that do make use of punishments tend to enjoy a competitive advantage over institutions that don't (Gürerk, Irlenbusch, & Rockenbach, 2006). Hence sanctions are economically rational on two accounts: they directly deter free riding, and they indirectly serve as an assurance that cooperation will pay off because of the negative incentive to defect.

Reputation benefits are likewise an effective means to elicit cooperation in social dilemmas. People are more likely to cooperate in public, and are less inclined to do so privately, because the publicity boosts their reputation of being generous. Numerous laboratory experiments have shown that reducing anonymity or introducing possible audience effects are very effective at increasing prosocial behavior in general (Kurzban, DeScioli, & O'Brien, 2007; Piazza & Bering, 2008). Thus cooperation may be a self-representation strategy by which people participate in "competitive altruism" to elicit indirect reciprocity from third parties (Nowak & Sigmund, 2005). If, in a group, person C observes person A doing a good deed to person B, person C may spread the word that person A is a virtuous person, deserving VIP treatment. Even if person B never reciprocated, A's reputation has become such that somewhere down the line person F or G may decide to provide A with extra benefits. Indeed, experiments have shown that more generous players in social dilemma games are more often chosen as game partners and enjoy a higher status in the group (Hardy & Van Vugt, 2006). In real life, people who donate generously to charity were found to enjoy higher sympathy ratings and were believed to be more trustworthy (Bereczkei, Birkas, & Kerekes, 2007). When in need, these generous people are likely to enjoy assistance or paybacks from indirect reciprocity.

What all these incentives (reciprocity, synergy, sanctions, and a good reputation) have in common is that, by aligning self- and collective interests, they prompt people to act prosocially to reap the benefits that emerge from (in)direct reciprocity or the synergy from joint efforts. The temptation to free ride is gone, and the rewards that they obtain give the individual a concrete advantage over others. Without these incentives, many people will be inclined to defect, at least if they adhere to the "I am selfish unless..." heuristic, a decision rule that fits well with the explanatory power of fitness and the selfish gene. It echoes Richard Dawkin's assertion that we are "survival machines."

1.3.2 Trust-Based Cooperation

Incentives can't explain all of human cooperation. Even in one-shot, anonymous interactions with no reputation advantages, some people still cooperate at least some of the time. This supposedly "irrational" behavior that goes against the predictions of the canonical self-interest model has been reported on all continents and in at least 15 different small-scale societies exhibiting a wide variety of economic and cultural conditions, including foraging groups (e.g., the Hadza in East Africa), slash and burn horticulturists (e.g., the Aché in South America), and nomadic herding groups (e.g., the Mongols in Central Asia). In a series of experiments, prosocial decisions in anonymous one- shot experimental games were observed over and over again, all over the world, even when the stakes were very high (gaining or losing up to a day's worth of wages). Cultural differences in cooperative behavior could not be attributed to individual economic or demographic variables, but instead appeared to depend on that particular society's economic structure and market integration. The more a society became economically interdependent and engaged in trade, the higher became the level of cooperation in one-shot games. In fact, decisions in these experimental games were generally consistent with behavior in daily lives. For example, the high degree of fairness shown by the Aché reflects that society's food-sharing practices: meat is typically distributed equally among many households, regardless of which hunter made the kill (Henrich et al., 2005).

One account for this seemingly irrational cooperative behavior that seems to be common to all cultures is to assume that some individuals are simple-minded and that they are confused because they treat single, anonymous interactions as if they were repeated. According to this "confusion hypothesis," humans misinterpret experimental one-shot games because social exchanges in ancestral environments occurred almost exclusively in small groups where everyone knew each other. So the behavioral rules that evolved in a context of recurrent interactions where reputation is always at stake are supposedly misapplied in the artificial, one-shot laboratory settings of today.

Many researchers, however, assert that over-applying the cooperative rule to one-shot situations does not necessarily mean that it is *mis*applied or that people are confused (e.g., Bowles & Gintis, 2003; Fehr & Henrich, 2003; Gintis et al., 2003). In dyadic laboratory prisoner's dilemma games, people are very good at distinguishing repeated from one-shot interactions, increasing their level of cooperation in the former and decreasing them in the latter. Cooperation levels furthermore drop drastically when players are informed that it is the last round in a multitrial game (e.g., Boone, De Brabander, & Van Witteloostuijn, 1999; Reuben & Suetens, 2012). Participants in laboratory experiments are also rational when it comes to splitting a sum of money between themselves and a partner. When there is a cost to being generous, participants adjust their donations to others accordingly: they give away less and keep more to themselves (Andreoni & Miller, 2002). In real life, being a good Samaritan and helping a stranded stranger in need is not a quirk. Neither are we confused when we send monetary aid to a foreign country that has just suffered from an environmental calamity. And most people will tip their waiter in a restaurant, even when away from home in a foreign city never to be traveled to again, provided, of course, that tipping is the local prevailing norm.

Next to the confusion hypothesis for cooperation in one-shot games, the "social exchange heuristic" posits that cooperative behavior is automatically triggered when we sense that we are in a social interaction. The social exchange heuristic is supported by error management theory, meaning that cooperation in one-shot anonymous interactions is favored because it is worth it to risk a single mistake (cooperating when the chance exists that it will not be reciprocated) than to lose out on a potentially fruitful long-term interaction (Haselton & Buss, 2000). Thus, people have become very sensitive to cues that are indicative of social exchanges. For example, Kiyonari, Tanida, and Yamagishi (2000) compared cooperation levels in a prisoner's dilemma game where participants made their decisions simultaneously, versus the same game where participants play sequentially. In the latter game, the decision of the first player is revealed to the second player who then has to decide whether or not to reciprocate. This sequence of events promotes a sense of contingency between the two players' choices, which was expected to trigger cooperation by heuristic processing. Indeed, cooperative decisions jumped from 38% in the simultaneously played game to 59% for first-mover decisions in the sequentially played game. This increase reflects the fact that players who are made aware of their interdependence with another player are more likely to bet that their partner will be cooperative. Second movers cooperated in 62% of the cases, supporting the idea that kindness begets kindness when people feel connected. Additional evidence for the social exchange heuristic hypothesis comes from the finding that applying time pressure in experiments increases cooperative decisions in some people (Rand et al., 2014). The shorter reaction times of cooperative decisions supposedly reveal their intuitive cooperative nature and lack of conscious deliberation.

The idea of a social exchange heuristic does not necessarily imply that we are "hard-wired" to always cooperate in reciprocal interactions, but – because it does not apply to everyone equally – it is compatible with the view that early life experiences and social learning can mold the brain to become very sensitive to cues that encourage people to engage in prosocial behaviors, at least within the boundaries of the close-knit group in which most of their social interactions are taking place. The social rewards they obtain in return may lead them to internalize the cooperative norm. Darwin already realized the power of social learning when he wrote in *The Descent of Man* that "a belief constantly inculcated during the early years of life, whilst the brain is impressible, appears to acquire almost the nature of an instinct; and the very essence of an instinct is that it is followed independently of reason" (Darwin, 1871/2007, p. 188). In a series of essays bundled under the title *Why We Cooperate*, Michael Tomasello (2009) elaborates further on the interplay of an intuitive cooperative inclination and socialization. He first summarizes the evidence showing that human children are born with a propensity to help, share, and inform each other, much more so than our chimpanzee cousins. However, around the age of three to four, these children learn more about how others behave and experience firsthand that their intent to be helpful is not always reciprocated. At the same time, they experience the temptation to be selfish and realize that they are also the target of others' judgments. As they learn who to imitate and who to avoid, their sense of self takes on the perspectives and values of the social group as a whole. From this emerges a sense of "we-ness and shared intentions." Tomasello describes the essence of norm internalization through social learning as follows:

> *As children transform themselves into public persons with their own identities in early childhood, they become concerned with their public reputations, and they are eager to follow and even enforce social norms [. . .]. Children do not only respect social norms, as is typically argued, due to the benefits of reciprocity and threat of punishment. Instead they are sensitive from a young age to their own interdependence with others in collaborative activities – a kind of "social rationality"[10] endemic to shared intentionality. (pp. 45–46).*

[10]Quotation marks added by author.

Cooperating for social rewards obtained from maintaining group ties can only be a sustainable strategy if people have some assertion that other group members will be loyal too. Toshio Yamagishi and colleagues show that people tend to be more altruistic toward ingroup members (allocating more money to ingroup members than to outgroup members) because they expect more loyalty from ingroup members than from outgroup members (Yamagishi, Terai, Kiyonari, Mifune, & Kanazawa, 2007). Therefore, it is not surprising that humans are very sensitive to ingroup/outgroup manipulations (e.g., Tajfel, Billig, Bundy, & Flament, 1971), and that they have devised all sorts of ways to protect the group from free riders, including monitoring, badmouthing, and even ostracizing those that ostensibly hurt the group (Williams, 2007). More amazing is the finding that people are even willing to incur the cost of sanctions themselves to punish free riding (Gintis et al., 2003). The occurrence of this so-called "altruistic punishment" has been demonstrated in a large-scale experimental study across 15 different small-scaled societies (such as the present day African Hadza and the !Kung). The researchers confronted individuals with experimental economic games (sometimes for high wages, amounting to a day's salary). Apparently, all populations demonstrated some willingness to administer costly punishment to defectors, and the magnitude of the punishment correlated positively with reports of altruistic behavior across populations (Henrich et al., 2006).[11] Importantly, the extra effort and cost to monitor and/or punish the behavior of others are often voluntary actions, and these have proven to be very successful, also in real life (Guala, 2012). Field studies on cooperative management of natural resources, such as agricultural lands or forests, have shown that the success of the commons depends in part on the number of cooperating individuals and the time they spend monitoring (Ostrom, 2009; Rustagi, Engel, & Kosfeld, 2010).

But even groups whose members have internalized prosocial norms (those that abide by *and* enforce social norms) are not immune to the destructive influences of selfishness, and a group of selfish individuals can easily induce a person with an internalized prosocial norm to defect (Camerer & Fehr, 2006). Inasmuch as such prosocial people like a mutually beneficial outcome the best (even if defecting would be

[11]It is worth noting that in cultures that lack strong social norms, antisocial punishment (punishing cooperators) has also been reported. When punishing is driven by vengeance that is not related to inequity aversion but aimed at hurting the "good guys," sanctions may be useless and would have no beneficial effect on cooperation (Herrmann, Thoni, & Gachter, 2008).

more profitable), they are also behavioral reciprocators who dislike an unfair or imbalanced outcome (Simpson, 2004). In many cultures, betrayal aversion has been shown to be an important motive for defection in social dilemma games (Bohnet, Greig, Herrmann, & Zeckhauser, 2008).

Thus, for internalized norms to pay off and for cooperation to become fruitful, it is essential that people trust each other. Trust subjectively transforms the fear of betrayal to expectations of reciprocity. Social cues that facilitate trust should therefore boost cooperation. This seems to be the case (see Balliet & Van Lange, 2013, for a meta-analysis). For example, reducing social distance increases trust and cooperation (Hoffman, McCabe, & Smith, 1996). It is also easier to trust someone who is like oneself, presumably because shared characteristics make it easier to predict someone's behavior. Consistently, people cooperate more with other people than with computers (Kiesler, Sproull, & Waters, 1996), with friends compared to strangers (Thompson, Kray, & Lind, 1998; Yamagishi & Sato, 1986), and with someone named "a partner" compared to an "opponent" (Burnham, McCabe, & Smith, 2000). Cooperation also increases when previously unknown interacting partners merely introduce themselves (Boone et al., 2008), perceive demographic similarity (Cole & Teboul, 2004), or even facial resemblance (DeBruine, 2002). Finally, a meta-analysis confirms that communication, which reduces uncertainty by letting partners assure each other of their loyalty, significantly increases cooperation in experimental social dilemma games (Balliet, 2010). Importantly, these cues that facilitate trust boost cooperative decisions even when economic incentives to cooperate are absent and when defecting would have yielded a clear advantage, as is the case in one-time interactions. Note that trust signals, the way we refer to them in this and subsequent chapters, is not the same as assurance. The latter also facilitates cooperation, but for a different reason. Sanctions, for example, facilitate cooperation because they provide tangible information that reduces uncertainty: we are assured that free-riders will be punished. In this way, sanctions serve as a negative incentive rather than a trust signal. In contrast, trust can be elicited by merely feeling comfortable around someone, and this feeling is experience- and culture-specific. Wearing a headscarf may be interpreted as a signal of trustworthiness in some cultural groups, while it creates distance among others.

1.4 RATIONALITY AND THE BRAIN

So far, we have described two different logics behind cooperation supported by two different heuristics. An implicit assumption is that these two heuristics can coexist within the same individual because they are *ecologically* and *boundedly* rational. By this we mean that the two decision rules "*I am selfish unless there are cooperative incentives*," and "*I cooperate unless my partner is untrustworthy*" are best seen as mental shortcuts, that are not designed for "optimizing," but for "satisficing,[12]" that is, they reframe a complex decision environment into one that is amenable to real-life human reasoning.

Bounded rationality opposes the classical economic theory of utility maximization and acknowledges that much of decision-making is not computed by complicated reasoning, probability theory, and Bayesian models, but, in Gerd Gigerenzer's words, that it is a process that "fits with reality." (Gigerenzer & Todd, 1999, p. 5). The starting point of bounded rationality is to accept that all human decision making takes place behind a veil of uncertainty. Its intent is to come up with new cognitive models that capture how real minds make decisions under real life constraints. Herbert Simon, the father of bounded rationality, described how a "boundedly rational" mind is the result of, on the one hand, the cognitive limitations of the brain, and on the other hand, the structure of the environment in which the mind is operating. The former constrains our ability to compute the best outcome, given limited time and knowledge. Even in a simple game such as the prisoner's dilemma, people are not likely to mathematically derive the *optimal* response or the Nash equilibrium, but they will rely on approximations to come up with what they feel is a *reasonable* response. Thus, even economically rational reasons to cooperate are not unconstrained. The latter part of Simon's bounded rationality theory (the structure of the environment) is at least as important and calls attention to the fact that rational decisions must also be appropriately adapted to the environment. This explains why there is not one single rational response to solving a prisoner's dilemma. While game theory may predict that an unboundedly rational agent will always defect in a prisoner's dilemma game, in reality people people may have all sorts of economically and/or socially well-grounded reasons to cooperate or defect, some of

[12]A term proposed by Herbert Simon to represent both the connotations of "satisfy" and "suffice."

which may be competing or interfering with each other. In most decision contexts, there are many sources of information that may influence the outcome of a decision, and converting them all to one common valuation currency (so as to be able to choose the best alternative) may be unduly complicated and effortful. Instead of undertaking the nearly impossible, a boundedly rational mind bases its decision on just one good reason that will satisfy an appropriate level of aspiration. Rationality need not be the same as optimization. Thus, defecting and cooperating can both be boundedly rational when they are the best and simplest solution we can come up with, given the structure of the decision-environment, our previous experiences, and our culturally learned values.

Gigerenzer et al. (1999) propose to "replace the image of an omniscient mind computing intricate probabilities and utilities with that of a bounded mind reaching into an adaptive toolbox filled with fast and frugal heuristics." (p. 5). These heuristics do not involve much computation; they are shortcuts created on the basis of recognition processes rather than lengthy information searches. When many competing reasons cannot be combined to a single currency for decision making, a fast and frugal heuristic may be the better strategy. The heuristics that support the two different logics to cooperate fit this description, but differ in how they are elicited. Following the first heuristic, "*I am selfish unless there are cooperative incentives*," the presence of extrinsic cooperative incentives makes cooperation *economically* (but still boundedly) rational. The second heuristic, "*I am cooperative unless my partner is untrustworthy*," depends on the implementation of an internalized social norm and becomes *socially* rational when there is sufficient trust that prevents compromising one's cooperative effort.

An important point to raise is that these two routes to cooperation should not be equated with dual-process accounts of decision making,[13] differentiating between an information-processing system that generates

[13]Dual-process theories of judgments and decision making (summarized in Evans, 2008) explain how information is processed via two distinct and alternative paths: the first one is typical of associative thinking and relies on "evolutionary old" neural networks, leading to *automatic*, sometimes unconscious decision outcomes; the second one is typical of rule-based inferential thinking, relies on "evolutionary new" neural networks, is more effortful, and generates *controlled* decision outcomes that are fully conscious. Following Kahneman's (2011) popularization in his book *Thinking Fast and Slow*, the former has been conveniently labeled "system 1," and the latter "system 2."

automatic and intuitive decisions, and a second system that relies on conscious deliberation and reasoning (often correcting the mistakes of the first system). Even if economically rational heuristics rely more on cost–benefit analyses (to evaluate the presence/absence of incentives), while socially rational heuristics may be more associated with socio-emotional processes, there is no one-to-one correspondence between these two types of heuristics and dual-processing systems. Both the economically and socially rational route to cooperation include elements of intuition and deliberation, and they will proceed automatically or controlled, depending on the amount and type of information in the environment, as well as the decision-makers' experience.

The heuristics literature, however, does not provide us with knowledge of how boundedly rational decision making corresponds to what is actually happening in the brain. Therefore, the second and main explanatory framework for how prosocial decisions are made will reside, we believe, in the growing field of neuroeconomics. The neuroeconomic approach combines the rigorous experimental paradigms from behavioral economics with psychological principles and neuroimaging techniques to identify the brain regions that are recruited during decision making (Camerer, 2008; Camerer, Loewenstein, & Prelec, 2005; Kahneman, 2003). By acknowledging the computational limits of memory systems and the role of affect, neuroeconomists aim to fine-tune theories of decision making. To them, deviations from the canonical self-interest model are clues to the underlying neurobiological basis of choice (De Martino, Kumaran, Seymour, & Dolan, 2006; Loewenstein, Rick, & Cohen, 2008). A recent finding in this respect is that prosocial and selfish decisions are processed much like any other choice that brings pleasure, and that they are the result of a reward-seeking brain (Fehr & Camerer, 2007). When choice behavior can further be shown to vary at the neural level in response to different experimental conditions, it may be possible to unravel the different psychological drivers of human decisions. This allows us to measure the relative contributions of emotions (e.g., compassion) versus cognition (e.g., strategizing) to the decision-making process.

In addition to opening the black box of the multiple motives that underlie the same behavior, neuroscience has begun to reveal how neural functioning is influenced by culture (Chiao & Cheon, 2010), individual differences (Nash, Gianotti, & Knoch, 2015), and values

(Declerck et al., 2013). Even evolutionary ancient limbic regions of the brain, as well as evolutionary conserved endocrine systems, show differential responses to environmental stimuli depending on one's culture, which again attests to the fact that brain circuits are malleable. In this way, neuroeconomics also corroborates that our genetic heritage lies not in hardwiring psychological processes, but in the capacity to learn them and to change them when necessary.

1.5 SUMMARY

To conclude this chapter, the ubiquity of foregoing personal gains in favor of moral sentiments such as sympathy or compassion suggests that prosocial behavior is unlikely to be irrational. But that does not mean that prosociality is our default *modus operandi*, or that self-interest is a myth. Both are part and parcel of our human nature. They exist in each and every one of us because evolution endowed us with multiple psychological motives which at times conflict. To solve the conflict, evolutionary old motivational-emotional systems in the brain are supported by heuristics that continue to be shaped by life experiences and remain sensitive to environmental cues. Two such heuristics lead to alternative routes to cooperation. The first route is economically rational and relies on extrinsic incentives that align self-and collective interest and thereby objectively achieve a goal transformation: cooperation that was once costly has become an attractive and lucrative option! Self-enhancement is the motivation to cooperate under the umbrella of economic rationality. The second route to cooperation is socially rational and the result of gene-culture co-evolutionary processes that shaped heuristics to facilitate cooperation by which to improve the welfare and survival chances of the group. These socially rational heuristics indirectly achieve group success by triggering decisions that fulfil an individual's immediate need to belong and provide pleasure from social interaction. Social inclusion yielding emotional gratification is the motivation to cooperate under social rationality. However, socially rational cooperation is contingent on trust. Social cues that induce trust subjectively transform situations of uncertainty to expectations of reciprocity and gratifying social relationships.

Thus, through evolution we inherited two core psychological motives and a flexible brain that makes it possible to value alternative decision outcomes *as if* we were computing expected utility functions.

The subjective value of the outcome will be based on boundedly rational decisions, following an economically rational cost/benefit analysis of the presence/absence of cooperative incentives, and a socially rational analysis of our relation to others and their degree of trustworthiness. Both self-interested decisions (economically rational) and selfless (socially rational) decisions can be based on heuristics or reflection, and may include elements of strategy and affect. In the chapters that follow, we will investigate how prosocial and self-interested choices are valued at the neural level and moderated in accordance with the presence or absence of extrinsic incentives, internalized social norms, and/or trust. We will show that we are wired for both types of rationality and that, for the brain, self-interest and prosocial behavior do not have to be paradoxical. We are all compassionate egoists.

REFERENCES

Andreoni, J., & Miller, J. H. (2002). Giving according to GARP: An experimental test of the consistency of preferences for altruism. *Econometrica*, *70*, 737–753.

Arrow, K. J. (1974). *The Limits of Organizations*. New York: Norton.

Axelrod, R., & Hamilton, W. D. (1981). The evolution of cooperation. *Science*, *211*, 1390–1396.

Balliet, D. (2010). Communication and cooperation in social dilemmas: A meta-analytic review. *Journal of Conflict Resolution*, *54*, 39–57.

Balliet, D., & Van Lange, P. A. M. (2013). Trust, conflict, and cooperation: A meta-analysis. *Psychological Bulletin*, *139*, 1090–1112.

Barclay, P. (2012). Proximate and ultimate causes of punishment and strong reciprocity. *Behavioral and Brain Sciences*, *35*, 16–17.

Baumeister, R. F., & Leary, M. R. (1995). The need to belong. Desire for interpersonal attachments as a fundamental human motivation. *Psychological Bulletin*, *117*, 487–527.

Bereczkei, T., Birkas, B., & Kerekes, Z. (2007). Public charity offer as a proximate factor of evolved reputation-building strategy: an experimental analysis of a real-life situation. *Evolution and Human Behavior*, *28*, 277–284.

Berg, J., Dickhaut, J., & McCabe, K. (1995). Trust, reciprocity, and social history. *Games and Economic Behavior*, *10*, 122–142.

Bohnet, I., Greig, F., Herrmann, B., & Zeckhauser, R. (2008). Betrayal aversion: Evidence from Brazil, China, Oman, Switzerland, Turkey, and the United States. *American Economic Review*, *98*, 294–310.

Boone, C., De Brabander, B., & Van Witteloostuijn, A. (1999). Locus of control and strategic behaviour in a prisoner's dilemma game. *Personality and Individual Differences*, *20*, 695–706.

Boone, C., Declerck, C. H., & Kiyonari, T. (2010). Inducing cooperative behavior among proselfs versus prosocials: The moderating role of incentives and trust. *Journal of Conflict Resolution*, *54*, 799–824.

Boone, C., Declerck, C. H., & Suetens, S. (2008). Subtle social cues, explicit incentives and cooperation in social dilemmas. *Evolution and Human Behavior*, *29*, 179–188.

Bornstein, G. (2003). Intergroup conflict: Individual, group, and collective interests. *Personality and Social Psychology Review*, *7*, 129–145.

Bowles, S., & Gintis, H. (2003). Origins of human cooperation. In P. Hammerstein (Ed.), *Genetic and Cultural Evolution of Cooperation* (pp. 429–443). Cambridge, Massachusetts: MIT Press.

Bowles, S., & Gintis, H. (2011). *A Cooperative Species. Human Reciprocity and its Evolution.* Princeton, New Jersey: Princeton University Press.

Boyd, R., & Richerson, P. (2000). The Pleistocene and the origins of human culture: Built for speed. *Perspectives in Ecology*, *13*, 1–45.

Brosnan, S. F., & Bshary, R. (2010). Cooperation and deception: From evolution to mechanisms. *Philosophical Transactions of the Royal Society. Series B, Biological Sciences*, *365*, 2593–2598.

Bshary, R., Hohner, A., Ait-El-Djoudi, K., & Fricke, H. (2006). Interspecific communicative and coordinated hunting between groupers and giant moray eels in the Red Sea. *PLoS Biology*, *4*, 2393–2398.

Burkart, J. M., Allon, O., Amici, F., Fichtel, C., Finkenwirth, C., Heschl, A., ... van Schaik, C. P. (2014). The evolutionary origin of human hyper-cooperation. *Nature Communication*, *5*, 4747.

Burnham, T., McCabe, K., & Smith, V. L. (2000). Friend-or-foe intentionality priming in an extensive form trust game. *Journal of Economic Behavior & Organization*, *43*, 57–73.

Camerer, C. F. (2008). Neuroeconomics: Opening the gray box. *Neuron*, *60*, 416–419.

Camerer, C. F., & Fehr, E. (2006). When does "economic man" dominate social behavior? *Science*, *311*, 47–52.

Camerer, C. F., Loewenstein, G., & Prelec, D. (2005). Neuroeconomics: How neuroscience can inform economics. *Journal of Economic Literature*, *43*, 9–64.

Caporael, L. R., Dawes, R. M., Orbell, J. M., & Vandekragt, A. J. C. (1989). Selfishness examined—cooperation in the absence of egoistic incentives. *Behavioral and Brain Sciences*, *12*, 683–699.

Chiao, J. Y., & Cheon, B. K. (2010). The weirdest brains in the world. (Commentary on Henrich, Heine, & Norenzayan, 2010). *Behavioral and Brain Sciences*, *33*, 88–90.

Cole, T., & Teboul, J. C. B. (2004). Non-zero-sum collaboration, reciprocity, and the preference for similarity: Developing an adaptive model of close relational functioning. *Personal Relationships*, *11*, 135–160.

Cronk, L., & Leech, B. L. (2013). *Meeting at Grand Central. Understanding the Social and Evolutionary Roots of Cooperation*. Princeton, New Jersey: Princeton University Press.

Dahrendorf, R. (1973). *Homo Sociologicus*. London: Routledge and Kegan Paul.

Darwin, C. (1871/2007). *The Descent of Man in Relation to Sex. The concise edition*. Selections and commentary by Carl Zimmer. Foreword by Frans De Waal. New York: PLUME, Penguin Group.

Dawkins, R. (1976). *The Selfish Gene*. Oxford: Oxford University Press.

DeBruine, L. M. (2002). Facial resemblance enhances trust. *Proceedings of the Royal Society of London Series B-Biological Sciences*, *269*, 1307–1312.

Declerck, C. H., Boone, C., & Emonds, G. (2013). When do people cooperate in social dilemmas? A review on the neuroeconomics of prosocial decision-making. *Brain & Cognition*, *81*, 95–117.

De Martino, B., Kumaran, D., Seymour, B., & Dolan, R. J. (2006). Frames, biases, and rational decision-making in the human brain. *Science*, *313*, 684–687.

Diamond, J. (2013). *The World Until Yesterday*. London: Allen Lane.

Evans, J. S. B. T. (2008). Dual processing accounts of reasoning, judgment, and social cognition. *Annual Review of Psychology*, *59*, 255–278.

Fehr, E., & Camerer, C. F. (2007). Social neuroeconomics: The neural circuitry of social preferences. *Trends in Cognitive Sciences*, *11*, 419–427.

Fehr, E., & Fischbacher, U. (2003). The nature of human altruism. *Nature*, *425*, 785–791.

Fehr, E., & Gachter, S. (2002). Altruistic punishment in humans. *Nature*, *415*, 137–140.

Fehr, E., & Henrich, J. (2003). Is strong reciprocity a maladaptation? On the evolutionary foundations of human altruism. In P. Hammerstein (Ed.), *Genetic and Cultural Evolution of Cooperation*. Cambridge, Massachusetts: MIT Press.

Fehr, E., & Rockenbach, B. (2004). Human altruism: Economic, neural, and evolutionary perspectives. *Current Opinion in Neurobiology*, *14*, 784–790.

Fehr, E., & Schmidt, K. M. (1999). A theory of fairness, competition, and cooperation. *Quarterly Journal of Economics*, *114*, 817–868.

Fiske, S. T. (2004). *Social beings: A Core Motives Approach to Social Psychology*. Hoboken, NJ: Wiley.

Frank, R. H. (2012). *The Darwin Economy. Liberty, Competition, and the Common Good.* Princeton, New Jersey: Princeton University Press.

Gigerenzer, G., Todd, P. M., & The ABC Research Group (1999). *Simple Heuristics that Make Us Smart*. New York: Oxford University Press.

Gintis, H., Bowles, S., Boyd, R., & Fehr, E. (2003). Explaining altruistic behavior in humans. *Evolution and Human Behavior*, *24*, 153–172.

Guala, F. (2012). Reciprocity: Weak or strong? What punishment experiments do (and do not) demonstrate. *Behavioral and Brain Sciences*, *35*, 1–59.

Gürerk, O., Irlenbusch, B., & Rockenbach, B. (2006). The competitive advantage of sanctioning institutions. *Science*, *312*, 108–111.

Haidt, J. (2012). *The Righteous Mind. Why Good People are Divided by Politics and Religion*. New York: Pantheon.

Hardin, G. (1968). The tragedy of the commons. *Science*, *162*, 1243–1248.

Hardy, C. L., & Van Vugt, M. (2006). Nice guys finish first: The competitive altruism hypothesis. *Personality and Social Psychology Bulletin*, *32*, 1402–1413.

Haselton, M. G., & Buss, D. M. (2000). Error management theory: A new perspective on biases in cross -sex mind reading. *Journal of Personality and Social Psychology*, *78*, 81–91.

Henrich, J., Boyd, R., Bowles, S., Camerer, C., Fehr, E., Gintis, H., ... Henrich, N. (2005). "Economic man" in cross-cultural perspective: Behavioral experiments in 15 small-scale societies. *Behavioral and Brain Sciences*, *28*, 795–855.

Henrich, J., Heine, S. J., & Norenzayan, A. (2010). The weirdest people in the world. *Behavioral and Brain Sciences*, *33*, 61–135.

Henrich, J., McElreath, R., Barr, A., Ensminger, J., Barrett, C., Bolyanatz, A., ... Ziker, J. (2006). Costly punishment across human societies. *Science*, *312*, 1767–1770.

Herrmann, B., Thoni, C., & Gachter, S. (2008). Antisocial punishment across societies. *Science*, *319*, 1362–1367.

Hoffman, E., McCabe, K., & Smith, V. L. (1996). Social distance and other-regarding behavior in dictator games. *American Economic Review*, *86*, 653–660.

Hrdy, S. B. (2009). *Mothers and Others. The Evolutionary Origins of Mutual Understanding*. Cambridge, Massachusetss: The Belknap Press of Harvard University Press.

Jacob, F. (1977). Evolution and tinkering. *Science*, *196*, 1161–1166.

Kahneman, D. (2003). Maps of bounded rationality: Psychology for behavioral economics. *American Economic Review*, *93*, 1449–1475.

Kahneman, D. (2011). *Thinking Fast and Slow*. New York: Farrar, Straus and Giroux.

Kiesler, S., Sproull, L., & Waters, K. (1996). A prisoner's dilemma experiment on cooperation with people and human-like computers. *Journal of Personality and Social Psychology*, *70*, 47–65.

Kiyonari, T., Tanida, S., & Yamagishi, T. (2000). Social exchange and reciprocity: Confusion or a heuristic? *Evolution and Human Behavior*, *21*(411), 427.

Kurzban, R., DeScioli, P., & O'Brien, E. (2007). Audience effects on moralistic punishment. *Evolution and Human Behavior*, *28*, 75–84.

Lewontin, R. C. (1970). The units of selection. *Annual Review of Ecology and Systematics*, *1*, 1–18.

Loewenstein, G., Rick, S., & Cohen, J. D. (2008). Neuroeconomics. *Annual Review of Psychology*, *59*, 647–672.

Nash, K., Gianotti, L. R., & Knoch, D. (2015). A neural trait approach to exploring individual differences in social preferences. *Frontiers in Behavioral Neuroscience*, *8*, 458.

Newson, L., & Richerson, P. J. (2009). Why do people become modern? A Darwinian explananation. *Population and Development Review*, *35*, 117–158.

Nowak, M. A., & Highfield, R. (2011). *SuperCooperators: Altruism, Evolution, and Why We Need Each Other to Succeed*. New York: Free Press.

Nowak, M. A., & Sigmund, K. (1998). Evolution and indirect reciprocity by image scoring. *Nature*, *393*, 573–577.

Nowak, M. A., & Sigmund, K. (2005). Evolution of indirect reciprocity. *Nature*, *437*, 1291–1298.

Olson, M. (1971/1965). *The Logic of Collective Action: Public Goods and the Theory of Groups (Revised edition ed.)*. Cambridge, Massachusetts: Harvard University Press.

Ostrom, E. (2009). A general framework for analyzing sustainability of social-ecological systems. *Science*, *325*, 419–422.

Panksepp, J., & Panksepp, J. B. (2000). The seven sins of evolutionary psychology. *Evolution and Cognition*, *6*, 108–131.

Persky, J. (1995). Retrospectives: The ethology of Homo economicus. *The Journal of Economic Perspectives*, *9*, 221–231.

Piazza, J., & Bering, J. M. (2008). Concerns about reputation via gossip promote generous allocations in an economic game. *Evolution and Human Behavior*, *29*, 172–178.

Pinker, S. (2012). The false allure of group selection. Edge. Retreived from <http://edge.org/conversation/the-false-allure-of-group-selection>.

Potters, J., & Suetens, S. (2006). Cooperation in experimental games of strategic complements and substitutes. *Review of Economic Studies*, *76*, 1125–1147.

Pruitt, D. G., & Kimmel, M. J. (1977). Twenty years of experimental gaming: Critique, synthesis, and suggestions for the future. *Annual Review of Psychology*, *28*, 363–392.

Rand, D. G., Peysakhovich, A., Kraft-Todd, G. T., Newman, G. E., Wurzbacher, O., Nowak, M. A., et al. (2014). Social heuristics shape intuitive cooperation. *Nature Communications*, *5*, 3677.

Rapoport, A., & Chammah, A. (1965). *The Prisoner's Dilemma*. Ann Arbor: University of Michigan Press.

Reuben, E., & Suetens, S. (2012). Revisiting strategic versus non-strategic cooperation. *Experimental Economics*, *15*, 24–43.

Richerson, P., Baldini, R., Bell, A., Demps, K., Frost, K., Hillis, V., ... Zefferman, M. (2015). Cultural group selection plays an essential role in explaining human cooperation: A sketch of the evidence. *Behavioral and Brain Sciences*, Available on CJO2014. http://dx.doi.org/10.1017/S0140525X1400106X.

Richerson, P. J., Boyd, R., & Bettinger, R. L. (2001). Was agriculture impossible during the Pleistocene but mandatory during the Holocene? A climate change hypothesis. *American Antiquity*, *66*, 381–411.

Rotter, J. B. (1980). Interpersonal trust, trustworthiness, and gullibility. *American Psychologist*, *35*, 1–7.

Rustagi, D., Engel, S., & Kosfeld, M. (2010). Conditional cooperation and costly monitoring explain success in forest commons management. *Science*, *330*, 961–965.

Simpson, B. (2004). Social values, subjective transformations, and cooperation in social dilemmas. *Social Psychology Quarterly*, *67*, 385–395.

Smaldino, P. E., Newson, L., Schank, J. C., & Richerson, P. J. (2013). Simulating the evolution of the human family: Cooperative breeding increases in harsh environments. *PLoS ONE*, *8*, e80753.

Sober, E., & Wilson, D. S. (1998). *Unto Others. The Evolution and Psychology of Unselfish Behavior*. Cambridge, Massachusetts: Harvard University Press.

Tajfel, H., Billig, M., Bundy, R. P., & Flament, C. (1971). Social categorization and intergroup behavior. *European Journal of Social Psychology*, *1*, 149–177.

Thompson, L., Kray, L. J., & Lind, E. A. (1998). Cohesion and respect: An examination of group decision making in social and escalation dilemmas. *Journal of Experimental Social Psychology*, *34*, 289–311.

Tinbergen, N. (1968). On war and peace in animals and man. *Science*, *160*, 1411–1418.

Tomasello, M. (2009). *Why We Cooperate*. Cambridge, Massachusetts: MIT Press.

Trivers, R. L. (1971). The evolution of reciprocal altruism. *Quarterly Review of Biology*, *46*, 35–47.

Williams, G. C. (1966). *Adaptation and Natural Selection*. Princeton University Press.

Williams, K. D. (2007). Ostracism. *Annual Review of Psychology*, *58*, 425–452.

Wilson, E. O. (1971). *The Insect Societies*. Cambridge, Massachusetts: Harvard University Press.

Yamagishi, T. (2011). *Trust, the Evolutionary Game of Mind and Society*. New York: Springer.

Yamagishi, T., & Sato, K. (1986). Motivational bases of the public goods problem. *Journal of Personality and Social Psychology*, *50*, 67–73.

Yamagishi, T., Terai, S., Kiyonari, T., Mifune, N., & Kanazawa, S. (2007). The social exchange heuristic: Managing errors in social exchange. *Rationality and Society*, *19*, 259–291.

Zahavi, A. (1975). Mate selection—a selection for handicap. *Journal of Theoretical Biology*, *53*, 205–214.

CHAPTER 2

The Neuroanatomy of Prosocial Decision Making: The Role of Valuation, Cognitive Control, and Social Cognition

Integrating neuroscience with the study of decision making has been a milestone in our understanding of human social behavior and has generated a wealth of new knowledge that is still steadily increasing as new research tools and techniques become available. The tradition of trying to understand the neural basis for social decisions finds its origin in the study of brain lesions, which made it possible to uncover basic brain-function relationships. A classic example is the 1848 case of the American railroad construction foreman, Phineas Gage, who survived a rock explosion that drove an iron rod through his left frontal lobe. This tragic accident left Gage's cognitive and motor functions intact, but it had a major impact on his personality and social conduct, causing him to lose his job and become socially estranged. Decades later, neurologists including Antonio and Hanna Damasio and Antoine Bechara recognized similar social deficits in psychiatric patients with brain lesions or tumors, prompting them to map the anatomical regions that make successful social interactions possible, thereby setting the stage for the field of decision neuroscience. Their aim was to "explore the neural *road map* for the physiological processes intervening between knowledge and behavior, and the potential interruptions that lead to a disconnection between what one knows and what one decides to do."[1]

Parallel to the developments in medical decision neuroscience, a small group of economists started to challenge the long-held view of classical economics that motives could not be observed and should therefore be excluded from the study of choice behavior. These behavioral economists drew attention to the fact that the assumptions of

[1]Quote from A. Bechara's personal webpage, University of Southern California Undergraduate Neuroscience program.

Neuroeconomics of Prosocial Behavior. DOI: http://dx.doi.org/10.1016/B978-0-12-801303-8.00002-1

modeling “rational decision making” with expected utility theory[2] are seldom met in real life. By acknowledging the importance of emotions, predispositions, and the computational limits of human memory, they wanted to account for the so-called anomalies in “rational” decision making. This led to the birth of neuroeconomics, a research field that combines imaging techniques with economic models to unravel how people *in real life* choose a course of action given multiple alternatives. As described below, neuroeconomics was inspired by three streams of thinking (see also Glimcher, Camerer, Fehr, & Poldrack, 2009):

1. Proponents of Herbert Simon’s idea of “bounded rationality” called for an ecological understanding of computation, whereby decision outcomes would not be *maximized*, but rather *satisficed*. Following an algorithm in the form of “always choose in terms of the *highest* utility” is too demanding for the human brain, given the tremendous amount of information that would need to be objectively considered to define what *highest* means. Within the framework of a computationally bounded mind, decisions can be guided by, often subconscious, evolutionary molded and/or experience based decision-rules or heuristics, which could bypass certain complex algorithmic decision-making processes and bias outcomes in favor of “quick and frugal” adaptive solutions.
2. The series of experiments by Daniel Kahneman and Amos Tversky convincingly demonstrated biases in decision making, revealing that decision makers were sensitive to “framing effects” across a wide range of situations (Kahneman & Tversky, 1984; Tversky & Kahneman, 1981). This defied once and for all the invariance principle (see footnote 2) and made clear that the choices people make are tremendously influenced by how these choices are described. Thus, decision makers’ expected utility functions needed to incorporate psychological and psychophysical parameters such as reference dependency. The clear message that emerged from their experiments is that when modeling decisions, context matters!

[2]Initiated by Daniel Bernouilli in the 1800s, the idea is that “rational” decisions (in the narrow sense of classical economics) with uncertain outcomes are made on the basis of their expected value, or the statistical expectation of an individual’s valuation of the outcome. Possible alternatives are then compared, and the outcome with the highest utility should always be chosen. The expected utility theory also supposes that rational decision making is defined by a number of axioms, such as the invariance principle. This is the most controversial one and states that the order in which alternatives are presented should not influence outcomes. Only if this and other axioms are satisfied can the decision makers’ preferences be modeled with classical economic utility functions.

3. Behavioral economists recognized that preferences need not be restricted to material self-interest, because many decision makers have social preferences and take into account the impact of their choice on others. Considering the dependency of humans on group living, the influence of social preferences on decision making is unlikely to be irrational from an ecological point of view. Instead, a prosocial decision (one that impacts others positively) would be favored if the *subjective* value an individual ascribes to the outcome of this decision outweighs the value ascribed to the outcome of an antisocial decision. The message here is that when analyzing choice behavior, individual differences also matter.

Neuroeconomics adds to the behavioral economics perspective by revealing that the underlying mechanisms of valuation is a reward-seeking brain whose function it is to integrate contextual information with personal values to arrive at a decision that matches one's anticipated individual expectation. In this chapter, we rely on the current state of the art in neuroeconomics to propose a conceptual model for prosocial decisions. The model is derived from the results of experiments that corroborate the influence of context on choice behavior. Before elaborating on the model, we first describe some of the more commonly used research tools used in neuroeconomics (Section 2.1.1) and we summarize some basic principles of brain organization (Section 2.1.2).

2.1 OPENING THE "BLACK BOX" OF DECISION MAKING

2.1.1 Neuroeconomic Methods

A major aim of neuroeconomics is to understand the physiological and neural mechanisms underlying decision making. This is done by conducting simple experiments whereby participants are asked to decide on alternative outcomes under very controlled conditions. When the decisions to be made are set in a social context, the experiments typically rely on game-theoretic paradigms such as the public goods game and prisoner's dilemma described in Chapter 1, in which incentives are provided. In a typical experiment, the proportion of prosocial versus antisocial decisions is then analyzed as a function of the experimental manipulations (such as the type of incentive) and the effect of this manipulation on decision making is then related to a biological measure (such as galvanic skin response, hormone levels, or brain activity). Joseph Kable offers a good review on the cognitive neuroscientist toolkits that are available to neuroeconomists (Kable, 2011).

The technology to produce functional brain images has made for much progress in neuroeconomics. The onset of functional magnetic resonance imaging (fMRI), in particular, has brought about a surge of data. This technique makes use of the fact that hemoglobin, the iron-containing oxygen-carrier in the blood, behaves differently under changing magnetic fields depending on whether blood is oxygenated or deoxygenated. Brain regions that are rich in oxygenated blood point to increased blood flow to that region and thus increased metabolic needs. From this correlation, neuronal activity is indirectly inferred. In an fMRI study, experimental subjects are asked to perform a choice task under the scanner and the change in blood flow (the hemodynamic response, or blood oxygen level dependent (BOLD) signal) is continuously imaged and matched with the time course of the experiment.

While fMRI is useful to visualize indirectly neuronal activity in the cell bodies, or gray matter, of the brain, it cannot reveal how different neurons are structurally connected. For this, diffusion tensor imaging (DTI) is the appropriate technique. These experiments are also conducted under an MRI scanner, but an image is created based on the diffusion perturbations of hydrogen molecules that are caused by axon bundles within the white matter of brain tissue. Based on measures of diffusion anisotropy, a tractography or visual representation of neural tracts within the brain can be generated.

Functional images of the brain can also be obtained by positron emission tomography, or PET scans, but this is a more invasive technique in comparison to MRI, and is thus less commonly used for research purposes. The three-dimensional PET image is produced by a computer detecting gamma rays indirectly emitted from a radionuclide that was introduced into the brain on a biologically active substrate (often a glucose analog). The concentrations of the tracer that are imaged in a particular brain region are indicative of metabolic activity in that region by virtue of its glucose uptake.

In contrast to functional imaging by means of fMRI or PET, which correlate decision outcomes with brain activity, repetitive transcranial magnetic stimulation (rTMS) is a technique used to ascribe a cause-and-effect function to a brain location. By holding an electromagnetic coil above an experimental subject's skull and transmitting repetitive electromagnetic pulses into the brain, neurons just a few centimeters below the magnet become depolarized or hyperpolarized, altering their function. The cognitive changes that occur while a specific part of the brain is being affected can then be noted.

Electroencephalography (EEG) and its variant, event-related potentials (ERP), are techniques that have been around much longer (before the 1950s). They continue to be used regularly in research because of their low cost, ease of application, and their very good temporal (within millisecond range) resolution. EEG measures the voltage fluctuations along the scalp that result from underlying electrical neuronal activity. With ERP, the EEG activity in response to a particular stimulus is averaged over many trials to differentiate the relevant waveform (the ERP) from random brain activity.

Lesion studies, which comprise the oldest of the neuroscientists' methodology, have continued to be a popular research tool. Their main advantage lies in the fact that they can provide proof of necessity of a particular brain region if damage to that region shows a breakdown of its presumed function. The damage can be derived from different sources, including stroke, degenerative diseases (e.g., Alzheimer's disease or frontotemporal dementia), neurosurgical tumor removals or corpus callostomy, and head injuries (e.g., the classic Phineas Gage example described at the beginning of this chapter). Typically, a group of patients with similar lesions are compared to both a group of healthy individuals (the "normal controls") and a group of patients with lesions in other brain regions that are not likely to be associated with the presumed function. The second control group serves to rule out potential confounds due to comorbidity. Practically, it is often difficult to obtain a sufficiently large population size to test hypotheses regarding the function of a specific and isolated brain region. But the technology has proven very successful in assessing differences in broad patterns, such as the difference between left- and right hemisphere functions.

Not all neuroeconomic methods target the brain. Often physiological measures such as heart rate, blood pressure, and skin conductance are useful as proxies for arousal and emotional responses, because they are indicative of sympathetic nervous system activity.

Finally, because the brain-function relationship does not entirely depend on brain anatomy but equally, or even more so, on brain chemistry, an entire stream of neuroeconomics focuses on neurotransmitter activity and/or endocrine effects. Neurochemical changes associated with decision making can be inferred by assaying hormone levels or neurotransmitter metabolites in response to certain stimuli, or by pharmacological manipulations of these chemical messengers. In particular, the neurotransmitters dopamine and serotonin, the opioids, and the hormones oxytocin, vasopressin, and testosterone are known to play an important role in social decision making. This will be the topic of Chapter 3.

2.1.2 Functional Organization of the Brain

The case of Phineas Gage (see introduction) was perhaps one of the first formal documentations of the relation between mind and brain, illustrating that damage to specific regions affect social behavior and may even induce lasting personality changes. Current theories on how the brain works include elements of modularity (i.e., the idea that there are a number of domain-specific regions in the brain that encapsulate a particular cognitive function) and distributive processing (i.e., the idea that cognitive functions are the result of integrated information-processing in highly interconnected brain regions). In order to better understand how the brain is functionally organized to make complex social decisions we outline in this section some of the very basic principles of brain anatomy.

The brain can superficially be divided into an outer portion, or cortex, and the subcortical regions lying below it (see Figure 2.1A). As one moves from the outer to the inner layers of the brain, the functions become increasingly more primitive (in the sense that we share these functions with all mammals) and require less conscious control. For example, the limbic system, which lies mostly subcortically, includes the amygdala, a major center of emotion processing and conditioned learning. The striatum, also lying beneath the cortex, comprises the putamen and the caudate which are primarily responsible for body movements and motor control. However, the caudate and ventral part of the striatum also have roles in motivation, learning, and emotion. The neocortex is the most recently evolved part of the brain and is essential for attention, sensory perception, memory, language, thought, and consciousness. In humans, 90% of the cortex consists of neocortex, which differs at the cellular level from the evolutionary older allocortex by having 6 layers. The neocortex may have expanded greatly during primate evolution as a response to living in increasingly larger groups which bring about more complex social interactions (Dunbar, 1998).

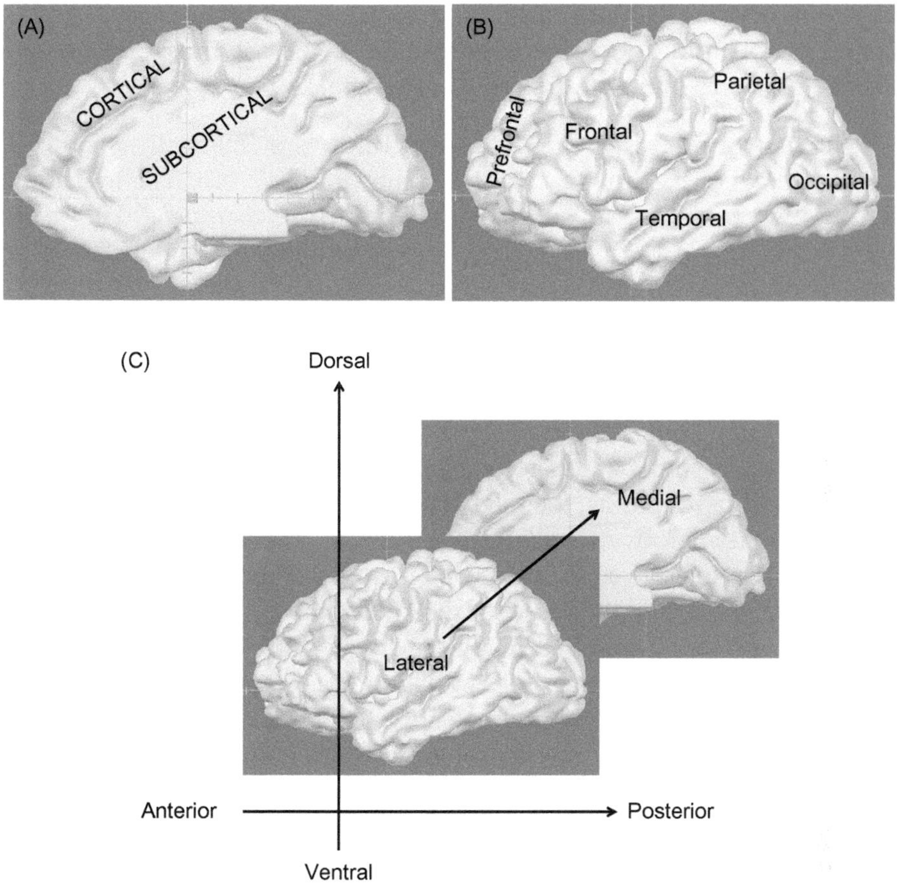

Figure 2.1 Principles of brain anatomy. (A) Evolutionary older subcortical regions lie below the cortex, the bulk of which comprises the phylogenetically newer neocortex. (B) The 5 lobes of the neocortex. (C) Principle brain axes.

The neocortex is subdivided into four lobes (Figure 2.1B). The occipital lobe, at the very back of the head, is entirely devoted to visual processing. Because it serves only this one function, it reflects most closely the modular specialization of the brain. The more dorsally located parietal lobe, (at the top of the head) integrates sensory information among many modalities, including spatial relations and touch. Below the parietal lobe lies the temporal lobe which processes auditory and visual stimuli. It is involved in the recognition of objects, memory, thought, and language. Finally, the frontal lobe includes the motor cortex and endows us with cognition and the capacity to self-regulate behavior. Especially the prefrontal area is of key importance when it comes to planning complex cognitive behavior (referring to the so-called "executive functions") and decision making.

The prefrontal cortex (PFC) is furthermore systematically organized around the three cardinal axes of the brain (Figure 2.1C). The longitudinal axis is known as the "anterior-posterior" (or "rostral-caudal") axis, the vertical axis runs from the top (known as the "dorsal" or "superior region" of the brain) to the bottom (known as the "ventral" or "inferior" region), and the transverse axis divides the brain between outer or "lateral" regions, and an inner or "medial" section. A functional map of the PFC reveals gradients, or systematic differences in functions associated with the locale along these axes (reviewed in O'Reilly, 2010), which may have important implications for understanding how we make decisions. Along the transverse axis, the medial areas tend to be more directly connected to limbic motivational/affective systems, whereas the lateral areas tend to be more involved in sensory/motor processing. This has led to the uncontroversial characterization of the lateral cortex as the site of "cold" cognition and the medial PFC as the site responsible for "hot" emotions and drives. The predominant interpretation of the anterior-posterior gradient is that more abstract and categorical information is processed in anterior regions, while the posterior regions are increasingly engaged as task- or rule complexity increases. Along the dorsal-ventral gradient of the PFC there appears to be some dissociation between the ventral parts which primarily process the meaning of incoming information ("what is it?") versus the dorsal parts that are concerned with turning perception into action ("how is it done?"). The functional differentiation along this axis emerges because the PFC interacts with the two distinct visual pathways[3] that run through the brain. A current interpretation is that the ventrolateral PFC exerts cognitive control on the ventral visual stream which runs through the temporal cortex, thereby facilitating the identification of "what" something is. It does this by exerting a top-down bias on the selection of semantic representations in the temporal cortex. The dorsolateral PFC, in contrast, exerts cognitive control on the dorsal visual stream which runs through the parietal cortex and is primarily concerned with spatial relationships. Because dorsolateral PFC regions are widely

[3]The ventral and dorsal visual pathways were proposed by Goodale and Milner (1992) to represent the "what" and "where" processing of visual information that exits the occipital lobe. The cellular basis of the ventrally located "what" and dorsally located "where" neural pathways were earlier described by Mishkin and Ungerleider (1982).

reported in action-selection and rule-based tasks, it is suggested that it provides a top-down bias transforming a wide range of sensory perceptions into appropriate motor actions (O'Reilly, 2010).

These differentiated and distinguishable top-down functions of the PFC are a prime example of the distributive processing properties of the brain. Human decision making is a complex function that draws heavily on integrating information through cortico-cortical connections between the dorsolateral PFC and the medial frontal cortex, as well as on subcortical projections from those two regions to the limbic system and the striatum. In particular, inputs from cortico-amygdala-striatal circuits (Cho, Ernst, & Fudge, 2013) may be crucial for decision-making in the social domain. In Table 2.1 we summarize some of the general functions of both cortical and subcortical regions that are likely functioning as "hubs" in these circuits and therefore implicated in deciding whether or not to act prosocially. We include in the table all those regions that are of importance in developing the model of prosocial decision-making in Section 2.2. In addition, we include the anterior insula, a region that is not further discussed in this chapter, but which will be mentioned several times later on in this book in relation to fairness considerations (Chapter 4) and empathic responding (Chapters 3 and 5). The insular cortex is considered by some researchers to be an entirely distinct lobe comprising 2% of the cortex. It is situated in the depth of the Sylvian fissure, in between the temporal and the parietal cortex, and is implicated in an astonishingly large number of functions, ranging from pain perception to speech production and processing of social emotions (Nieuwenhuys, 2012).

2.2 A MODEL FOR (PRO)SOCIAL DECISION MAKING BASED ON INCENTIVES AND TRUST

In Chapter 1 we described how prosocial decisions are valued on two accounts: (1) the self-enhancing value of the prosocial act, based on a material cost–benefit analysis, (2) the value placed on one's relationship with the beneficiaries of the prosocial act, based on social rewards rather than profits. The decision outcome of valuation (1) is economically rational and facilitated by a simple decision rule: "*I am selfish unless there are cooperative incentives.*" The valuation behind (2) reflects a more socially oriented rationality yielding affective (rather than economic) rewards. As described in Chapter 1, this heuristic only works if there are sufficient others in the group deciding by the same rule.

Table 2.1 Legend: Functions Related to Prosocial Behaviors that are Attributed to Brain Regions Discussed in this Chapter and in the Rest of this Book

Brain Region		Function in Prosocial Behavior	Relevant Reference
frontal lobe	dorsal ACC	conflict detection and monitoring; recruits lateral PFC to resolve conflicts; link with cognitive control during empathic response.	Carter & van Veen, 2007; Carter, Botvinick, & Cohen, 2004.
	lateral PFC	working memory and executive functions; planning and cost/benefit analysis; top-down modulation of motivational processes; impulse control.	Miller & Cohen, 2001; McClure et al., 2004 ; Mesulam 1998; Weisman, Perkins, & Woldorff, 2008.
	dorsomedial PFC	trait inferencing; mentalizing about other's thoughts and intentions; representing and integrating different types of social information with cognitive decision-making.	Amodio & Frith, 2006; Frith & Frith, 2006; Van Overwalle, 2009; Van Overwalle & Baetens, 2009.
	ventromedial PFC / orbitofrontal cortex	integrates affective, homeostatic, and sensory information into response selection; emotion regulation; encoding the salience of a reward; computing expected value of decision-outcome.	Bartra et al., 2013; Fellows, 2007; Kringelbach & Rolls, 2004; Levy & Glimcher, 2012.
insular cortex	anterior insula	homeostatic alerting to emotional stimuli; perceiving one's own and other's pain; empathy; fairness considerations and betrayal aversion.	Aimone, Houser, & Weber, 2014; Buckzolz & Marois, 2012; Nieuwenhuys, 2012; Palminteri et al., 2012; Sanfey, Rilling, Aronson, Nystrom, & Cohen 2003.
temporal / parietal junction	superior temporal sulcus (STS)	inferring intentions of others at a more perceptual level; implicit impression formation; moral judgments.	Van Overwalle, 2009; Van Overwalle & Baetens, 2009; Frith & Frith, 2006; Winston et al., 2002; Singer et al., 2004.
subcortical	amygdala	enhancing perceptual processing, especially of threatning signals; processing happy and angry faces; assessing trustworthiness; fear conditioning	Anderson & Phelps, 2001; Engell et al., 2007; Le Doux, 2003.
	ventral striatum (nucleus accumbens)	valuation; comparing actual with expected rewards; computing experienced decision utility; generating the "warm glow of giving."	Abler et al., 2006; Bartra et al., 2013; Fehr & Camerer, 2007; Harbaugh et al., 2007.
	dorsal striatum (caudate nucleus)	instrumental and value-based learning; updating behavior.	O'Doherty et al., 2004; Cools, Clark, Owen, & Robbins, 2002; Waegeman et al., 2014.

Therefore, to be ecologically rational, realizing the expected outcome based on (2) requires trust. In other words, the subjective value expected from a prosocial act needs to be weighed by the presence of social signals that reduce the fear of betrayal in a social interaction and provide some assurance of the beneficiary's loyalty. The decision rule in this case is "*I am cooperative unless my partner is not trustworthy.*" Trust signals are vital because they help to evaluate the outcome of a cooperative decision that endorses group welfare more than it yields benefits to the self. The outcome in this case is weighed in terms of the subjective expected social rewards, rather than the material benefits.

Trust signals probably do not contribute much to prosocial decisions when extrinsic cooperative incentives are present (e.g., incentives that make cooperation economically rational by providing synergy or a good reputation). This is at least suggested by the results of an experiment that used a repeated dyadic public goods game paradigm with real monetary incentives (Boone, Declerck, & Suetens, 2008). All participants were given an initial endowment and asked if they wanted to contribute a fraction of it to a common pool (the public good). The contributions were then multiplied by a factor according to an *a priori* determined payoff structure, and redistributed among the participants. After each trial, participants received feedback about their and their partner's decisions, and thus they were well aware of the profits that accrued, both for themselves and for their partner. In this particular public goods game, payoff structures for both partners were either strategic complements (in which the optimal contribution consisted of imitating the expected contribution of the other player) or strategic substitutes (in which the optimal contribution was to decide in the direction opposite of what one expects the other player to contribute). The Nash equilibrium[4] in both games was kept the same, but only the complements game offered synergy from cooperation, thus this game elicited a strong incentive to cooperate. The experiment was set up so that half of the participants were able to meet in small groups, introduce themselves, and shake hands with their potential partners prior to the game. This short interaction was found to boost trust and significantly increased cooperation in the substitutes game. These same trust signals had no effect on the games with strategic complements where cooperation was naturally incentivized and

[4]The Nash equilibrium is the solution developed by game theorist to represent the set of strategies in non-cooperative games (e.g., the public goods or prisoner's dilemma game) whereby no player has an incentive to change strategy given the strategy of the other player. Players do not know each other's choices but they can infer other players' strategy from the pay-off matrix of the game. The Nash equilibrium is reached when all players have chosen a strategy whereby no-one can improve their own pay-off by changing strategy if others' strategies remain unchanged.

already at a high level. Therefore, it appears that trust signals (shaking hands prior to a subsequent strategic interaction) and extrinsic cooperative incentives (a payoff structure in the form of strategic complements) are independent and alternative drivers of cooperative behavior.

Can this proposal—that extrinsic incentives and trust signals are two independent drivers of cooperative decision making (one based on economic rationality, the other on social rationality)—be justified by neuroeconomic data? In a recent publication (Declerck, Boone, & Emonds, 2013), we developed a multilevel model for prosocial decision making based *ex post* on an exhaustive literature review. The model, reproduced in Figure 2.2, aims to specifically explain how extrinsic incentives (that align self- and collective interest) and trust signals (that minimize the chance of exploitation) are processed by the brain to yield cooperative versus noncooperative decisions in strategic interactions. The main proposition implicit in the model is that, for the brain, economic

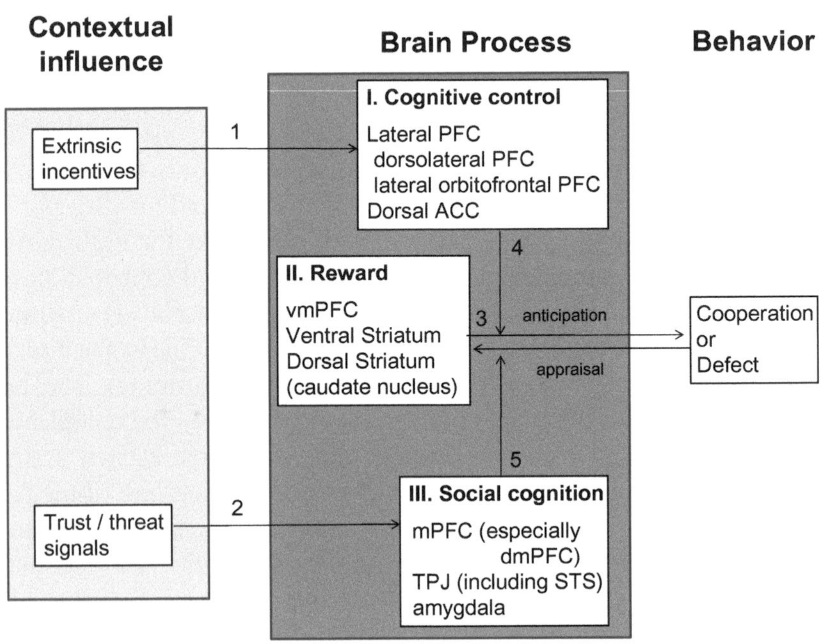

Figure 2.2 Published in: Declerck et al. (2013), Brain and Cognition 81 *(2013) 95–117 ISSN:* **0278-2626.** *A theoretical model identifying the neural networks recruited to solve social dilemmas: a cooperative or defect decision is driven by the brain's valuation system that computes a common currency based on anticipated economic and social rewards. Activation of the reward system is modulated by the presence or absence of extrinsic cooperative incentives, processed by cognitive control regions in the brain, and by trust/threat signals, processed by social cognition regions. Numbered arrow labels are explained in the text. ACC = anterior cingulate cortex; PFC = prefrontal cortex; mPFC = medial prefrontal cortex; vmPFC = ventromedial prefrontal cortex; dmPFC = dorsomedial prefrontal cortex; TPJ = temporoparietal junction, STS = superior temporal sulcus.* Copied with permission from Elsevier.

and social rationality do not have to be contradictory, in that they are rooted in different neural networks that operate in concert and independently modulate decision making. Because these decisions are made with the anticipation of generating positive feelings, they are always motivated choices that yield either economically valuable or social rewards.

To substantiate the model, we conducted a literature search by entering keywords in the Web of Science search engine and by examining the reference section of current review articles to locate as many neuroimaging studies as possible on cooperation in interactive game settings and/or altruism. Figures 2.2 and 2.3 identify those brain regions that are consistently reported to be activated when people make prosocial versus antisocial decisions in social dilemma-type situations (i.e., when torn between a cooperative versus a self-serving choice). However, this list is not meant to be an exhaustive representation of the neural correlates of prosociality. The aim of the model is to conceptually understand how these brain regions fit into networks or systems that can independently process extrinsic incentives or trust signals and modulate motivational processes so as to make cooperation more or less desirable.

Three such brain systems appear to be consistently recruited when people are faced with social dilemmas, namely the neural networks dedicated to processing reward, cognitive control, and social cognition (e.g., Fehr & Camerer, 2007; Fehr & Rockenbach, 2004; Sanfey, 2007; Tabibnia & Lieberman, 2007; Walter, Abler, Ciaramidaro, & Erk, 2005). The specific brain regions that are associated with the reward system, cognitive control, and social cognition, respectively, are illustrated in Figure 2.3. The reward system (Figure 2.2, box II) generates the *motivation* to act in a certain way by encoding the saliency of the reward associated with a particular decision outcome and by computing the likelihood that the decision will generate the desired outcome (Bartra, McGuire, & Kable, 2013; Levy & Glimcher, 2012; O'Doherty et al., 2004). But the reward system[5] is impartial with respect to the direction of the decision.

[5]The term "reward system" stems back to research in the 1950's conducted by James Old and Peter Milner: they discovered regions in the rat's brain that, when stimulated, would cause pleasure. The rats would keep on repeating those actions that caused the stimulation in the first place. These regions, known in humans to constitute the mesolimbic motivational systems, are at the core of reinforcement learning. More recently, neuroeconomic research has introduced the term "valuation system" to refer to the same mesolimbic pathway regions and its connection with the ventromedial prefrontal cortex. Activation in these regions are necessary to compute and compare the rewarding value of alternative decision outcomes. We use the terms "reward system," "motivational system" and "valuation system" interchangeably. We also point out that we interpret "reward" in the broad sense: avoiding punishment can also be rewarding, and be hence a valued outcome.

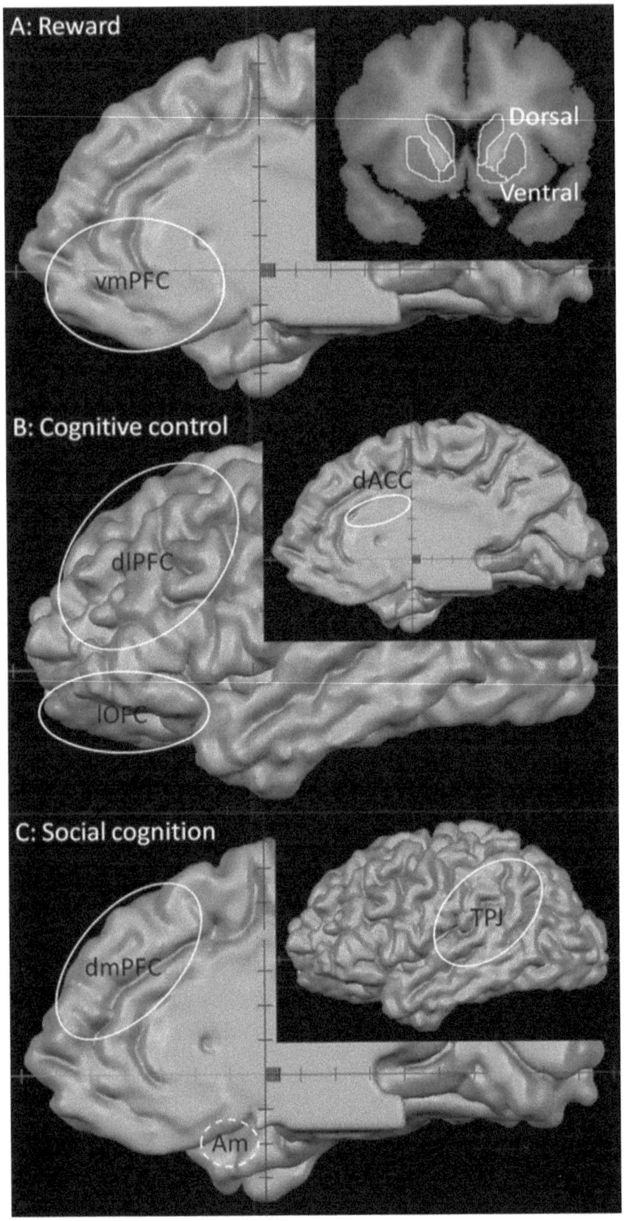

Figure 2.3 Published in: Declerck et al. (2013), Brain and Cognition 81 *(2013) 95–117 ISSN:* ***0278-2626.*** *(A) Medial view of an average brain showing regions of the reward system including; insert: coronal slice at y = 6. (B) Lateral view of an average brain showing regions associated with cognitive control; insert: medial view. (C) Medial view of an average brain showing regions associated with social cognition; insert: lateral view. Abbreviations: vmPFC: vetromedial prefrontal cortex; dlPFC: dorsolateral prefrontal cortex; lOFC: lateral orbitofrontal cortex; dACC: dorsal anterior cingulate cortex; dmPFC dorsomedial prefrontal cortex; Am: amygdala; TPJ: temporoparietal junction.* Copied with permission from Elsevier.

Both cooperative and noncooperative decisions, once their subjective values have been computed, are motivated decisions that, when chosen, are expected to feel good!

Several studies have corroborated that there is extensive overlap in activation of the striatum (in the part that is located within the reward system) when people receive rewards for themselves (e.g., receiving a sum of money) and when they are rewarding others, such as when they are voluntarily giving away money to charity (Fehr & Camerer, 2007; Izuma, Saito, & Sadato, 2010). Thus, for the brain, it seems that extrinsic lucrative rewards are equivalent to the intrinsic affective feeling ("the warm glow of giving") stemming from socially motivated decisions.[6] By computing the economic *and* social values of such decisions, the reward system forms anticipatory expectations of a decision outcome (Knutson, Taylor, Kaufman, Peterson, & Glover, 2005). It is furthermore involved in appraising whether or not these expectations are met following the decision (Bartra et al., 2013; Peterson, 2005); thus the reciprocal arrow 3 in Figure 2.2.

The model in Figure 2.2 also proposes that activity in the reward system is modulated by activity in the cognitive control system (box I), which processes prevailing extrinsic incentives (arrow 1), and the social cognition system (box III), which processes the extent to which surrounding social cues signal (un)trustworthiness (arrow 2). Via these two systems, reward expectations and the (un)willingness to cooperate are determined (arrows 4 and 5): cognitive control can lead to both cooperate or defect decisions depending on what type of extrinsic incentives are present. When cooperation is perceived to be lucrative (through synergy, long-term payoffs, or reputation benefits) it becomes economically

[6]A recent debate emerged as to whether there is a single unified "reward system" that fires in response to both social and nonsocial stimuli, or whether the valuation of these two types of stimuli each have their own dedicated neural processes (see Ruff & Fehr, 2014). According to the "extended common currency schema," a single neural circuit determines the motivational significance of all stimuli. Social and nonsocial decisions would then result in identical activity in reward-related brain areas. Most experimental evidence so far points in this direction. However, some studies are consistent with a "social valuation-specific schema," whereby the neural valuation of social and nonsocial stimuli engages neural processes that follow similar computational principles, but are implemented in distinct neuronal populations. The specialized neurons that evolved to deal specifically with social information may be located in different brain areas, or be in very close proximity, even within a value-processing brain region such as the striatum. In either case, the functional interactions with other brain regions that process peripheral information and exert modulatory influences on decision making (see Section 2.3.2) would be similar for both social and nonsocial type valuation neurons.

rational. When extrinsic incentives are absent, cooperation can still be valued because of its social rewards. In that case, cooperation becomes socially rational provided that there are sufficient social cues that are indicative that the interacting party is trustworthy. When no incentives are present and/or partners are perceived to be untrustworthy, the likelihood of prosocial decisions declines drastically.

In the remainder of this chapter we summarize the results of neuroeconomic studies that are consistent with the model proposed in Figure 2.2 (some of these studies are also reviewed in Declerck et al., 2013; Engelmann & Hein, 2013; and Rilling & Sanfey, 2011).

2.3 REWARD SYSTEM COMPUTES THE SUBJECTIVE EXPECTED VALUE OF (PRO)SOCIAL DECISIONS

In classical economic theory, decision making is often equated with the process of value maximization. This process is easy to comprehend when deciding between two alternatives with similar qualitative properties and one assumes that more is always better: e.g., two apples will then be chosen over one apple. But how to choose between two euros and one apple? Or an apple now versus a bag of popcorn later? These choices are likely to depend on subjective preferences (whether one likes apples, popcorn, or money better) and other contextual values such as how hungry one is or how easily one can delay gratification. Prosocial decisions may additionally have values that go beyond the material qualities of an outcome. A hungry person may still decide to share her popcorn with friends because she expects gratitude, something he or she greatly appreciates.

Since the seminal work of Paul Samuelson (1937), economists have argued that decision makers who are internally consistent act *as if* the values of the outcomes they considered were mapped on a single common scale for comparison. The idea that there is a common currency that guides all choices has prompted neuroeconomists in the last decade to search for the root of all value, that is, to find where in the brain value representations of fundamentally different reward types become integrated (Levy & Glimcher, 2012). As a result, numerous fMRI studies have been conducted to find out how both the magnitude of a reward and the subjective value an individual places on that reward are related to brain activity. Research in this domain has also distinguished how the brain computes outcome expectations based on reward properties (sometimes called "decision utility") and how decision outcomes are evaluated (also referred to as "experienced utility").

From two recent meta-analyses on fMRI experiments, it appears that two brain regions form the core of the valuation system: the ventromedial prefrontal cortex (vmPFC) and the ventral striatum. First, Levy and Glimcher (2012) reviewed 13 studies and came to the conclusion that a small subregion of the vmPFC tracks the expected subjective value on a common currency appropriate for guiding choices between different rewards. In a typical behavioral choice experiment of this sort, participants under the fMRI scanner have to choose between monetary rewards of different sizes or between disparate kinds of rewards (for example, money versus food items). Researchers then try to identify those brain areas where the size of the rewards, or the preference expressed for one type of reward over another, correlates with the BOLD signal. If the BOLD signal in a particular brain region is equal for two different types of rewards, it would indicate that both rewards are equally appealing and that the individual is indifferent between them. Importantly, in many studies reported so far, it does not appear to matter if the rewards are material or social. This was corroborated during a gambling task in which the choices made in some trials had financial consequences (losing or gaining a dollar), while in other trials the choice made led to either a social reward (seeing the picture of a happy face and hearing an accompanying positive word, such as "excellent" or "bravo") or a social punishment (a picture of an angry face accompanied by a negative word such as "stupid" or "moron"). The results of this study once again corroborated that activity in a small region of the vmPFC correlated with both the monetary and the social subjective value (Lin, Adolphs, & Rangel, 2012).

It is unlikely that the vmPFC, which emerged as the most important region encoding common currency in the meta-analysis of Levy and Glimcher, would be the only region implicated in valuation. Many previous studies have also indicated the involvement of the striatum and other brain regions in choice tasks. Bartra et al. (2013) conducted a meta-analysis of 206 studies and identified the vmPFC *and* the ventral striatum as the two most important regions where brain activity correlates positively with subjective value. These two regions were responsive both when decisions between different types of rewards were made ("decision utility") as well as when those rewards were delivered ("experienced utility"). The authors nevertheless acknowledge that finer-grained anatomical distinctions between brain regions that encode subjective value during decision and outcome phases are likely to exist. In line with this, their meta-analytical results show that the subjective value response foci are more densely clustered in the vmPFC during the decision phase than during the outcome phase, reinforcing the idea that the vmPFC especially supports value-based decision making (Levy & Glimcher, 2012; Rangel & Hare, 2010), while the ventral striatum may play a more important role in experienced utility and learning. This would mean that the vmPFC and ventral striatum work in concert and in a dynamic fashion: computing the expected value of an outcome (vmPFC) is a prerequisite of decision making, while the value of a received outcome (ventral striatum) can be used to guide future expectations and decisions (Kable & Glimcher, 2009).

This need for a dynamic interplay between the vmPFC (computing decision utility) and the ventral striatum (computing experienced utility) illustrates that motivated decision making encompasses more than valuation. The expected subjective value of a decision does not arise out of the blue, but it is derived based on previous experiences and must furthermore be flexible enough to be modified when reward contingencies change. Therefore, in dynamic social interactions, the process of encoding the saliency of a reward must be closely linked with learning processes. Consistently, both associative and reinforcement learning have already been shown to activate the striatum.

A breakthrough in this domain came with the pioneering work of Wolfram Shultz, who described how dopamine neurotransmission in the ventral striatum could generate the motivation to repeat those decisions that lead to reward and interrupt this process when rewards are worse than expected. Dopamine neurons in the nucleus accumbens portion of the ventral striatum fire in response to the magnitude of the obtained reward and code the quality (positive or negative) of the so-called dopamine prediction error. A better-than-expected reward elicits a positive prediction error signal, while the omission of an expected reward yields a negative signal (Schultz, 1997, 2002). The value of this prediction error also corresponds to neural activity in the ventral striatum, which can be measured with fMRI (Abler, Walter, Erk, Kammerer, & Spitzer, 2006).

Finally, while the vmPFC and ventral striatum form anticipatory expectations via error predictions and determine both decision and experienced utility, the dorsal striatum also appraises the rewarding value of a decision and is known to be involved in reinforcement and reversal learning (O'Doherty et al., 2004; Tricomi, Delgado, & Fiez, 2004; Tricomi, Delgado, McCandliss, McClelland, & Fiez, 2006; Tricomi & Fiez, 2008). The dorsal striatum is, more than the ventral striatum, involved in the agency behind the decision rather than in valuation per se (O'Doherty et al., 2004). Theoretical models of reinforcement learning have identified two components to reinforcement learning: a "critic," which forms expectations regarding future rewards, and an "actor," which maintains information about the rewarding outcomes to assess the status quo and modify future behavior as needed. O'Doherty et al. (2004) showed with fMRI that the "critic" component is associated with the ventral striatum, while the "actor" relates to activity in the dorsal striatum. These researchers compared a Pavlovian and instrumental learning task under the scanner and corroborated that the caudate nucleus (located within the dorsal striatum) becomes activated only during instrumental learning (associating a reward with a particular response) and not during a Pavlovian task (associating a stimulus with a forthcoming reward). Thus, an active caudate nucleus would explain why decisions with a better or worse outcome will tend to be repeated or attenuated. From this experiment it appears that the roles of the ventral and dorsal striatum are dissociated, with the former being more important in forming stimulus-reward contingency associations and the latter playing a more important role in updating decision making in accordance with new contingencies.

The results of the experiments described so far bolster the conclusion that the vmPFC and ventral striatum form the core of a "valuation system" believed to play a critical role in value-based learning and motivated decision making, while the dorsal striatum appears to be important in monitoring contingencies between decisions and outcomes. In addition, the dorsal striatum may have a role in implementing behavioral updates when necessary (Waegeman, Declerck, Boone, Seurinck, & Parizel, 2014). The studies summarized in the next subsection corroborate that these conclusions hold in the domain of prosocial decision making.

2.3.1 Neuroeconomic Studies that Corroborate the Role of the Ventromedial Prefrontal Cortex and Ventral Striatum in (Pro) Social Decision Making

The prisoner's dilemma game lends itself well to testing if the reward system is involved in the process of learning to value prosocial decisions, and this is exactly what Rilling and colleagues (Rilling et al., 2002; Rilling, Sanfey, Aronson, Nystrom, & Cohen, 2004) set out to do. In this classic, non-zero-sum game, two anonymous players have to independently choose between two options: one denoting cooperation (option C), the other defection (option D). A monetary reward is offered in function of the combination of options chosen by both partners. There are four possible outcome combinations: both players cooperate (C1C2), both defect (D1D2), player 1 cooperates and player 2 defects (C1D2), or vice versa (D1C2). The payoffs for player 1 are always such that D1C2 > C1C2 > D1D2 > C1D2. Both players are better off when they mutually cooperate than when they mutually defect. But a player who defects when the other cooperates has an even greater advantage. And a player who cooperates risks the worse possible outcome when the other defects. If the game is played only once, defect is the dominant strategy because, irrespective of the choice of the other player, a rational player has no incentive to deviate from this choice (see also Chapter 1). The greed to earn more (D1C2) as well as the fear to lose out (C1D2) drive this game to the D1D2 Nash equilibrium.

In one reported fMRI experiment (Rilling et al., 2004), the authors tested if evaluating the outcome of a cooperative decision in a one-shot prisoner's dilemma game possibly involves a dopamine prediction error in the ventral striatum. Each participant played 10 one-shot games under the scanner, supposedly with 10 different partners, and thus with no prospects for future repayments by establishing a mutually beneficial relationship. In each trial, a player would have to estimate again and again what the likelihood of reciprocation might be, given that human behavior is far from 100% predictable. After the decision is made, feedback regarding the decision of the other player is given, and this can be better or worse than expected. If reciprocation is better than expected, the discrepancy between reward estimate and actual outcome would generate a positive dopamine prediction error. Brain contrasts between reciprocated and unreciprocated cooperation indicated that reciprocated cooperation resulted in a positive BOLD response in the ventral striatum and vmPFC, while unreciprocated cooperation resulted in a negative BOLD response. Because the ventral striatum and vmPFC receive mesolimbic dopamine projections, the authors therefore interpret the increased activation as an indication of a positive prediction error while the decreased activation indicates a negative prediction error. From this discrepancy in reward expectation a player can learn whether to keep on cooperating or switch to a different strategy.

When, however many trials of the prisoner's dilemma game are repeated with the same partner, the profits from mutual cooperation would become much larger than those of mutual defection, so each partner would benefit from learning to value mutual cooperation and believing that the other one does so too. In another fMRI experiment (Rilling et al., 2002), participants played a repeated prisoner's dilemma game with the same partner. Most participants reported that they found mutual cooperation the most personally satisfying outcome (despite the fact that the game structure was such that in each trial they could earn more by defecting), and mutual cooperation was again associated with increased activity in the vmPFC and ventral striatum. Interestingly, when the game was played with a computer rather than a human partner, no increase in ventral striatum activity was observed. This suggests that the mere fact of establishing mutual cooperation with another person has a rewarding value over and above the material rewards obtained from cooperation.

That cooperation without remuneration has rewarding value and activates the ventral striatum and the vmPFC has been illustrated with fMRI numerous times in other, more mundane, settings than the prisoner's dilemma game. In a computer task whereby players had to construct a target pattern either alone, with another person (cooperation), or against another person (competition), it appeared that, cooperation as compared to competition activated the vmPFC and the posterior cingulate cortex (Decety, Jackson, Sommerville, Chaminade, & Meltzoff, 2004). Another fMRI study reported on the "warm glow of giving" associated with charity donations (Harbaugh, Mayr, & Burghart, 2007). Ventral striatum activity increased when participants witnessed mandatory money transfers (including from their own accounts) into the charity's account. This suggests that people like to see a charity receive money. Those who showed more activation in the ventral striatum were also more likely to subsequently contribute voluntarily to charity and also reported more satisfaction from giving. In the charitable donation study by Moll et al. (2006), striatal regions were activated both when donating and when receiving monetary rewards, corroborating that obtaining economic and social rewards are processed in the same (or very proximate) anatomical brain substrates. Decisions to donate also activated the oxytocin-rich subgenual area, a brain region connected to the reward system and implicated in bonding and social attachment (Bartels & Zeki, 2004; Depue & Morrone-Strupinsky, 2005). This is consistent with the proposition that the rewarding value of cooperation and altruistic acts stem from the psychological satisfaction of establishing a commonality with another individual (Decety et al., 2004). When decision outcomes are not remunerative (and thus not economically rational), the reward value can be strengthened by positive affect and feelings of social affiliation.

Results of lesion studies are furthermore consistent with a role of the vmPFC in generating positive affect from social interactions. Compared to normal controls and patients with other brain lesions, vmPFC lesion patients are found to be less generous and less trustworthy when they are engaged in a battery of economic games (Krajbich, Adolphs, Tranel, Denburg, & Camerer, 2009). They also show less reciprocity behavior (Moretto, Sellito, & di Pellegrino, 2013). Most probably, this antisocial trend in their decision-making strategy stems from a failure to appreciate the intrinsic social rewards due to impairments in a valuation system that is also attuned to mediating social interaction with kin or group members (Bechara & Damasio, 2005; Fellows, 2007; Rolls, 2000).

These examples do not imply that people are consciously striving for hedonic feelings when they are behaving altruistically. True altruism can be the result of many different motives, such as empathy, categorical imperatives, or internalized social norms. Some of these motives may be acting in concert, facilitating prosociality. For example, fairness considerations apparently strengthen affective feelings, and this is again accompanied by increased activation in the vmPFC and ventral striatum. This is true for benefactors as well as for recipients, as illustrated in an fMRI study that compared the neural response of "fair" and "unfair" offers of equal magnitude in a dictator game. In this game, a participant (outside the scanner) receives an amount of money and is asked if he or she wants to offer any part of it to an anonymous partner who has received nothing and has no power to respond. For the receiving party (inside the scanner), "fair" offers were associated with higher happiness ratings and increased activation in the vmPFC and ventral striatum compared to "unfair offers" that had the same monetary value (Tabibnia, Satpute, & Lieberman, 2008). A follow-up experiment furthermore showed that these same regions become activated when a player under the scanner observes that unfair offers to another person are subsequently reduced by transferring additional funds into the account of the underprivileged party (Tricomi, Rangel, Camerer, & O'Doherty, 2010).

2.3.2 Context Modulates Valuation and Activity in the Reward System

So far we have reviewed how the valuation system, including the vmPFC and striatum, converts different sorts of values to a common currency to form expectations, evaluate outcomes, and steer future decision making. But to arrive at this common currency of disparate reward types that may include monetary or reputation gains as well as warm feelings of affect, multiple brain regions must undoubtedly be involved. Furthermore, the rule set by which values are assigned are not written in stone but varies with changing conditions, contrary to the assumptions of "unbounded" rationality. Alternative choice options, a shift in reference point, and different social contexts have not only been shown to modulate behavior, but they also exert their influence on valuation itself and associated neural responsiveness (Engelmann & Hein, 2013).

When experimental tasks activate the vmPFC and the striatum, modulation of the BOLD signal by other brain regions is often reported (Engelmann & Hein, 2013). Not only are vmPFC and striatum themselves highly interconnected by dopamine neurons, they also independently receive input from various other cortical and subcortical regions, particularly the amygdala and temporal parietal junction implicated in social cognition (Hare, Camerer, Knoepfle, & Rangel, 2010). By monitoring and appraising large amounts of sensory data, the vmPFC and striatum serve as prime integration zones to affect subsequent brain functions (Levy & Glimcher, 2012; Staudinger, Erk, Abler, & Walter, 2009). The result of this external input into the brain's valuation system is that values are relative and that they will influence subsequent behavior depending on context. A good example is the observation that a food eaten to satiety decreases the reward value of that food, and that, once satiated, the odor of that particular food (relative to another food item) will be associated with decreased activation in the orbitofrontal/ventromedial cortex (O'Doherty et al., 2000). Findings such as these indicate that external stimuli can alter the response of vmPFC neurons so that the reward value becomes modulated by an individual's motivational state (Engelmann & Hein, 2013). Thus, it is likely that the subjective expected value of a prosocial decision that is based on different (economic and social) types of reward (e.g., economic vs social) will also depend on outside information.

A number of studies have indeed shown that the neural response elicited by *economic rewards* is relative and affected by the presence of alternatives. For example, the BOLD response in regions of vmPFC and ventral striatum appears to be greater when a stimulus preceding the receipt of a financial reward predicts a gain (when the alternative was of a lesser value) compared to when the same reward predicts a relative loss (when the alternative was of greater value, see Elliott, Agnew, & Deakin, 2008; Nieuwenhuis et al., 2005). Social comparison can also affect reward-related brain activity, as shown in the study by Fliessbach et al. (2007). Participants performed a simple estimation task (estimating the number of dots on a screen) in pairs of two in return for monetary compensation while they were being scanned using two adjacent fMRI scanners. Activity in the ventral striatum (following compensation) varied according to how much *the other participant* was financially rewarded for his or her performance on the same task. The authors interpret this to mean that outperforming someone else contributes to the increased neural response in addition to the expected reward from being correct. Hence the mere information about another person performing the same task can have an immediate effect on motivation-related brain processes.

Similarly, valuation of *social rewards* in the vmPFC and ventral striatum are also affected by context. People tend to value compliance in judgments, reassuring themselves of their group inclusion by not deviating from the group norm. It turns out that valuation of music fragments (Campbell-Meiklejohn, Bach, Roepstorff, Dolan, & Frith, 2010) and facial attractiveness (Klucharev, Hytonen, Rijpkema, Smidts, & Fernandez, 2009) can also be modulated by cues that indicate conformity. Activity in the ventral striatum again increases when judgments conform to the group norm (for facial attractiveness) or are in agreement with experts' opinion (for music). A classic experiment by Plassmann, O'Doherty, Shiv, and Rangel (2008) furthermore revealed that the neural representation of the experienced pleasantness of tasting wine is modulated by its price. When the price of the wine increased (indicating that the wine is highly socially approved), so did the subjective experience of the flavor, and this was accompanied by an increased BOLD signal in the orbitofrontal cortex. Finally, in a study by Janowski, Camerer, and Rangel (2013), empathic choices (choices that enhance the well-being of others, such as the sacrifices parents make for their children) were shown to engage regions of the vmPFC involved in valuation, and this activity was in turn modulated by activity in the inferior parietal lobule, a region known to play a role in processing social cues.

In the next two sections we will continue to focus on how neural activity in the reward system is modulated by two types of contexts that are very relevant to prosocial decision making (see also Figure 2.2): the presence or absence of incentives and the types of social cues.

2.4 COGNITIVE CONTROL SYSTEM PROCESSES EXTRINSIC INCENTIVES

Appreciating the economic value of cooperation requires cognitive resources, and some authors (e.g., Stevens & Hauser, 2004) believe that reciprocal (or costly) cooperation is rare among animals because they lack the cognitive capacity to weigh the future benefits of cooperative versus noncooperative decisions. In a long-term relationship, the accrual of mutual benefits generates incentives that turn the temptation to free ride into an opportunity to elicit reciprocity. People understand, better than animals, that a long-term, mutually cooperative relationship is economically more advantageous (and therefore rational) compared to unilateral defection. Even in situations with a high degree of uncertainty regarding one's partner, it may still be worth it to pay the initial cost of cooperation rather than forsaking the possibility of establishing a fruitful future relationship (Haselton & Buss, 2000; Yamagishi, Jin, & Kiyonari, 1999). This capacity for suppressing selfish impulses and managing decisions in a time horizon emerged only late in primate evolution with the great cortical expansion of the lateral dopaminergic neural pathway (Previc, 1999; Stevens & Hauser, 2004). This pathway links the caudate nucleus in the dorsal striatum with the dorsolateral prefrontal cortex (PFC). In concert with the dorsal anterior cingulate cortex (dorsal ACC), the dorsolateral PFC sustains the so-called "executive functions," which made deliberate processing of incentives possible.

More specifically, the dorsolateral PFC is an important component of working memory (Miller & Cohen, 2001), and is involved in resolving conflicts signaled by the dorsal ACC. The latter is interconnected with the dorsolateral PFC and the ventral striatum (Alexander, DeLong, & Strick, 1986) and is activated whenever there are conflicting motives, such as those generated by a social dilemma (Carter, Botvinick, & Cohen, 1999; Rilling et al., 2002). The lateral orbitofrontal cortex is considered to be part of the cognitive control system because of its role in evaluating punishment threats (Kringelbach & Rolls, 2004), and avoiding punishment can be a strong incentive to cooperate. Finally, an additional role of the dorsolateral PFC is the provision of impulse control to resist immediate urges in favor of greater rewards at a later time (McClure, Laibson, Loewenstein, &

Cohen, 2004). We next illustrate the involvement of these three cognitive control functions (conflict resolution, evaluating punishments, and impulse control) with respect to prosocial decision making next.

2.4.1 Neuroeconomic Studies that Corroborate the Role of the Dorsolateral Prefrontal Cortex, Dorsal Anterior Cingulate Cortex, and Lateral Orbitofrontal Cortex in Appraising Incentives that Lead to (Un)Cooperative Decisions

First we present the evidence that cognitive control is necessary to resolve the issue of conflicting motives presented by social dilemmas. When cooperation leads to synergy and all cooperating parties benefit equally, there is no conflict between self- and collective interest, and no advantage to free ride. Such synergetic incentives are expected to relax the need for cognitive control and deactivate the lateral PFC, in comparison to decisions made in mixed-motive social dilemmas. This was tested in an fMRI experiment that contrasted brain activity elicited by a one-shot prisoner's dilemma game (a mixed motive game) and a coordination game (Emonds, Declerck, Boone, Vandervliet, & Parizel, 2012). In a coordination game (also called an assurance game or stag hunt), the payoff for unilateral defection is the same or less than for mutual cooperation. This seemingly small change aligns self- and collective interest and has a quantum effect on behavior: people cooperate much more in a coordination game than in a prisoner's dilemma (Knez & Camerer, 2000; Kollock, 1998; Liebrand, 1983; Skyrms, 2004). Because the payoff-dominant Nash equilibrium in the coordination game is also Pareto efficient (it is the best outcome for everyone), no one has an incentive to deviate from it. In contrast, in the prisoner's dilemma, players are torn between choosing the most efficient distribution of payoffs (the cooperative option) and the awareness that every player (including themselves) can personally benefit by defecting. As expected, the fMRI results are consistent with the proposition that cognitive control is needed to resolve the conflict elicited by the mixed motives of the prisoner's dilemma. The dorsolateral PFC and dorsal ACC were significantly more activated by the prisoner's dilemma than by the coordination game. Because the experiment offered no chance to develop a long-term partnership, the best response in the prisoner's dilemma was to defect. Accordingly, in this game, cognitive control monitors the absence of cooperative (synergetic) incentives and modulates the decision-making process toward the economically rational best response, which is to not cooperate.

Second, when punishment threats are present in a social dilemma, cooperation does become rational (see the experiments by Fehr and Gachter, 2002, which illustrate how the punishment of defectors is a powerful motive for cooperation). According to the model in Figure 2.2, registering the presence of sanctions would also require cognitive control. This was corroborated by an fMRI study conducted by Spitzer, Fischbacher, Herrnberger, Gron, and Fehr (2007). Participants played two versions of a dictator game. In the "no punishment condition," player 1 (inside the scanner) received a sum of money to be split in any proportion between himself or herself and another player (outside the scanner). In the "punishment condition," player 2 could impose a monetary sanction if the allotment was perceived to be unfair. On average, the presence of the punishment threat doubled the level of generosity. Brain contrasts between the two conditions (no punishment versus punishment) indicated that the threat of punishment is associated with increased activity (bilaterally) in the dorsolateral PFC, the lateral orbitofrontal cortex, and the adjacent ventrolateral PFC.

A subsequent study by Rilling et al. (2008) corroborates that the lateral orbitofrontal cortex is involved in monitoring punishments in a repeated prisoner's dilemma game. These authors found that activity in the lateral orbitofrontal cortex following a defect decision of a partner could predict a player's subsequent defect decision. This makes sense, considering that a cooperative person who experiences nonreciprocity in a repeated social interaction needs to switch strategies. Presumably, this can only be possible if the lateral orbitofrontal cortex communicates with the caudate nucleus in the reward system (dorsal striatum) that the current decision-making strategy should be updated, because there is no longer an incentive to cooperate.

Third, the need to control impulses to make rational decisions, and the involvement of the lateral PFC to accomplish this, is illustrated in an experiment by Knoch, Schneider, Schunk, Hohmann, and Fehr (2009). They used repetitive transcranial magnetic stimulation (rTMS) to show that controlling the selfish impulse to benefit from reputation gains in a trust game is causally related to a fully functional lateral PFC. In a trust game (first described by Berg, Dickhaut, & McCabe, 1995), player 1 (the "investor") receives an amount of money and can decide how much of this amount to transfer to player 2 (the "trustee"). The transferred money is then tripled. Next, player 2 is given the choice to keep the tripled endowment or to return a portion of it to player 1.

Thus, the decision of player 1 to transfer money relies heavily on the expectation that player 2 is trustworthy. In the experiment by Knoch et al. (2009), there were two conditions in which this trust game was played: an anonymous condition, in which the decision of player 2 is not revealed to anyone but player 1, and a reputation condition, in which the decision of player 2 (the trustee) is made available to future investors. Not surprisingly, considering that reputation can be a strong incentive to cooperate, back transfers from the trustee to the investor were twice as much in the reputation condition compared to the anonymous condition. By means of rTMS, the researchers were able to block out the lateral PFC. They found that, when activity in the right dorsolateral PFC was interrupted by rTMS, the trustees lacked the necessary impulse control to resist the temptation to keep all of the money to themselves. The back transfers in the reputation condition were therefore significantly lower under rTMS, even when the trustees knew that defecting was irrational because it would put their reputation at stake and most likely reduce future transfers into their accounts.

2.5 SOCIAL COGNITION SYSTEM PROCESSES TRUST AND THREAT SIGNALS

Social cognition refers to our ability to understand others. This became essential in the evolutionary history of humans when they adopted group living. As groups grew larger and interactions more complex, individuals needed a way of bookkeeping the (dis)honorable activities of other group members. Mental processes such as face recognition, trait inferences, and mind reading became necessary to navigate through the social world, as they provided extra information about the likelihood that cooperative endeavors would not be exploited by selfish others.

The primate brain evolved in a social environment, where it needed to constantly exchange signals with other brains. Thus, primate brains were likely shaped by natural selection to be social (Dunbar, 1998). The result is that we, the primates with the largest brains and living in the largest social groups, have become very much attuned to social cues, such as facial expressions and gestures, and that we are constantly adapting our beliefs and decisions in concordance with our interpretation of those cues. Interest in the neural basis of social cognition was stirred by psychiatrist Leslie Brothers who borrowed the metaphor of the fictitious Robinson Crusoe, who, despite being shipwrecked and abandoned on a desolate island, remained a product of society. With her point that there is no Crusoe without Friday,[7] she wanted to convince neuroscientists to abandon studying brain functions in isolation. Based on single cell recordings of macaque monkeys and lesion studies, she described how the amygdala and regions of the temporal and frontal cortex respond specifically to social stimuli, which she collectively called "the social brain" (Brothers, 1990).

Since Brother's first conception of the social brain, numerous imaging studies have confirmed that a distributed corticolimbic network is activated when people form beliefs or expectations of others. In particular, meta-analyses of more than 200 fMRI studies (Van Overwalle, 2009, 2011; Van Overwalle & Baetens, 2009) reveal that two brain regions are crucial and specific for mentalizing about other's intentions, beliefs, or moral traits: the temporoparietal junction (TPJ) and the medial prefrontal cortex (mPFC). The TPJ extends from the superior temporal sulcus (STS) to the inferior parietal lobule. The mPFC incorporates the entire medial area of the PFC, including the anterior cingulate cortex (but it does not include the frontal poles, the posterior part of the medial PFC or the posterior cingulate cortex). Moreover, there may be a functional dissociation between the TPJ and the mPFC (Van Overwalle, 2009): the TPJ infers goals and intentions at a more perceptual level. It elicits automatic processing and is consistent with the idea of a mirror system for inferring intentionality in the human brain (Keysers, 2011). In contrast, the mPFC may integrate different types of social and emotional information at a more abstract, cognitive level (Van Overwalle, 2009). It is a rather large brain structure that can further be subdivided into a posterior, ventral, and dorsal part. It is the dorsal part of the medial PFC (dmPFC) that is the most associated with trait inference and mentalizing tasks (Amodio & Frith, 2006; Frith & Frith, 2006).

In addition to the role of the TPJ and the mPFC, evidence that the amygdala is essential to process social information has accumulated as well. Amygdala damage in childhood can have enduring effects on theory of mind development in adults, making it more difficult for afflicted individuals to acquire false belief understanding (realizing that an individual's representation of the social world may conflict with reality) and to be able to infer other people's thoughts and feelings from facial expressions (Stone, Baron-Cohen, Calder, Keane, & Young, 2003). People with

[7]Friday is the name of the freed prisoner who, after many years, became Crusoe's companion.

autism or Asperger syndrome show similar deficits in social cognition. When they are asked to make mentalistic inferences from pictures of eyes, they do not activate the amygdala in fMRI studies, while people without autism do (Baron-Cohen et al., 2000).

We have suggested that the most important way by which the social cognition system may influence prosocial decision making is by processing trust (and threat) signals to temper (or worsen) the fear of betrayal so that the desired outcome can be pursued safely (Acevedo & Krueger, 2005; Boone et al., 2008; Boone, Declerck, & Kiyonari, 2010; Simpson, 2004). These processes may occur explicitly, by mentalizing, or implicitly, by automatically responding to trust signals and withdrawing from threat signals. Both spontaneous (implicit) as well as intentional (explicit) impression formation have been shown to involve activation in the TPJ, the mPFC, and the amygdala (Ma, Vandekerckhove, Van Overwalle, Seurinck, & Fias, 2011), as illustrated next.

2.5.1 Neuroeconomic Studies that Corroborate the Role of the Medial Prefrontal Cortex, Temporoparietal Junction, and Amygdala in Evaluating Trustworthiness

Since Le Doux's (2003) classic research on fear conditioning, the amygdala has been known to play a role in processing threatening stimuli, and human lesion studies have corroborated that the amygdala is essential for enhancing perceptual awareness of emotionally significant events (Anderson & Phelps, 2001). Such sentience is especially important to a decision maker in a precarious situation. The actual neural correlates of trustworthiness judgments were for the first time investigated with fMRI by Winston, Strange, O'Doherty, and Dolan (2002). When participants of the experiment were asked to judge the trustworthiness of pictures of faces presented to them under the scanner (explicit evaluations), the TPJ showed increased activation. In addition, the right amygdala was activated more when viewing untrustworthy faces compared to trustworthy faces. The involvement of the right amygdala during implicit evaluation of threatening faces was later on replicated in a study by Engell, Haxby, and Todorov (2007).

Implicit evaluation of trustworthy faces (as opposed to untrustworthy faces) appears to activate the left amygdala (as opposed to the right amygdala), as well as the bilateral TPJ (Singer, Kiebel, Winston, Dolan, & Frith, 2004). In this experiment, participants first played a series of sequentially played prisoner's dilemma games with different partners.

The participant was always the first mover in the games, and his or her decision was revealed to the partner, who could then respond by reciprocating, betraying, or responding neutrally. To enhance the moral saliency of the partner's response, half of the partners were said to act "intentionally" (they deliberately chose to reciprocate or betray) or "unintentionally" (they followed a predetermined response sequence). In the second phase of the experiment, the participant was placed under the fMRI scanner and shown pictures of the faces of these partners and were asked to make gender judgments. The authors predicted that seeing faces of people who previously betrayed or reciprocated their cooperative decision would implicitly activate brain regions involved in social cognition, and that this would be more pronounced for intentional than unintentional responders. Their results confirmed that this was true when evaluating faces of intentional cooperators (compared to neutral faces). In addition to the TPJ and amygdala activation, there was also activity in the ventral striatum of the reward system, which was consistent with the high likability ratings of the faces of cooperators.

In Section 2.3.2 we discussed how contextual signals, including trust signals, can modulate neural activity in the reward system. Two studies are particularly interesting because they show that, by changing the neural signal in the dorsal striatum, they affect the decision to cooperate. First, King-Casas et al. (2005) performed a hyperscan fMRI study whereby they concurrently scanned two participants playing a repeated trust game (described earlier). They wanted to find out how trust develops and can change over time during a continuous exchange between two partners. As player 1 (the investor) increases his investments, player 2 (the trustee) increases repayments. Increases in investments were associated with greater activation of the head of the caudate nucleus in the trustee's brain. Additionally, an interesting pattern in the timing of caudate nucleus activation emerged. At first, the increase in caudate nucleus activation in the trustee's brain occurred after the investment of the investor was revealed to the trustee (which the authors called "reactive activity"). As the experiment progressed, the caudate nucleus activation shifted to a time preceding the revelation of the investment (called "anticipatory activity"). The authors interpret these results to mean that the caudate nucleus integrates information about the fairness of a partner's decision with the intention to repay this decision with trust. Through reinforcement learning in the caudate nucleus, the reputation of the investor is developed over time and serves as the input for the trustee's future decision-making scheme.

The second experiment by Delgado, Frank, and Phelps (2005) investigated how trust decisions in a trust game are affected by contextual information regarding the partner's (the trustee's) moral status. The player in the scanner received an endowment which could be "kept" on any given trial or "shared" with one of several partners outside the scanner. Prior to the scanning session, the players had been given vivid descriptions of each partner's character, which could reflect a neutral, praiseworthy, or immoral nature. The results showed that good partners consistently elicited more "sharing" than either neutral or bad partners, even if the good partners frequently violated the trustworthy expectations of the player. Interestingly, this disregard for the norm violation of a so-called good partner appears to be related to diminished activity in the caudate. When the partner was perceived to be neutral, the caudate nucleus showed the expected differential response to sharing decisions that were reciprocated and sharing decisions that were dishonored. But when the partner was perceived to be either good or bad, the differential neural response to feedback was not as robust or was completely nonexistent. The "good" moral profile not only created positive expectations of reciprocity, it also led players to discount feedback information by which they may have updated the beliefs about their partner. Similarly, the negative expectations of partners with a "bad" moral profile inhibit players to alter their behavior when these partners actually turn out to be reciprocal. Thus, artificially manipulated trustworthiness signals interfere with the caudate nucleus response to feedback, which may lead to socially motivated but economically unwarranted decisions.

Meta-analytical connectivity modeling, a robust tool for developing models of connectivity from neuro-imaging data, corroborates that there is significant co-activation between on the one hand the caudate nucleus, and on the other hand the amygdala, and regions of the prefrontal cortex where the construal of trust and moral profiles are likely taking place (Robinson et al., 2012). In addition, this study shows that it is especially the head of the caudate (as was the case in the study of King-Casas et al., 2005) that receives input from emotion- and cognition-specific circuits, such as the amygdala and prefrontal cortex.

2.6 SUMMARY

The findings corroborate that trust is an important contextual moderator of the expected value of a prosocial decision, and that this occurs through changing the neural signal in the caudate nucleus of the reward system. In addition to the signal change in the caudate, a widely distributed social cognition system in the brain processes social cues in facial gestures or written vignettes so as to infer the trustworthiness of the partner. When trust is manifested, it facilitates heuristic prosocial decisions following a simple decision rule "I cooperate as long as my partner is trustworthy." Trust in this case makes cooperation socially rational. Similarly, we presented evidence that synergetic benefits resulting from mutual cooperation activate the ventral striatum in the reward system, yielding positive affect. A decision rule that specifies "not cooperating unless there are incentives that align self-and collective interest" can be economically rational if people have the capacity to recognize situations with and without cooperative incentives. We reviewed the evidence that this capacity can be accomplished by the cognitive control functions of the lateral prefrontal cortex. Because cognitive control and social cognition can independently modulate the neural signal in the valuation (reward) system to compute the decision outcome which will generate the greatest pleasure (even if the expected rewards that are to be compared are of a different kind) the brain appears to be anatomically wired for two routes to cooperation: one is socially rational and trust-based, yielding mostly social rewards, the other is economically rational and incentive-based, steering decision making towards tangible and lucrative rewards.

But anatomy systems alone do not lead to decision making. The neural activity that is recorded with fMRI in the gray matter of the brain represents the firing of cells that release the neurotransmitters that are responsible for neural impulses. In the next chapter we describe in more detail some of the neurotransmitters that are so far known to contribute to humans' great capacity for cooperation.

REFERENCES

Abler, B., Walter, H., Erk, S., Kammerer, H., & Spitzer, M. (2006). Prediction error as a linear function of reward probability is coded in human nucleus accumbens. *NeuroImage*, *31*, 790–795.

Acevedo, M., & Krueger, J. I. (2005). Evidential reasoning in the prisoner's dilemma. *American Journal of Psychology*, *118*, 431–457.

Aimone, J. A., Houser, D., & Weber, B. (2014). Neural signatures of betrayal aversion: An fMRI study of trust. *Proceedings of the Royal Society B: Biological Sciences*, *281*(1782).

Alexander, G. E., DeLong, M. R., & Strick, P. L. (1986). Parietal organization of functionally segregated circuits linking basal ganglia and cortex. *Annual Review of Neuroscience*, *9*, 357–381.

Amodio, D. M., & Frith, C. D. (2006). Meeting of minds: The medial frontal cortex and social cognition. *Nature Reviews Neuroscience*, *7*, 268–277.

Anderson, A. K., & Phelps, E. A. (2001). Lesions of the human amygdala impair enhanced perception of emotionally salient events. *Nature*, *411*, 305–309.

Baron-Cohen, S., Ring, H. A., Bullmore, E. T., Wheelwright, S., Ashwin, C., & Williams, S. C. R. (2000). The amygdala theory of autism. *Neuroscience and Biobehavioral Reviews*, *24*, 355–364.

Bartels, A., & Zeki, S. (2004). The neural correlates of maternal and romantic love. *NeuroImage*, *21*, 115–1166.

Bartra, O., McGuire, J. T., & Kable, J. W. (2013). The valuation system: A coordinate-based meta-anamysis of BOLD fMRI experiments examining neural correlates of subjective value. *NeuroImage*, *76*, 412–427.

Bechara, A., & Damasio, A. R. (2005). The somatic marker hypothesis: A neural theory of economic decision. *Games and Economic Behavior*, *52*, 336–372.

Berg, J., Dickhaut, J., & McCabe, K. (1995). Trust, reciprocity, and social history. *Games and Economic Behavior*, *10*, 122–142.

Boone, C., Declerck, C. H., & Kiyonari, T. (2010). Inducing cooperative behavior among proselfs versus prosocials: The moderating role of incentives and trust. *Journal of Conflict Resolution*, *54*, 799–824.

Boone, C., Declerck, C. H., & Suetens, S. (2008). Subtle social cues, explicit incentives and cooperation in social dilemmas. *Evolution and Human Behavior*, *29*, 179–188.

Brothers, L. (1990). The social brain: A project for integrating primate behavior and neurophysiology in a new domain. *Concepts in Neurocience*, *1*, 27–51.

Campbell-Meiklejohn, D. K., Bach, D. R., Roepstorff, A., Dolan, R., & Frith, C. D. (2010). How the opinion of others affects our valuation of objects. *Current Biology*, *20*, 1165–1170.

Carter, C. S., Botvinick, M. M., & Cohen, J. D. (1999). The contribution of the anterior cingulate cortex to executive processes in cognition. *Reviews in the Neurosciences*, *10*, 49–57.

Carter, C. S., & van Veen, V. (2007). Anterior cingulate cortex and conflict detection: An update of theory and data. *Cognitive Affective & Behavioral Neuroscience*, *7*, 367–379.

Cho, Y. T., Ernst, M., & Fudge, J. L. (2013). Cortico-amygdala-sriatal circuits are organzied as hierarchical subsystems through the primate amygdala. *The Journal of Neuroscience*, *33*, 14017–14030.

Cools, R., Clark, L., Owen, A. M., & Robbins, T. W. (2002). Defining the neural mechanisms of probabilistic reversal learning using event-related functional magnetic resonance imaging. *Journal of Neuroscience*, *22*(11), 4563–4567.

Decety, J., Jackson, P. L., Sommerville, J. A., Chaminade, T., & Meltzoff, A. N. (2004). The neural bases of cooperation and competition: An fMRI investigation. *NeuroImage*, *23*, 744–751.

Declerck, C. H., Boone, C., & Emonds, G. (2013). When do people cooperate? The neuroeconomics of prosocial decision-making. *Brain & Cognition*, *81*, 95–117.

Delgado, M. R., Frank, R. H., & Phelps, E. A. (2005). Perceptions of moral character modulate the neural systems of reward during the trust game. *Nature Neuroscience*, *8*, 1611–1618.

Depue, R. A., & Morrone-Strupinsky, J. V. (2005). A neurobehavioral model of affiliative bonding: Implications for conceptualizing a human trait of affiliation. *Behavioral and Brain Sciences*, *28*, 313–395.

Dunbar, R. I. M. (1998). The social brain hypothesis. *Evolutionary Anthropology*, *6*, 178–190.

Elliott, R., Agnew, Z., & Deakin, J. F. W. (2008). Medial orbitofrontal cortex codes relative rather than absolute value of financial rewards in humans. *European Journal of Neuroscience*, *27*, 2213–2218.

Emonds, G., Declerck, C. H., Boone, C., Vandervliet, E. J. M., & Parizel, P. M. (2012). The cognitive demands on cooperation in social dilemmas: An fMRI study. *Social Neuroscience*, *7*, 494–509.

Engell, A. D., Haxby, J. V., & Todorov, A. (2007). Implicit trustworthiness decisions: Automatic coding of face properties in the human amygdala. *Journal of Cognitive Neuroscience*, *19*, 1508–1519.

Engelmann, J. B., & Hein, G. (2013). Contextual and social influences on valuation and choice. *Progress in Brain Research*, *202*, 215–237.

Fehr, E., & Camerer, C. F. (2007). Social neuroeconomics: The neural circuitry of social preferences. *Trends in Cognitive Sciences*, *11*, 419–427.

Fehr, E., & Gachter, S. (2002). Altruistic punishment in humans. *Nature*, *415*, 137–140.

Fehr, E., & Rockenbach, B. (2004). Human altruism: Economic, neural, and evolutionary perspectives. *Current Opinion in Neurobiology*, *14*, 784–790.

Fellows, L. K. (2007). Advances in understanding ventromedial prefrontal function. *Neurology*, *68*, 991–995.

Fliessbach, K., Weber, B., Trautner, P., Dohmen, T., Sunde, U., Elger, C. E., & Falk, A. (2007). Social comparison affects reward -related brain activity in the human ventral striatum. *Science*, *318*, 1305–1308.

Frith, C. D., & Frith, U. (2006). How we predict what other people are going to do. *Brain Research*, *1079*, 36–46.

Glimcher, P. W., Camerer, C. F., Fehr, E., & Poldrack, R. A. (2009). Introduction: A brief history of neuroeconomics. In P. W. Glimcher, C. F. Camerer, E. Fehr, & R. A. Poldrack (Eds.), *Neuroeconomics. Decision Making and the Brain* (pp. 1–11). London: Elsevier, Academic Press.

Goodale, M. A., & Milner, A. D. (1992). Separate visual pathways for perception and action. *Trends in Neuroscience*, *15*, 20–25.

Harbaugh, W. T., Mayr, U., & Burghart, D. R. (2007). Neural responses to taxation and voluntary giving reveal motives for charitable donations. *Science*, *316*, 1622–1625.

Hare, T. A., Camerer, C. F., Knoepfle, D. T., & Rangel, A. (2010). Value computations in ventral medial prefrontal cortex during charitable decision making incorporate input from regions involved in social cognition. *Journal of Neuroscience*, *30*, 583–590.

Haselton, M. G., & Buss, D. M. (2000). Error management theory: A new perspective on biases in cross-sex mind reading. *Journal of Personality and Social Psychology*, *78*, 81–91.

Izuma, K., Saito, D. N., & Sadato, N. (2010). Processing of the incentive for social approval in the ventral striatum during charitable donation. *Journal of Cognitive Neuroscience*, *22*, 621–631.

Janowski, V., Camerer, C., & Rangel, A. (2013). Empathic choice involves vmPFC value signals that are modulated by social processing implemented in IPL. *Social Cognitive and Affective Neuroscience*, *8*, 201–208.

Kable, J. W. (2011). The cognitive neuroscience toolkit for the neuroeconomist: A functional overview. *Journal of Neuroscience, Psychology, and Economics*, *4*, 63–84.

Kable, J. W., & Glimcher, P. W. (2009). The neurobiology of decision: Consensus and controversy. *Neuron*, *63*, 733–745.

Kahneman, D., & Tversky, A. (1984). Choices, values and frames. *American Psychologist*, *39*, 341–350.

Keysers, C. (2011). *The Empathic Brain. Kindle E-books*. Social Brain Press.

King-Casas, B., Tomlin, D., Anen, C., Camerer, C. F., Quartz, S. R., & Montague, P. R. (2005). Getting to know you: Reputation and trust in a two-person economic exchange. *Science*, *308*, 78–83.

Klucharev, V., Hytonen, K., Rijpkema, M., Smidts, A., & Fernandez, G. (2009). Reinforcement learning signal predicts social conformity. *Neuron*, *61*, 140–151.

Knez, M., & Camerer, C. (2000). Increasing cooperation in prisoner's dilemmas by establishing a precedent of efficiency in coordination games. *Organizational Behavior and Human Decision Processes*, *82*, 194–216.

Knoch, D., Schneider, F., Schunk, D., Hohmann, M., & Fehr, E. (2009). Disrupting the prefrontal cortex diminishes the human ability to build a good reputation. *Proceedings of the National Academy of Sciences*, *106*, 20895–20899.

Knutson, B., Taylor, J., Kaufman, M., Peterson, R., & Glover, G. (2005). Distributed neural representation of expected value. *Journal of Neuroscience*, *25*, 4806–4812.

Kollock, P. (1998). Social dilemmas: The anatomy of cooperation. *Annual Review of Sociology*, *24*, 183–214.

Krajbich, I., Adolphs, R., Tranel, D., Denburg, N. L., & Camerer, C. F. (2009). Economic games quantify diminished sense of guilt in patients with damage to the prefrontal cortex. *Journal of Neuroscience*, *29*, 2188–2192.

Kringelbach, M. L., & Rolls, E. T. (2004). The functional neuroanatomy of the human orbitofrontal cortex: Evidence from neuroimaging and neuropsychology. *Progress in Neurobiology*, *72*, 341–372.

Le Doux, J. (2003). The emotional brain, fear, and the amygdala. *Cellular and Molecular Neurobiology*, *23*, 727–738.

Levy, D. J., & Glimcher, P. W. (2012). The root of all value: A neural common currency for choice. *Current Opinion in Neurobiology*, *22*, 1027–1038.

Liebrand, W. B. G. (1983). A classification of social dilemma games. *Simulation & Gaming*, *14*, 123–138.

Lin, R., Adolphs, A., & Rangel, A. (2012). Social and monetary reward learning engage overlapping neural substrates. *Social Cognitive and Affective Neuroscience*, *7*, 274–281.

Ma, N., Vandekerckhove, M., Van Overwalle, F., Seurinck, R., & Fias, W. (2011). Spontaneous and intentional trait inferences recruit a common mentalizing network to a different degree: Spontaneous inferences activate only its core areas. *Social Neuroscience*, *6*, 123–138.

McClure, S. M., Laibson, D. I., Loewenstein, G., & Cohen, J. D. (2004). Separate neural systems value immediate and delayed monetary rewards. *Science*, *306*, 503–507.

Miller, E. K., & Cohen, J. D. (2001). An integrative theory of prefrontal cortex function. *Annual Review of Neuroscience*, *24*, 167–202.

Mishkin, M., & Ungerleider, L. G. (1982). Contribution of striate inputs to the visuospatial functions of parieto-preoccipital cortex in monkeys. *Behavior and Brain Research*, *6*, 57–77.

Moll, J., Krueger, F., Zahn, R., Pardini, M., de Oliveira-Souzat, R., & Grafman, J. (2006). Human fronto-mesolimbic networks guide decisions about charitable donation. *Proceedings of the National Academy of Sciences*, *103*, 15623–15628.

Moretto, G., Sellito, M., & di Pellegrino, G. (2013). Investment and repayment in a trust game after ventromedial prefrontal damage. *Frontiers in Human Neuroscience*, *7*. Article #UNSP 593.

Nieuwenhuis, S., Heslenfeld, D. J., von Geusau, N. J. A., Mars, R. B., Holroyd, C. B., & Yeung, N. (2005). Activity in human reward-sensitive brain areas is strongly context dependent. *NeuroImage*, *25*, 1302–1309.

Nieuwenhuys, R. (2012). The insular cortex: A review. *Progress in Brain Research*, *195*, 123–163.

O'Doherty, J., Dayan, P., Schultz, J., Deichmann, R., Friston, K., & Dolan, R. J. (2004). Dissociable roles of ventral and dorsal striatum in instrumental conditioning. *Science*, *304*, 452–454.

O'Doherty, J., Rolls, E. T., Francis, S., Bowtell, R., McGlone, F., Kobal, G., ... Ahne, G. (2000). Sensory-specific satiety-related olfactory activation of the human orbitofrontal cortex. *Neuroreport, 11*, 893–895.

O'Reilly, R. C., & Randall, C. (2010). The what and how of prefrontal cortical organization. *Trends in Neurosciences, 33*, 355–361.

Palminteri, S., Justo, D., Jauffret, C., Pavlicek, B., Dauta, A, Delmaire, C., ... Pessiglione, M. (2012). Critical roles for anterior insula and dorsal striatum in punishment-based avoidance learning. *Neuron, 76*, 998–1009.

Peterson, R. L. (2005). The neuroscience of investing: fMRI of the reward system. *Brain Research Bulletin, 67*, 391–397.

Plassmann, H., O'Doherty, J., Shiv, B., & Rangel, A. (2008). Marketing actions can modulate neural representations of experienced pleasantness. *Proceedings of the National Academy of Sciences, 105*, 1050–1054.

Previc, F. H. (1999). Dopamine and the origin of human intelligence. *Brain and Cognition, 41*, 299–350.

Rangel, A., & Hare, T. (2010). Neural computations associated with goal directed choice. *Current Opinion in Neurobiology, 20*, 262–270.

Rilling, J. K., Goldsmith, D. R., Glenn, A., Jairam, M. R., Elfenbein, H. A., Dagenais, J. E., ... Pagnoni, G. (2008). The neural correlates of affective response to unreciprocated cooperation. *Neuropsychologia, 46*, 1256–1266.

Rilling, J. K., Gutman, D. A., Zeh, T. R., Pagnoni, G., Berns, G. S., & Kilts, C. D. (2002). A neural basis for social cooperation. *Neuron, 35*, 395–405.

Rilling, J. K., & Sanfey, A. G. (2011). The neuroscience of social decision-making. *Annual Review of Psychology, 62*, 23–48.

Rilling, J. K., Sanfey, A. G., Aronson, J. A., Nystrom, L. E., & Cohen, J. D. (2004). Opposing BOLD responses to reciprocated and unreciprocated altruism in putative reward pathways. *Neuroreport, 15*, 2539–2543.

Robinson, J. L., Laird, A. R., Glahn, D. C., Blangero, J., Sanghera, M. K., Pessoa, L., ... Young, K. A. (2012). The functional connectivity of the human caudate: An application of meta-analytic connectivity modelling with behavioral filtering. *NeuroImage, 60*, 112–129.

Rolls, E. T. (2000). The orbitofrontal cortex and reward. *Cerebral Cortex, 10*, 284–294.

Ruff, C. C., & Fehr, E. (2014). The neurobiology of rewards and values in social decision-making. *Nature Reviews Neuroscience, 15*, 549–562.

Samuelson, P. (1937). A note on measuring utility. *The Review of Economic Studies, 4*, 155–161.

Sanfey, A. G. (2007). Social decision-making: Insights from game theory and neuroscience. *Science, 318*, 598–602.

Sanfey, A. G., Rilling, J. K., Aronson, J. A., Nystrom, L. E., & Cohen, J. D. (2003). The neural basis of economic decision-making in the ultimatum game. *Science, 300*, 1755–1758.

Schultz, W. (1997). Dopamine neurons and their role in reward mechanisms. *Current Opinion in Neurobiology, 7*, 191–197.

Schultz, W. (2002). Getting formal with dopamine and reward. *Neuron, 36*, 241–263.

Simpson, B. (2004). Social values, subjective transformations, and cooperation in social dilemmas. *Social Psychology Quarterly, 67*, 385–395.

Singer, T., Kiebel, S. J., Winston, J. S., Dolan, R. J., & Frith, C. D. (2004). Brain responses to the acquired moral status of faces. *Neuron, 41*, 653–662.

Skyrms, B. (2004). *The Stag Hunt and the Evolution of Social Structure*. Cambridge, U.K: Cambridge University Press.

Spitzer, M., Fischbacher, U., Herrnberger, B., Gron, G., & Fehr, E. (2007). The neural signature of social norm compliance. *Neuron, 56*, 185–196.

Staudinger, M. R., Erk, S., Abler, B., & Walter, H. (2009). Cognitive reappraisal modulates expected value and prediction error encoding in the ventral striatum. *NeuroImage, 45*, 713–721.

Stevens, J. R., & Hauser, M. D. (2004). Why be nice? Psychological constraints on the evolution of cooperation. *Trends in Cognitive Sciences, 8*, 60–65.

Stone, V. E., Baron-Cohen, S., Calder, A. J., Keane, J., & Young, A. (2003). Acquired theory of mind impairments in individuals with bilateral amygdala lesions. *Neuropsychologia, 41*, 209–220.

Tabibnia, G., & Lieberman, M. D. (2007). Fairness and cooperation are rewarding—Evidence from social cognitive neuroscience. *Annals of the New York Academy of Sciences, 1118*, 90–101.

Tabibnia, G., Satpute, A. B., & Lieberman, M. D. (2008). The sunny side of fairness—Preference for fairness activates reward circuitry (and disregarding unfairness activates self-control circuitry). *Psychological Science, 19*, 339–347.

Tricomi, E., Delgado, M. R., McCandliss, B. D., McClelland, J. L., & Fiez, J. A. (2006). Performance feedback drives caudate activation in a phonological learning task. *Journal of Cognitive Neuroscience, 18*, 1029–1043.

Tricomi, E., & Fiez, J. A. (2008). Feedback signals in the caudate reflect goal achievement on a declarative memory task. *NeuroImage, 41*, 1154–1167.

Tricomi, E., Rangel, A., Camerer, C. F., & O'Doherty, J. P. (2010). Neural evidence for inequality-averse social preferences. *Nature, 463*, 1089–1091.

Tricomi, E. M., Delgado, M. R., & Fiez, J. A. (2004). Modulation of caudate activity by action contingency. *Neuron, 41*, 281–292.

Tversky, A., & Kahneman, D. (1981). The framing of decisions and the psychology of choice. *Science, 211*, 453–458.

Van Overwalle, F. (2009). Social cognition and the brain: A meta-analysis. *Human Brain Mapping, 30*, 829–858.

Van Overwalle, F. (2011). A dissociation between social mentalizing and general reasoning. *NeuroImage, 54*, 1589–1599.

Van Overwalle, F., & Baetens, K. (2009). Understanding others' actions and goals by mirror and mentalizing systems: A meta-analysis. *NeuroImage, 48*, 564–584.

Waegeman, A., Declerck, C. H., Boone, C., Seurinck, R., & Parizel, P. M. (2014). Individual differences in behavioral flexibility in a probabilistic reversal learning task: An fMRI study. *Journal of Neuroscience, Psychology, and Economics, 7*, 203–218.

Walter, H., Abler, B., Ciaramidaro, A., & Erk, S. (2005). Motivating forces of human actions—Neuroimaging reward and social interaction. *Brain Research Bulletin, 67*, 368–381.

Weisman, D. H., Perkins, A. S., & Woldorff, M. G. (2008). Cognitive control in social situations: A role for the dorsolateral prefrontal cortex. *NeuroImage, 40*, 955–962.

Winston, J. S., Strange, B. A., O'Doherty, J., & Dolan, R. J. (2002). Automatic and intentional brain responses during evaluation of trustworthiness of faces. *Nature Neuroscience, 5*, 277–283.

Yamagishi, T., Jin, N., & Kiyonari, T. (1999). Bounded generalized reciprocity: Ingroup favoritism and ingroup boasting. *Advances in Group Processes, 16*, 161–197.

CHAPTER 3

Neurochemistry of Prosocial Decision Making: The Role of Dopamine, Serotonin, and Oxytocin

So far we have argued that proximate explanations for variation in prosocial behavior must be sought in the modulatory influences on the brain's valuation system. At the cellular level, neural modulation is accomplished through the release of neurotransmitters in synapses that connect neurons from disparate brain regions. There they target very specific receptors to which they bind and affect the efficacy of neural transmission and the firing pattern of the postsynaptic neuron. Through their excitatory or inhibitory properties, different neurotransmitters may have their own profound influence on moment-to-moment behavior. Thus, a discussion of the underlying processes that are responsible for the swaying in prosocial decision making would not be complete without considering the potential contributions of neurochemistry. In this chapter we will discuss the behavioral influences of three well-studied neurotransmitters—dopamine, serotonin, and oxytocin—and we will present some evidence that they have differential roles in generating economic versus socially rational decisions.

All three (dopamine, serotonin, and oxytocin) are phylogenetically old molecules with neuromodulating functions in the central nervous system. Their chemical structure is shown in Figure 3.1. Dopamine and serotonin are both monoamines derived from the amino acids tyrosine and tryptophan respectively while oxytocin is a small protein-like molecule (a neuropeptide) comprising 9 amino acids. The defining feature of a neuromodulator is that it is an indirect signal transduction mechanism, triggering a chain of biochemical events inside the cell. Signal transduction occurs when neuromodulators bind to metabotrophic receptors (or G-protein coupled receptors) located on the membrane of the postsynaptic cell, altering the configuration of the receptor and activating a primary effector (the G-protein), which can then go on to activate secondary messengers. The end effect is to open or close ion channels (letting more or less charged chemicals into the cell), which changes the membrane excitability and impacts the

Neuroeconomics of Prosocial Behavior. DOI: http://dx.doi.org/10.1016/B978-0-12-801303-8.00003-3

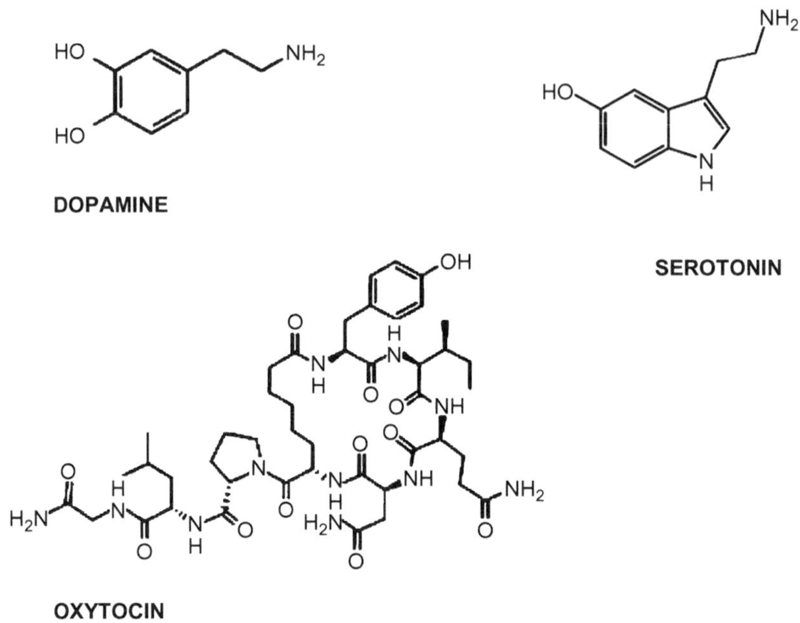

Figure 3.1 The chemical structure of dopamine, serotonin, and oxytocin. Dopamine (3,4-dihydroxyphenethylamine) and serotonin (5-hydroxytryptamine, abbreviated as 5-HT) are both neurotransmitters in the monoamine family. Dopamine is a catecholamine (i.e., containing a benzene ring with two hydroxyl groups) derived from the amino acid tyrosine Serotonin is an indolamine (i.e., containing an indole ring with one hydroxyl group) derived from tryptophan. Oxytocin is a neuropeptide acting as a neurotransmitter in the central nervous system and as a hormone in the periphery. It contains the following nine amino acids: cysteine-tyrosine-isoleucine-glutamine-asparagine-cysteine-proline-leucine-glycine.

amount of current that is needed for action potentials to be fired along the cell's membrane. Metabotrophic receptors differ from the other class of neurotransmitter receptors, known as ionotrophic receptors, which are basically gated ion channel pores. When a neurotransmitter binds to an ionotrophic receptor, it directly opens a channel that allows ions such as Na^+, K^+, or Cl^- to flow inside the cell. The main difference between gating ion channels by ionotrophic and metabotropic receptors is that the latter involves a number of secondary messengers, which will make for much longer-lasting effects that are also more widespread.

By altering the pattern of neuronal spiking in a given population of neurons, neuromodulators allow the brain to regulate control over sensory perceptions and action readiness. The inhibitory properties of dopamine, for example, reduce the signal-to-noise ratio for firing of nearby neurons, thereby directing more focused attention to the stimuli that are relevant for the task or decision at hand (Tucker & Williamson, 1984). In the following sections, however, we focus not so much on the cellular events, but on the overall patterns of behavior that are influenced by specific neuromodulators.

3.1 DOPAMINE

As one of the catecholamine neurotransmitters, dopamine (DA) has a simple structure derived from the amino acid tyrosine. Its exact functions are, however, more dependent on its location in the brain than on its structure. DA neurotransmission occurs along specific pathways of neurons that originate in the tegmentum of the midbrain. Two pathways are particularly relevant for human decision making: the mesolimbic dopaminergic pathway (from here on referred to as the *medial system* because of its more medial position in the brain) and the nigrostriatal and mesocortical dopaminergic pathways (which we will refer to jointly as the *lateral system*, consistent with their more lateral position).

The terms *medial* and *lateral* dopaminergic pathways, denoted by Previc (2009), also emphasize the divergence of these two subcortical-frontal dopamine systems during primate evolution. Using fluorescent dye tracings and immunohistochemistry, Williams and Goldman-Rakic (1998) showed that the different functional DA projections can be related to different origins in the midbrain. While the medial system emanates from cell groups in the ventral tegmental area in the midbrain, the lateral system has a more lateral cellular origin, a more dorsal striatal innervation, and expands into more lateral regions of the prefrontal cortex (especially the evolutionary recent dorsolateral prefrontal cortex). The lateral system appears to be unique to primates (Williams & Goldman-Rakic, 1998). Its fibers connect the substantia nigra in the midbrain with the dorsal striatum and then innervate the prefrontal cortex (Cummings, 1995; Tekin & Cummings, 2002). In humans its projections are especially prominent in the left hemisphere (Tucker & Williamson, 1984). Dopaminergic projections of the medial system, in contrast, loop around the limbic nuclei, the nucleus accumbens in the ventral striatum, and connect to the ventromedial prefrontal cortex (Cummings, 1995; Le Moal & Simon, 1991; Tekin & Cummings, 2002).

As one of the most commonly studied and well-known neurotransmitters, DA has been linked to several physical and mental disorders and is implicated in diverse functions including motor behavior, emotions, and cognition. Not surprisingly, DA has been labeled as an "everyman's transmitter" because it does everything (Previc, 2006, citing Koob, Riley, Smith, & Robbins, 1978). Perhaps the most plausible, overarching function of DA is that (despite its mostly inhibitory properties at the cellular level) it *activates*. More specifically, it enables motor readiness and stimulates approach behavior. The medial and the lateral dopaminergic systems furthermore appear to be differentiated in this respect: the medial system is known to facilitate appetitive behavior (Depue & Morrone-Strupinsky, 2005; Rolls, 2000; Schultz, 2002) and incentive motivation (Depue & Collins, 1999; Le Moal & Simon, 1991), and has been inferred to play an important role in the valuation system by contributing to the computation of expected (decision) utility (Berridge, 2012). In contrast, the lateral system is implicated in cognitive control by supporting executive functions such as working memory and flexibility, both of which are crucial to accomplish goal-directed behavior (Depue & Morrone-Strupinsky, 2005; Previc, 2009; Tekin & Cummings, 2002). As there is crosstalk between the two systems, it becomes difficult to isolate the contributions of either system alone to decision making. Most likely it is the relative balance of lateral versus medial DA activity that is key to understanding variations in behavior when overall DA levels remain basically the same (Previc, 2009). By connecting the lateral prefrontal cortex (PFC) with the dorsal striatum, the lateral system may exert cognitive control over incentive salient cues (e.g., Figner et al., 2010; Hare, Camerer, & Rangel, 2009). This means that decisions driven by immediate salient rewards (coded as such by medial DA neurons) may be overridden by lateral DA activity instigated by cues that indicate rewards in the distant future.

3.1.1 Medial Dopamine System and Incentive Salience

That the medial (mesolimbic) DA system plays an important role in reward processing has long been known. But the original impression, that DA was responsible for generating the pleasant feelings of a reward, was challenged about 20 years ago as researchers noted that humans and animals with hardly any dopamine in their brain could still experience normal pleasure (Berridge & O'Doherty, 2014). This means that DA is unlikely to play a role in the *experienced utility* of a decision, but more likely forms a necessary part of *decision utility* (see Chapter 2). Today, evidence has accumulated that "liking," "wanting," and "learning" are dissociable components of rewards, with "liking" being dependent mostly on opioids and endocannabinoids, while "wanting" and "learning" involve medial DA to some extent (Berridge & O'Doherty, 2014; Berridge, Robinson, & Aldridge, 2009). Consistently, pharmacological suppression of medial DA reduces "wanting" (e.g., cravings for a substance) but not "liking." Similarly, amplification of "wanting" by amphetamine stimulation may enhance cravings, but does not appear to alter "liking" (Berridge et al., 2009). While the brain usually likes what it wants, sometimes it may want something that it no longer likes, or not want something that is still liked.

If medial DA does not change the experience of pleasure following choice behavior, what then would be its exact role in valuation? Some authors (O'Doherty et al., 2004; Schultz, 2002) describe DA as an error prediction mechanism of reward learning. That is, DA facilitates remembering past rewards associated with a particular stimulus, and then helps to form expectations of future rewards associated with that same stimulus. However, while many experiments have corroborated the role of DA in some types of reward learning, including both Pavlovian and instrumental learning, the involvement of DA does not always appear to be necessary for learning to associate a reward with a stimulus or a goal-directed response. Boosting DA pharmacologically often fails to improve learning, even among those people that would mostly benefit from it. Therefore, other authors (Berridge, 2007) maintain that the evidence for DA in reward learning is inconclusive and that DA only enhances the *motivation* to earn the reward. This may at times lead to irrational decision making, such as consciously overpaying for a beverage for which one has a (perhaps unconsciously induced) craving (Berridge, 2012). Trying to reconcile the many, sometimes conflicting findings of DA's involvement in decision utility, Berridge and O'Doherty came to a consensus in a joint paper, agreeing that the medial DA system is definitely involved in incentive salience, while its role in learning may be more subtle and in need of further study (Berridge & O'Doherty, 2014). Also the dynamics of DA release should be examined in more detail: phasic and tonic DA release are known to have different properties, whereby phasic DA could represent reward prediction errors, while tonic DA could be involved in modulating the vigor of instrumental learning, similar to the "motivation" hypothesis just described (Niv, Daw, Joel, & Dyan, 2007).

What does all this mean with respect to prosocial decision making? Because medial DA is not involved in liking (or in experienced utility), it is unlikely to have any links with social rationality or with the numerous findings corroborating that a prosocial decision per se can be associated with pleasure (see Chapters 1 and 2). If medial DA is involved in learning, it could potentially still contribute to economically rational decisions, by facilitating a tit-for-tat strategy or "learning to cooperate" (see Rilling et al., 2002). However, if it turns out to be so that the only role of medial DA is to modulate incentive salience, even to the point that "wants" no longer have to correspond to "likes," the medial DA system is more likely to contribute to impulsive and selfish decisions, and it is unlikely to be related to insightful, long-term prosocial decision making, even when that would be the rational choice.

3.1.2 Lateral Dopamine System and Cognitive Control

A link between DA and economic rationality is more plausible via the lateral system, which heavily innervates the dorsolateral prefrontal cortex and the anterior cingulate gyrus, two regions that sustain the *frontal executive functions*, including working memory, planning, and shifting ability. Together with the striatum, these regions function to regulate behavior by updating the original goal held in memory with new contextual information, making goal-directed behavior possible. This evolutionary unequaled capacity to shift actions and strategies is what Mesulam (1998) referred to when he wrote that the prefrontal cortex makes no contributions to routine behaviors, but that it is a "luxury dividend that phylogeny offered primates and that catalyzed the ability to transcend stimulus-bound existence."

In his book *The Dopaminergic Mind in Human Evolution and History*, Fred Previc (2009) argues that the role of DA in goal-directed behavior clearly goes beyond purely enhancing motivation, and that it can be tied to several cognitive skills that are all, directly or indirectly, involved with attending to distant space and time. For all mobile animals, orienting in space is an important and ubiquitous task and, arguably, this may be the single-most important organizing principle shaping the major neural pathways in the brain (Previc, 1998). There is sufficient evidence (summarized in Previc, 2009) that DA activation increases the attention to and exploration of distant space. Throughout evolution, this role of DA may have become extended, starting with whole-body locomotion in rodents, to include oculomotor scanning in primates and, finally, abstract thought in humans (Previc, Declerck, & De Brabander, 2005). If, Previc argues, DA did not show this bias for processing spatially and temporally distant cues, allowing us to surpass the here and now and engage in offline, abstract thinking, its role in generating goal-directed behavior would have been much more limited. For example, working memory (sustained by DA) is essential to goal directed-behavior to keep the spatial location and representation of the future goal in immediate memory while working toward obtaining it. Planning ahead, another of the executive functions, requires keeping old and new information concurrently in working memory, so as to carry out the sequential steps needed to achieve future goals. Finally, cognitive flexibility allows us to change course as we move along toward that distant goal.

DA is the principal neurotransmitter involved in all the above-mentioned executive functions (Previc, 1999) and can be blocked by dopamine inhibitors (D'Esposito & Grossman, 1996; Diamond, 1996; Robbins, 2000; Welsh, 1996). Research with psychiatric patients furthermore indicates that mental afflictions that accompany disorders characterized by DA imbalances (e.g., a deficit of DA reported in Huntington's and Parkinson's disease, and above-average levels of DA in autism and schizophrenia) often come with impaired executive functioning. However, not all DA-effects related to mental disorders compromise executive functions, as patients suffering from autism may have an extraordinary working memory ability (one of the most important central executive functions) and high intelligence, yet they may at the same time have problems functioning in ordinary daily life activities, especially social activities. Some of these DA-affected patients hover between, on the one hand, hallucinatory imaginations in distant time and space and, on the other, being locked-in in the present.

The DA bias to distant space and time is also helpful to establish a causal association between events in the future and what they are worth to us, an ability necessary to overcome the habit of time discounting, or the tendency to weigh the attractiveness of a reward inversely to its delay. Postponing a given reward in favor of a better one is associated with increased activity in the dorsolateral prefrontal cortex (McClure, Laibson, Loewenstein, & Cohen, 2004; Waegeman, Declerck, Boone, Van Hecke, & Parizel, 2014), and it appears that DA systems are likely required for such cost–benefit analyses: when DA neurotransmission in rodents is blocked by haloperidol treatment, they no longer tolerate a delay. They more often choose 2 food pellets now rather than waiting for 10. Similarly, they are also less inclined to exert more effort for a better reward. After having been trained to climb a barrier in a T maze to obtain a food reward of 4 pellets, haloperidol-treated rats preferred the easier path without a barrier that leads to only a 2-pellet reward (Denk et al., 2005; see also Puumala & Sirvio, 1998, for a similar study).

The contributions of the lateral DA system to abstract thinking and computation (such as is needed in strategic planning and switching) may be well established, but its role in strategic *social interactions*, however, is less clear. Studies investigating how pharmacological manipulations of DA neurotransmission affect the social behavior of people are rare. An exception is the recent study by Pedroni, Eisenegger, Hartmann, Fischbacher, and Knoch (2014) who investigated the influence of administering a single dose of the drug Levodopa (or L-DOPA) on decisions made in two types of economic bargaining games. L-DOPA is a tyrosine-derived biochemical precursor of DA, and it is known to enhance DA neurotransmission in the brain. One of the bargaining games was similar to a dictator game, where the experimental subject acted as the proposer who could transfer a part of his or her monetary endowment to an anonymous recipient. The second game was similar to an ultimatum game where the recipient could punish the participant if the proposed offer was perceived to be unfair. This experimental setup allows us to uncover whether or not DA facilitates adapting behavior in an economically rational way, which would be accomplished by reducing offers in the dictator game and increasing them in the ultimatum game.[1] In the latter game, a prosocial decision is rational because, by complying to the fairness norm, pecuniary sanctions are likely avoided. Contrary to expectations, the data indicated no interaction effect between drug administration (L-DOPA versus placebo) and game condition (dictator game without sanctions versus ultimatum game with sanctions). All subjects were significantly more norm abiding when there was an actual punishment threat, with no observable difference between the L-DOPA versus placebo group. Furthermore, L-DOPA had no observable effect on punishment

[1]Note that this experimental setup is similar to the experiment by Spitzer, Fischbacher, Herrnberger, Gron, and Fehr (2007) described in Chapter 2. These researchers found that the dopamine-rich dorsolateral prefrontal cortex was more activated when participants transferred money in the ultimatum-like game compared to the dictator-like game. Thus it was plausible to expect that DA would have facilitated norm compliance in the ultimatum game which offers sanctions for noncooperation.

avoidance in the ultimatum game. In the dictator game, however, L-DOPA significantly reduced monetary transfers compared to the placebo condition. This is again consistent with the role of DA in reward seeking and selfish, short-sighted decision making.

Pharmacological manipulations of brain level DA do not, however, allow us to distinguish behavioral differences mediated by the lateral system from those of the medial system. With the Pedroni study, for example, we have to assume that both systems showed enhanced DA neurotransmission. The results are nevertheless thought-provoking, because they seem to imply that, under the given experimental conditions, boosting DA especially affected immediate reward-seeking behavior (thus engaging the medial system) and that its effect on cognitive control to establish the absence or presence of sanctions was less pronounced or even absent. If the lateral system were more engaged, we suspect that DA-treated individuals would also have responded to a punishment threat (by obeying the fairness norm) in the same way that they responded to a reward. The finding that DA only affected the response to reward (by keeping virtually all the money to themselves) is interesting because it suggests that, in a social context, DA may be more involved in impulsive selfishness than in strategic prosocial behavior, which is basically what we would expect from the medial system. The research findings by Pedroni et al. (2014) did not support the hypothesis that boosting DA would facilitate the detection of incentives that align self-interest and other interests in the ultimatum game.

The selfishness that results from DA activity is consistent with a left hemisphere bias for self-centered behavior. As the left hemisphere processes more piecemeal information in a logical and sequential way (e.g., Hellige, 2001), it may be predisposed to facilitate economic rationality without considerations of others. A recent hypothesis by McGilchrist (2009) pictures the left hemisphere as the "emissary," whose capacities became more important as complexity increased and the need for more detailed information processing grew, but which lost touch with the right hemisphere "master" holding the more global view. As the lateral dopaminergic system increased in importance throughout evolution and expanded, especially into the left hemisphere (Tucker & Williamson, 1984), a predominantly left-sided dopaminergic overactivation would have led to "internal control, ego-strength, technological abstraction and diminution of outside thoughts [...] all at the expense of empathy toward others and maintenance of the emotional self" (Previc, 2009, p. 128). As a corollary to the preponderance of selfish tendencies ascribed to the left hemisphere, there is also a vast literature on brain lesions from which it can be deduced that the right hemisphere is favored in prosocial interactions (reviewed in Hecht, 2014). Brain lesion studies seem to corroborate that patients with right-sided lesions in the parietal cortex have impaired considerations of others and weakened empathic responses (Shamay-Tsoory, Tomer, Goldsher, Berger, & Aharon-Peretz, 2004).

In conclusion, through enhancing incentive salience and reward-seeking decisions, and through increased attention for distant cues, DA could possibly facilitate an economic rationality, at least when it comes to computing cost benefits in nonsocial situations (such as in time-discounting tasks). In the social domain, however, this economic rationality apparently translates only to selfish decisions without much consideration of others. DA appears to have neither a special role in gauging social norms, nor in avoiding social punishments.[2] It is still possible, of course, that, when it comes to social interaction, rationality is determined by the concerted actions of DA, serotonin, and oxytocin. We will discuss later in this chapter how oxytocin increases DA release in the nucleus accumbens, and this mechanism might account for the linking of the experience of pleasure to social approach motivation. Moreover, the serotonergic inhibition of DA is one of the most widespread neurochemical interactions in the brain, so that greater DA concentrations in certain regions may produce less serotonin, and vice versa (Damsa et al., 2004; Previc, 2006, 2007, 2009). Drugs that increase serotonin tend to act therapeutically against the symptoms associated with a hyperdopaminergic condition, such as the social isolation reported for autism. Conversely, individuals with chronically low serotonin levels, or transient depletion of serotonin, are more prone to develop hyperdopaminergic psychopathologies such as schizophrenia (Previc, 2009). Finally, whereas DA can be linked to incentive-based

[2]Experimental studies that have looked directly at the specific effects of DA itself may be sparse, but they support the view that DA promotes selfishness with little regard for others or the outcome of social interactions. Additional research shows that amphetamines (DA agonists) diminish social behavior in voles (Young, Liu, Gobrogge, Wang, & Wang, 2014). In humans, drugs that block DA action are most effective to treat the symptoms of autism (which improves their social abilities), whereas DA agonists exacerbate autistic traits (Volkmar, 2001). Because we do not know exactly where drugs target the brain, it is also possible that these effects are due to interactions with other neurotransmitters (Volkmar, 2001).

positive emotional states, such as grandiosity, elation, and even euphoria (Panksepp, 2006; Previc, 2009), it is also associated with emotional detachment and social isolation (Previc, 2009). High serotonin levels, in contrast, are typical of proximal, affiliative interactions (Depue & Morrone-Strupinsky, 2005). In the next section we address more precisely the role of serotonin modulation in social decision making.

3.2 SEROTONIN

For the indolamine serotonin (5-hydroxytryptamine, or 5-HT) there is more direct evidence for a link with economic rationality and, more specifically, economically rational prosocial behavior. In this section we will try to make the case that, in the domain of decision making, 5-HT, more than DA, supports the decision heuristic "*I am selfish but I cooperate when there are cooperative incentives.*" Specifically, we will present some evidence that 5-HT is a necessary factor in the process of assessing whether or not it is worth it to cooperate, given the available incentives. In that case, the regulatory properties of 5-HT will provide the necessary control to inhibit selfish urges. When there is a deficiency of 5-HT, the strategic benefits of cooperation are not realized, leading to asocial and/or selfish behaviors that are not rational and eventually result in failure or economic losses.

As is the case for the other monoamines, 5-HT is again an evolutionary conserved molecule, derived from the amino acid tryptophan. It is synthesized in the raphe nuclei located on the midline of the brain stem, and the multiple 5-HT receptors lie along ascending neurons that extend over the entire brain. 5-HT is released into synapses of neurons that are arranged into a distinct serotononergic system connecting, among others, the limbic, insular, and prefrontal cortex regions. Although only a small percentage of total body serotonin is found in the brain (with around 90% found in the digestive tract), this messenger has well-known and profound effects on behavior. In the central nervous system, 5-HT is implicated in regulating a diverse array of functions, including appetite, sleep, sexual arousal, learning, and mood. Above and beyond these properties, 5-HT is generally thought of as producing happiness or well-being, which explains why manipulating 5-HT in the central nervous system levels has become an important target for treating mental health disorders. For a reference to the diverse functions of central serotonin, we refer to Soubrie (2010).

The relation between general well-being and 5-HT is a clue that this neurotransmitter plays a role in regulating social behavior, as social integration is indispensable to happiness. For many animal species including primates, there is overwhelming evidence that low 5-HT is related to aggression, and in particular, emotion-driven aggression (rather than predatory aggression). Retributional aggressive behavior (often related to vengeance) is typically unconstructive and inappropriately expressed and can therefore lead to social isolation and subsequent antisocial behavior. High 5-HT, on the contrary, is related to high social rank. For many species, attaining high social ranks requires strategic prosocial behaviors. For example, Raleigh and colleagues showed that, in stable groups of vervet monkeys, individual differences in affiliative behaviors (e.g., grooming) were positively associated with several indices of serotonergic functioning (Raleigh et al., 1981) and that these behaviors could be altered by pharmacological intervention of 5-HT (Raleigh, Brammer, McGuire, & Yuwiller, 1985).

In a clever follow-up experiment, these researchers showed that affiliative behaviors are expressed strategically to acquire dominance. First, they disturbed the social ranking of the group by removing the dominant males of 12 social groups. Then, for four consecutive weeks, one of the remaining subdominant males received drugs to either facilitate or diminish serotonergic function. The dietary supplement tryptophan (the precursor of 5-HT) and the serotonin reuptake inhibitor fluoxetine were used to augment 5-HT levels. These males soon engaged in more prosocial behavior: in comparison to untreated males, they approached, groomed, and stayed in closer proximity of conspecifics, and they also aggressed less. During the second week of the experiment, and probably as a result of the increase in affiliation, the females differentially directed their coalitional support toward the treated males. This was a critical step, because support from high-ranking females is essential for males to attain dominance. Finally, by the end of the fourth week, each one of the tryptophan- or fluoxetine-treated males achieved dominance status. In contrast, none of the males that had been treated with drugs to decrease brain 5-HT concentrations (fenfluramine or cyproheptadine) reached high dominance, and throughout the experimental period these males had shown a decline in approach, grooming, and proximity, while they became more active and engaged in more aggressive behavior (Raleigh, McGuire, Brammer, Pollack, & Yuwiller, 1991). These results are a convincing demonstration that activation of the serotonergic system is necessary to attain dominance via strategic prosocial behavior. Acquiring a dominant social status, in this case, appears to be the incentive to cooperate.

Inspired by the vervet monkey study, Moskowitz, Pinard, Zuroff, Annable, and Young (2001) tried to replicate the findings in a human population. Using a within-subject design, they treated 98 experimental subjects for several days with tryptophan (to augment 5-HT levels) and a placebo (in random order), and asked them to report on the various behaviors they had been engaged in during their everyday social interactions. Similar to the monkeys, participants reported that they were less quarrelsome and that they showed more dominance-type behaviors when receiving tryptophan compared to the placebo.

While the Moskowitz study is informative because it was conducted in a natural human setting (social interactions occurring in daily lives), it is difficult to draw a cause-and effect conclusion between the 5-HT manipulations and the self-reported behaviors. The uncontrolled setting allows for many spurious variables to affect state fluctuations in behavior, and the nature of self-report questionnaires makes it difficult to avoid answers that are tainted with social desirability. To fill this void, a number of experiments have been conducted in laboratory settings using the prisoner's dilemma paradigm. In two studies, Tse and Bond (2002a, 2002b) showed that, compared to a placebo treatment, boosting 5-HT functioning with selective serotonin reuptake inhibitors increased cooperative behavior in a repeated mixed motive game (a modified prisoner's dilemma game). In addition to making their decisions, participants were allowed to send each other communicative messages halfway through the trials. Again, the 5-HT treatment elicited significantly more cooperative messages (such as "I enjoy working with you"), which seems a very reasonable thing to do, at least when one has the economically rational intent to elicit cooperation from the partner (Tse & Bond, 2002a). In the second study, the authors found less evidence for cooperation when the partner (a confederate of the study) behaved in a non-sociable manner. The authors conclude that 5-HT helps the participants to protect themselves against the negative consequences of social interactions (Tse & Bond, 2002b).

The converse, that reducing 5-HT levels decreases cooperative behavior, was shown in an experiment where participants were temporarily deprived of dietary tryptophan, a procedure that is known to affect central nervous system 5-HT levels and associated cognitive functions (Wood, Rilling, Sanfey, Bhagwagar, & Rogers, 2006). To implement a within-subject design, the experiment was conducted on two different days. On each day participants were either given a tryptophan-containing beverage to restore normal 5-HT levels or a beverage without tryptophan (maintaining the depleted state). Next participants engaged in the iterated version of the prisoner's dilemma game, playing a series of games twice against a computer programmed to respond in a tit-for-tat manner. The participants, however, thought they were playing against real partners. On the first day of the experiment, tryptophan depletion reduced cooperative responses by 31%. Given that the tit-for-tat strategy is known to be an effective way to elicit cooperation from a partner (Sheldon, 1999), it is remarkable that cooperative response in the depleted condition remained so low, even following a mutually cooperative outcome. In addition, pairwise within-subject comparisons indicated that depleted individuals who cooperated little on day 1 of the study significantly increased their level of cooperation when tryptophan was restored on day 2. In contrast, those individuals in the control condition who cooperated much on day 1 continued to cooperate on day 2, when tryptophan was depleted. In other words, tryptophan depletion did not have a significant effect on the second day of the experiment, when participants had already learned through experience that cooperation was strategically the best outcome. The authors interpret this to mean that disruption of 5-HT impairs the *acquisition* of cooperative behaviors, even when the strategies of the game partners (playing tit for tat) are geared to elicit reciprocity.[3]

Tryptophan depletion in humans has previously been associated with an impaired ability to learn and relearn stimulus-reinforcement associations (Park et al., 1994) and with a compromised capacity to delay gratification (Denk et al., 2005; Soubrie, 2010). There is also accumulating evidence that 5-HT modulates various aspects of reward processing, including the circuitry encompassing the ventral striatum and ventromedial prefrontal cortex (Robbins & Everitt, 1996;

[3]The finding that the effect of an increase or decrease in the level of 5-HT is only significant when a task is performed for the first time (as it was in the first part of the study) and that its effect is less pronounced the second time around (as in the second part of the study) has been reported several times (e.g., Moskowitz et al., 2001; Park et al., 1994). Thus 5-HT treatment can have different effects on behaviors depending on how much previous experience and learning went on prior to taking the drug.

Sasaki-Adams & Kelley, 2001), which would indicate a role of 5-HT in experiencing the rewarding outcome of cooperation.

The capacity to link stimuli to a rewarding outcome is critical to function effectively in many social environments. In an iterated prisoner's dilemma game, economically rational decision making requires that the link be made between the repeated nature of the game and the long-term rewards that accrue. From the experiments described previously it appears that lowering 5-HT interferes with this ability, leaving the individual selfishly tempted by short-term impulses. In contrast, activating 5-HT makes people strategically cooperative. But to ascertain the role of 5-HT in economic rationality, we would also need to show that, without incentives, 5-HT makes a person strategically selfish. For this we would need a study that looks at the effect of 5-HT on behavior in a one-shot, anonymous interaction where there are no lingering long-term implications of a (non)cooperative decision. A study with the ultimatum game points in this direction.

In the ultimatum game, a proposer (the first player) receives a monetary endowment that can be shared in any proportion with a receiver (the second player). The second player has the choice to either accept the offer, in which case the proposed split is implemented, or reject the offer, in which case neither player receives anything. A rich amount of empirical data collected on all continents indicated that proposers are likely to give away around 50% of their endowment, that offers of 20% or less are rejected more than half the time, and that rejection rates increase as offers become smaller (Camerer, 2003; Thaler, 1988). A rational receiver is expected to accept any offer, because any positive amount of money is better than no money at all. Accepting an unfair offer in the ultimatum game is therefore the economically rational thing to do: it provides a benefit to others as well as to the self. Rejecting an unfair offer serves as a punishment for the proposer and may express the responder's taste for fairness, but it involves a personal cost. Rejection may also serve as a signal to the remainder of the group that unfair behavior is not tolerated and that violators of the fairness norm are punished. In this sense, rejecting an unfair offer may be considered socially rational, but it is definitely not economically rational. Because neither party benefits when an offer is rejected, and because the decision to reject is driven by negative emotions and not by a cooperative intent, rejection is here considered an antisocial rather than a prosocial behavior. Indeed, rejection in a ultimatum game has been shown to be driven by anger and spite (Pillutla & Murnighan, 1996) and heightened physiological arousal (van't Wout, Kahn, Sanfey, & Aleman, 2006). Rejection rates drop drastically when receivers are able to express their negative emotions to the proposer in a communicative message (Xiao & Houser, 2005). This seems to be sufficient to resolve the issue of punishing norm violators and to restore economically rational decision making.

Molly Crockett used the tryptophan depletion procedure and showed that, as expected, lowering 5-HT increases the rejection of unfair offers (Crockett, Clark, Tabibnia, Lieberman, & Robbins, 2008). Lowering 5-HT did not affect the normal tendency to accept fair offers more often than unfair offers, suggesting that 5-HT does not interfere with the reward computation mechanisms itself. Neither could the results be explained by changes in mood. Crockett noted that the effect of lowering 5-HT on rejection was similar to the decisions made by ventromedial prefrontal cortex (vmPFC) patients. As the vmPFC is highly innervated by dorsal raphe 5-HT projections, this suggests that the increase in rejection may be the result of modulation of vmPFC neuronal activity. She later described three possible mechanisms by which 5-HT modulation might affect the decision to accept or reject unfair offers (Crockett, 2009). First, 5-HT may play a role in altering behavior when response contingencies change: it downregulates the emotional reaction associated with previously rewarded, but now punished responses. Impairing 5-HT through tryptophan depletion may interfere with the vmPFC's role of downregulating the negative emotions following unfair offers. Second, given that 5-HT promotes calmness and emotional resilience, lowering 5-HT neurotransmission in the limbic system and insula may heighten the reactivity to emotional events (such as being treated unfairly). Third, low 5-HT levels may have altered the connectivity pattern between the prefrontal cortex and the limbic system/insula. This last proposition is consistent with a recent functional magnetic resonance imaging (fMRI) finding indicating an inverse relation between activity in the ventrolateral prefrontal cortex and the insula in the brain of responders facing an unfair offer in the ultimatum game. These offers have a higher chance of being rejected as insula activation increases, and prefrontal cortex activity decreases (Tabibnia, Satpute, & Lieberman, 2008).

The resulting increase in rejecting unfair offers with lowered 5-HT levels depletion is again suggestive of our proposal that serotonergic functions are involved in driving economically rational decision heuristics. In the ultimatum game, accepting an unfair offer is the nicer, and also the more lucrative, decision, but when strong emotions obscure the advantage of "having something against having nothing," impulsive decision making overrides. With deficient 5-HT modulation, the link between the cooperative decision (in this case, accepting) and the incentive (each gets his share of the deal) is not made, and the person abides by the "I am selfish" heuristic, resorting to a spiteful outcome (so that both people lose).[4]

Under normal 5-HT functioning, people realize that suppressing the urge to punish is profitable (despite the fact that it is unfair) and therefore an incentive to be nice. This is not so different from the deduction of Philippe Soubrie (2010), who attributed to 5-HT an overarching role in behavioral inhibition. In a *Behavioral and Brain Sciences* article, he summarizes the human and animal evidence suggesting that the inhibition caused by 5-HT cannot solely be due to its supposed relief of mental anxiety. In addition, central serotonergic activity would guard a person against the urge to remove the obstacles that typically prevent the immediate attainment of an anticipated reward. He proposes that serotonergic neurons are involved in "enabling the organism to arrange or to tolerate delay before acting" (p. 319). From the evidence we have summarized in this section, this applies also to social interactions. Decreasing 5-HT will therefore increase the impulsive but socially inappropriate response that is usually suppressed, to the point that behavior is no longer economically rational.[5]

[4]This scenario treats rejection as an impulsive, emotion-driven response, for which there is much evidence. However, individuals tend to be inconsistent in their pattern of punishments (punishing in some types of games and not in others), and punishment is also very sensitive to moment-to-moment fluctuations in moods and in framing effects. Therefore, there may be multiple motivations to reject unfair offers in an ultimatum game, some of which may be driven out of a concern for the wellness of the group. Our main proposition here is that these more socially rational motivations to reject are not driven by the serotonergic system.

[5]Although we do not review the role of norepinephrine, there are reasons to accept that its functions in promoting prosociality may be similar to those of serotonin (Tse and Bond, 2002b). Structurally, norepinephrine is a cathecholamine derived from dopamine and differing only in having an additional hydroxyl group. Both catecholamines increase sympathetic nervous system activity, but whereas dopamine and serotonin activate by focusing attention, the primary function of norepinephrine lies in sensory arousal, promoting vigilant attention. Therefore it is perhaps not surprising that norepinephrine is also often implicated in studies on social behavior, as social interactions are typically arousing. Nelson and Panksepp (1998) report that norepinephrine may play a role in the formation of odor-based social memory in rodents (similar to oxytocin). The work of Tse and Bond shows that, in humans, enhancing norepinephrine with drug treatment boosts social assertiveness and agreeableness, which are sometimes related to cooperation (Tse & Bond, 2002b, 2003, 2006).

The findings suggesting that 5-HT promotes economically rational prosocial behavior (i.e., that the prosocial intent is pre-meditated and serves an economic purpose) do not necessarily discount the possibility that 5-HT might also mediate prosociality at a more basal level, or that it might play a role in affiliative bonding. We already mentioned earlier that 5-HT may have a modulatory role in experiencing rewards from social interaction through its influences on the ventral striatum and ventromedial prefrontal cortex (Robbins & Everitt, 1996; Sasaki-Adams & Kelley, 2001), which may explain the reports that enhancing 5-HT with drugs leads to increased social confidence and feelings of connectedness with others (Nelson & Panksepp, 1998, citing Kramer, 1993). Rats that experience prolonged social isolation have greatly reduced brain 5-HT levels, further suggesting a role in regulating bonding and affiliative behavior (Jones, Hernandez, Kendall, Marsden, & Robbins, 1992). Research on the prosocial side-effects of MDMA ("ecstacy") indicates that taking the drug is associated with increased plasma levels of prolactin, which is a marker of serotonergic activity (Hysek et al., 2014). But so is oxytocin, hence the role of 5-HT in "feeling connected" may only be of secondary significance compared to the impact of other neurotransmitters. In the next section we will show that oxytocin probably underscores one of the most important mechanisms facilitating *socially* rational prosocial behavior, far more so than serotonin.

3.3 OXYTOCIN

The last decade has seen a surge of studies addressing the role of oxytocin in regulating human social behavior, so dramatic that even the media caught on and promptly labeled it the "cuddle hormone," advocating it as a therapeutic, almost magic love potion. While this should be a hint toward a role in promoting socially rational behavior, the next section will make clear that the media's portrayal has been shortsighted, and that by now many antisocial properties of oxytocin have also been reported, making it not so cuddly after all. Nevertheless, even the "dark side of oxytocin" points to a hormone that appears to facilitate group living by enhancing trust, generosity, and loyalty in an ecologically sensible way and by creating personally satisfying human relationships. In fact, the combination of the disparate functions and behavioral outcomes that have been ascribed to oxytocin suggest that this small molecule may have played a tremendous role in the evolution of social rationality.

Oxytocin (OT) is a nine-amino-acid peptide, produced in the hypothalamus of the brain. It is known to activate only a single type of oxytocin receptor (OTR) distributed throughout the central nervous system and periphery. Stored in the pituitary and released into the bloodstream, it also acts as a hormone affecting a variety of bodily functions, mostly related to reproduction. Perhaps oxytocin is best known for triggering the letdown reflex in breastfeeding mothers and causing uterine contractions during the later stages of labor, thus its name "rapid birth" in Greek. Its structure is evolutionary conserved in all vertebrate taxa, and originally it may have served to support osmotic regulation and egg-laying (Choleris, Pfaff, & Kavaliers, 2013). In mammals, these functions may have become co-opted to regulating maternal and social behavior as well, including social recognition and memory, pair-bonding, alloparental behavior, flocking and grooming, sharing, trusting, and cooperating (see recent reviews such as Anacker & Beery, 2013; Bos, Panksepp, Bluthé, & van Honk, 2012; Broad, Curley, & Keverne, 2006; Ebitz & Platt, 2013; Meyer-Lindenberg, Domes, Kirsch, & Heinrichs, 2011; Olff et al., 2013). Considering the importance of these behaviors to group living, several researchers put forth the hypothesis that, during primate evolution, the ancestral role of OT in sexual and maternal behaviors became extended to facilitate bonding between sexual partners and, eventually, between more distant group members. This would set the stage for extended group care and cooperation. However, a recent body of research investigating the effects of exogenous OT administration to humans also revealed antisocial consequences, such as competitiveness and ethnocentricity (Declerck, Boone, & Kiyonari, 2010; De Dreu, 2012), aggression (Campbell, 2008), lying (Shalvi & De Dreu, 2014), envy, and *schadenfreude* (Shamay-Tsoory et al., 2009).

These counterexamples prompted researchers to identify those conditions where OT promotes prosociality and those where it does not, or even acts against it. The neuroeconomic approach in these studies is threefold: searching for the factors that trigger endogenous OT release, understanding how an increase in central OT affects the neural firing patterns in the brain, and, finally, finding out how these OT-mediated changes in neural activity alter behavior.

3.3.1 Neural and Behavioral Responses to a Change in Central Oxytocin

Endogenous OT release in a mammalian "receiver" occurs as a natural response to honest, affiliative social signals sent out by a "signaler" attempting to provide information about the likelihood that a social interaction will turn out to be friendly as opposed to antagonistic (Ebitz & Platt, 2014). In humans, social signals that have been shown to correlate with a subsequent rise in plasma levels of oxytocin include suckling (Heinrichs, Neumann, & Ehlert, 2002), touch (Morhenn, Park, Piper, & Zak, 2008), and massage (Morhenn, Beavin, & Zak, 2012). Similarly, plasma oxytocin levels have been reported to rise in both men and women following orgasm (Carmichael et al., 1987), when playing with one's child (Strathearn, Fonagy, Amico, & Montague, 2009), or simply when receiving someone's trust (Zak, Kurzban, & Matzner, 2004). While it is still not exactly clear how a boost of endogenous OT release in the periphery translates to a change in central OT, there is plenty of evidence that social signals such as those just described also affect behavior through a cascade of OT neuromodulatory effects in the receiver's brain (Meyer-Lindenberg et al., 2011; Ross et al., 2009).[6]

From neuroscience, we know that OT receptors are distributed throughout the brain, although a clear mapping is still lacking (Bethlehem, van Honk, Auyeung, & Baron-Cohen, 2013; Zink & Meyer-Lindenberg, 2012). A major difference with dopamine and serotonin neurotransmission is that OT release is not restricted to synaptic connections of neurons that are arranged in functional neural pathways (as is the case for the mesolimbic dopaminergic pathway discussed earlier). Instead, OT can be released from all parts of a neuron into the extracellular space and diffuse over a much wider range of the brain, affecting a broader spectrum of functions. Thus, compared to classical neurotransmitters, the spatial and functional specificity of OT is much smaller (Meyer-Lindenberg et al., 2011). Nevertheless, neuroimaging studies that have investigated the influence of intranasal OT administration in double blind experiments have drawn our attention to a number

[6]Many of the behavioral effects observed with OT result, in fact, from interactions with sex hormones and cross reactions with vasopressin, a nanopeptide whose amino-acid sequence differs in only two positions from oxytocin. Bos et al. (2012) review how steroid hormones and neuropeptides influence different and overlapping aspects of social behavior, with vasopressin interacting primarily with testosterone, and oxytocin with estrogen.

of brain regions that are *consistently* affected when subjects under the scanner are asked to evaluate social signals or make social decisions. These studies point overwhelmingly to the role of subcortical regions, including the striatum and the amygdala. In addition, the insular and subgenual anterior cingulate cortex are also prime targets of OT. The role of the amygdala is not surprising, considering that the amygdala plays a critical role in social cognition (see Chapter 2) and in extracting trustworthiness information from faces (Adolphs, 2010).

The amygdala has long been known to process fear and threatening signals and provides the major link with the peripheral autonomic nervous system. The presence of neurons that respond both excitatory and inhibitory to OT binding was first shown by Huber, Veinante, and Stoop (2005), a finding that was then corroborated by a number of fMRI studies indicating that exposure to exogenous OT (compared to a placebo) attenuates amygdala activation when viewing pictures of threatening faces (Kirsch et al., 2005; Petrovic, Kalisch, Singer, & Dolan, 2008) or emotional faces in general (Domes et al., 2007a). Other studies showed that different parts of the amygdala become either activated or deactivated when viewing respectively happy or angry faces (Gamer, Zurowski, & Buechel, C., 2010). Sex differences are noted as well: when females view threatening stimuli, exogenous OT appears to activate, rather than attenuate the amygdala response (Domes et al., 2010; Lischke et al., 2012). Such findings point to interactions with sex hormones and reinforce the importance of taking individual differences into account when interpreting the behavioral effects of OT, a point we return to later in this section.

In addition to the amygdala, regions of the striatum (the dorsally located caudate nucleus and the more ventral nucleus accumbens) may also be critical in shaping the behaviors that follow a rise in central OT. Changes in the reactivity of the caudate nucleus after OT inhalation (compared to a placebo) have been reported in two studies. First, participants in the study by Baumgartner, Heinrichs, Vonlanthen, Fischbacher, and Fehr (2008) played the part of "investor" in a trust game while their brains were scanned with fMRI. In this game, the investor is asked how much of an endowment he or she is willing to send to a trustee. The invested money is tripled, after which the trustee may send back a portion of the gains. Thus, the investor has to trust that his or her investment will pay off and that the trustee does not keep all the money to him or herself. Participants who received oxytocin showed reduced activation in the amygdala and caudate. Consistent with the caudate' role in updating behavior (Chapter 2), those who received a placebo significantly changed their trusting behavior in subsequent games. In contrast, no-one in the oxytocin group changed their willingness to invest after being informed that their initial investments were repaid only 50% of the time. Thus, it seems that a boost of OT signals that the trustee in this game is trustworthy, thereby reducing the need to learn from feedback. Such a drastic behavioral response of OT was not found in a similar study conducted by Rilling et al. (2012). Here participants played a repeated prisoner's dilemma game (see Chapters 1 and 2), where two players have to independently decide to cooperate or defect in a number of trials. The monetary rewards in each trial are determined by the combination of their choices. When cooperation was reciprocated, intranasal OT administration increased amygdala and caudate activity. In this case, OT apparently stimulated feedback learning, which would facilitate positive reciprocation. This shows that the type of paradigm (trust vs. prisoner's dilemma game) used in an experiment greatly impacts how OT will affect brain activity. In both of the cases described, however, the end result seems to suggest that OT acts to sustain a continued cooperative relationship.

Considering that OT has often been associated with positive affect, its documented influence on the nucleus accumbens in the ventral striatum is perhaps not surprising. Secure breastfeeding mothers show greater ventral striatum activity when viewing pictures of the face of their own baby under the scanner (Strathearn et al., 2009). OT may furthermore modulate neural activity in the reward system by stimulating mesolimbic DA release in the nucleus accumbens, thereby connecting the DA-mediated incentive motivation to the experience of pleasure (Depue & Morrone-Strupinsky, 2005; Skuse & Gallagher, 2008).[7] Thus, OT might facilitate social encounters by linking them to feeling rewarded from interaction with others (Campbell, 2008; Guastella, Mitchell, & Mathews, 2008).

[7]There is some evidence from research with mice that the rewarding properties of social interaction may also require the coordinated actions of oxytocin and serotonin in the nucleus accumbens (Dolen, Darvishzaden, Huang, & Malenka, 2013). However, there is also research with mice showing inhibitory interactions between dopamine and oxytocin (Qi et al., 2008), so oxytocin may not unequivocably stimulate dopamine release in the nucleus accumbens.

Finally, a number of studies have shown that, under certain conditions, intranasal administration of OT increases empathic concern for others (Abu-Akel, Palgi, Klein, Decety, & Shamay-Tsoory, 2015; Hurlemann et al., 2010; Krueger et al., 2013), leading some authors to hypothesize that OT affects the neural circuitry of emotional empathy (Decety, Norman, Berntson, & Cacioppo, 2012; De Dreu, 2012), which includes the insula, anterior medial cingulate cortex, and inferior frontal gyrus (Lamm, Batson, & Decety, 2007). Consistently, when scanned with fMRI, women who were given OT showed increased BOLD signals in the insula and inferior frontal gyrus in response to listening to an infant crying (Riem, Pieper, Out, Bakermans-Kranenburg, & van Ijzendoorn, 2011). The increased insular response supposedly indicates that the experimental signal (an infant cry) causes a subjective emotional discomfort (Decety et al., 2012), which can be interpreted as eliciting maternal care toward offspring (Riem et al., 2011).[8]

In summary, the altered neural activity patterns induced by OT[9] can be categorized into three general classes of influences, all of which would eventually increase prosocial behavior (see also De Dreu, 2012; Kemp & Guastella, 2011): (1) reduced social anxiety by attenuating activity in the amygdala; (2) increased pleasure in social interactions by (in)direct effects on the reward system (involving the caudate and ventral striatum); and (3) increased concern for others by enhancing activity in the neural circuitry of emotional empathy.

Inasmuch as these three generalizations will hold in the face of future research, it is safe to conclude that OT, in many instances, does promote prosociality. But to qualify as a neuromodulator that promotes *socially rational behavior*, the bias toward prosocial decisions needs to be ecologically warranted. If OT were to indiscriminately favor prosocial decisions, this would create an infinite spiral of prosocial signaling and responding that could easily burst. Any hard-wired mechanism that sustains prosocial behavior is bound to be selected against, as it would be prone to mimicking behavior to obtain benefits without giving anything in return. To fit with the principles of

[8]The increased empathic response and insular activation was, however, not found in a sample of males who received intranasal OT and were scanned with fMRI while observing their partners receiving a painful stimulation to the hand (Singer et al., 2008).

[9]Importantly, OT can also change the functional connectivity of the above-mentioned brain regions in response to social signals. See Bethlehem et al., 2013, and Zink & Meyer-Lindenberg, 2012 for reviews on the subject.

ecological rationality, OT should not modulate decision making independent from the context in which the decision is made. Therefore, many authors have called for an interactionist approach to the study of OT (Bartz, Zaki, & Ochsner, 2011a; Declerck et al., 2010; Ebitz & Platt, 2014), whereby the behavioral effects of increased OT levels would depend on the evolutionary history of the species, the current ecological demands, and individual differences in personality. These contingencies are the focus of the next sections. We will describe studies that corroborate that OT elicits an adaptive decision bias and that it is therefore a good candidate underlying the heuristic "*I cooperate unless there are indications that my partner is untrustworthy.*"

3.3.2 Effect of Oxytocin Depends on a Species' Evolutionary History

In all mammals, from mice to sheep to primates, pregnancy and parturition are characterized by hormonal changes preparing the animal not only for the physiological changes that make birth and lactation possible, but also for the behavioral changes that will be necessary for the survival of the offspring. To accomplish this, evolution favored a conservatory use of biochemical pathways that coordinate peripheral physiology with behavioral motivations (Ross & Young, 2009). In many species (including humans), the onset of parental behaviors correlates with rising OT levels. However, the particularities of these behaviors appear to be species specific. In rodents, maternal behaviors include nest building, licking, grooming, and hovering over pups—behaviors that are absent in virgin or nulliparous females. These behaviors are similarly absent in OTR gene knockout mice, or in rats that have just given birth but were injected with an OT antagonist. The maternal behaviors of rodents are, however, not specific to their own pups but could be displayed to any genetically unrelated pup placed in her nest. The ecological implications of this nonspecificity are likely to be trivial, because rodents have altricial young and therefore the probability that this would actually happen in nature is rather low. This is different from sheep, who live in large herds and give birth en masse to precocial young that are sufficiently mobile to get stranded into a foreign nest. A ewe will reject a lamb that is not her own, a behavior that has been attributed to OT released during labor. This happens because OT facilitates the formation of olfactory memories, allowing the ewe to recognize and differentiate between the odors of different lambs. This ability may help species with precocial young to secure a very selective mother–infant bond and prevent wasting energy on offspring that are not genetically their own (Ross & Young, 2009).

The role of forming long-lasting pair bonds and the extent of alloparenting (including father care) has been most extensively studied in voles because, within the same genus, there are different social structures that are related to distinct neuroanatomical substrates. The monogamous prairie vole, for example, provides biparental care and has a much greater density of OTR in the nucleus accumbens and the caudate nucleus compared to the nonmonogamous meadow vole or montane vole (the latter living in mountainous or other high-elevation terrain). OT antagonists that are injected into the nucleus accumbens block alloparenting and mate preferences in the prairie voles (Young, Lim, Gingrich, & Insel, 2001). Using viral vector transfer, researchers were furthermore able to show that partner preference formation can be accelerated when OTR in the nucleus accumbens becomes overexpressed. However, increasing OTR expression in the nucleus accumbens of the meadow vole is not sufficient to induce partner preference, suggesting that the mechanism by which OT underscores a particular social structure does not work in its same, unmodified state in another species. Changing the expression of the vasopressin (rather than OT) receptor in the ventral striatum, however, does seem to facilitate partner preference formation in the meadow vole (Lim, Wang, Olazabal, Terwilliger, & Young, 2004), suggesting that multiple neurochemical differences are probably responsible for social bonding among different species of voles.

Thus, it seems that evolutionarily, the behavioral effects of OT are shaped by neural plasticity in the expression of OTR in very specific brain regions, which may in part be determined by species-specific differences in ecology. While the social structure of rodents and sheep is determined mostly by olfaction, humans rely much more on visual cues, and this is likely to affect which brain regions will be targeted by OT and which behaviors will emerge when these regions are activated.

3.3.3 Effect of Oxytocin Depends on Context

Lactating Wistar rats may show very affectionate care toward their pups. However, if they have been bred for high anxiety related behaviors, they will behave very aggressively toward virgin intruders, and this maternal aggression correlates positively with central OT.

Blocking the OTR with an antagonist reduces aggression among rats with high anxiety, but increases aggression in low anxiety rats, corroborating that OT stimulates defense-motivated aggression toward intruders, helping anxious rats (those who need it most) to protect their offspring (Bosch, Meddle, Beiderbeck, Douglas, & Neumann, 2005).

In human social behavior, there are many similar reports that intranasally administered OT fosters considerate or cooperative behavior toward familiar others, and competitive behavior toward strangers. One of the first studies to show this was a double-blind experiment where participants played a coordination game either with other participants they had briefly met prior to the experiment or with completely anonymous others (Declerck et al., 2010). Game partners had to independently and simultaneously choose between a cooperative and a competitive outcome in a game, and (as in typical social dilemma games) they received a monetary reward based on the combination of their decisions. The incentive structure of the coordination game was such that the highest payoff could be obtained if both partners chose to cooperate (a pareto-optimal, Nash equilibrium). As one can never be 100% sure that the partner will actually be cooperative, the risk averse decision is to compete. Participants given intranasal OT cooperated significantly more than those given a placebo, but this was only true in the prior contact condition. When partners remained anonymous, OT significantly decreased cooperation! Thus, some form of relationship needs to be in existence before OT can exert its prosocial effects. Similar results had already been obtained with the trust game, with individuals given OT being more trusting than those given a placebo, as long as the partner was portrayed as familiar or benign (Kosfeld, Heinrichs, Zak, Fischbacher, & Fehr, 2005; Mikolajczak et al., 2010). Thus, it seems that OT facilitates cooperation only when there is a positive expectation that one's cooperative effort will be reciprocated. Otherwise, OT appears to have either no effect or a negative effect that may serve a protective function.

De Dreu and colleagues elaborated on the idea that OT functions to form and maintain protective social ties, even to the point that it may facilitate parochialism. The roots of parochialism lie in the human propensity for ingroup–outgroup categorization, and this may have served the group well by increasing its survival chances at the detriment of other groups, a phenomenon that probably occurred in ancestral as well as contemporary societies. As evidence accumulates that OT influences perceptual processes (Churchland & Winkielman, 2012), facilitates the recognition of emotional expressions (Domes, Heinrichs, Michel, Berger, & Herpertz, 2007b), and improves the accuracy of evaluative judgments (Di Simplicio, Massey-Chase, Cowen, & Harmer, 2009; Lambert, Declerck, & Boone, 2014; Striepens et al., 2012), it seems logical that OT would also motivate people to cooperate more with partners who share the same ethnicity, which is exactly what De Dreu, Greer, Van Kleef, Shalvi, and Handgraaf (2011) found.

Parochialism is not only sustained by ingroup love, but also by outgroup derogation. To discern between these two motives, De Dreu et al. (2010) observed what happened when participants in their studies played an intergroup prisoner's dilemma game after they had inhaled either oxytocin or a placebo. Participants received a monetary endowment that they could keep to themselves, invest in the ingroup at no cost to the outgroup, or invest in the ingroup to hurt the outgroup. The results were consistent with the proposal that OT encourages ingroup love: whereas participants in the placebo group kept the bulk of their monetary endowment to themselves, significantly more participants in the OT group allocated money to the ingroup, without hurting the outgroup. These individuals also expected other members of their group to show ingroup love. Evidence for outgroup hate was only observed when the payoff structure was manipulated in such a way that the outgroup composed a real threat to the within-group accrual of money. In that case, OT significantly increased noncooperation with members of the outgroup, ostensibly hurting them to protect vulnerable ingroup members (De Dreu et al., 2010, 2011; De Dreu, Shalvi, Greer, Van Kleef, & Handgraaf, 2012a).

The increased desire to see the group prosper when given exogenous OT manifests itself in other ways. When shown pictures of potential allies, males will select the more dominant-looking ones into their teams, asserting that they would be more useful (De Dreu, Greer, Handgraaf, Shalvi, & Van Kleef, 2012b). Finally, a recent study revealed that OT increased lying in group settings, but only when the group stands to benefit from the lie. Individuals do not personally gain anything from lying; its only advantage is to allow the group to gain money. The additional finding that OT also lowered the response time of lying in the group's best interest furthermore suggests that OT facilitates automatic processes in social interaction (Shalvi & De Dreu, 2014).

Thus, it seems that through intuitively lying and helping, cooperating and competing, nurturing and protecting, OT may have contributed to the plethora of behaviors that shape human morality. From history, we know that moral conduct is inherently plastic and context-dependent. For example, a Ku Klux Klan member in favor of racial cleansing will spend his Sundays in church praying to an all-loving God. His hate crimes as well as his worship are likely fostered by group belonging, and both types of behaviors seem rational to him given the social rewards he will experience from participating in each group's rituals. What the studies in this section suggest is that OT may play a role in promoting this type of plasticity by enhancing the tendency to engage in those behaviors that will guarantee group inclusion.

3.3.4 Effect of Oxytocin Depends on Personality

The interactionist approach furthermore emphasizes that the behavioral effects driven by OT also vary between people. On the one hand, this can be the result of individual differences in *endogenous* levels of OT, or in the individual's intrinsic propensity to produce or respond to OT. Consequently, peripheral OT concentrations often correlate with the extent to which people naturally engage in social behaviors. For example, individuals who suffer from autism spectrum syndrome and who are generally socially withdrawn tend to have lower plasma levels of OT (Modahl et al., 1998). The same is true for stable individual differences in parenting styles (Feldman, Gordon, Schneiderman, Weisman, & Zagoory-Sharon, 2010; Gordon, Zagoory-Sharon, & Leckman, 2010) and the tendency to develop major depression (Parker et al., 2010). Possibly such individual differences may have genetic roots and could be related to central OTR densities (which would determine the magnitude of central OT-receptor binding) and/or polymorphisms in the OTR gene. Several prosocial traits (such as empathy) have already been associated with single nucleotide substitutions (Bakermans-Kranenburg & van Ijzendoorn, 2008; Riem et al., 2011; Rodrigues, Saslow, Garcia, Oliver, & Keltner, 2009; Tost et al., 2010), and the stable personality trait known as "social value orientation" can be characterized by a specific haplotype of the OTR gene (Israel et al., 2009), which appears to be a significant predictor of the prosocial–proself dichotomy.

On the other hand, OT might also affect people differently because of idiosyncratic differences in the nervous system that make for different reactions to *exogenous* boosts of OT. This means that OT administration should have different effects depending on individual predispositions. An interesting hypothesis in this respect is that exogenous OT would have a greater marginal effect on those individuals that are in some way deficient in one of the functions facilitated by OT. Indeed, the enhanced prosocial effects of intranasally administered OT are especially pronounced for individuals suffering from socioemotional deficits (Andari et al., 2010; Luminet, Grynberg, Ruzette, & Mikolajczak, 2011). For example, individuals with Asperger syndrome will maintain more eye contact and initiate more social encounters when given OT compared to a placebo. Similarly, OT improves the recognition of kinship and intimacy, but only in schizophrenia patients who are normally less socially competent compared to otherwise healthy people (Fischer-Shofty, Shamay-Tsoory, & Levkovitz, 2013). Among borderline patients, those that are anxiously attached (but not necessarily avoidant) respond with increased cooperation when given OT (Bartz et al., 2011b). This is consistent with the proposition that the observed attenuated amygdala activation induced by OT may normalize baseline hyperactivity in some people (Labuschagne et al., 2010), which would further indicate that OT helps to regulate internal homeostasis.

Finally, sometimes tangible effects of OT may depend on the *combination of* context and individual differences. This was shown in a study that investigated how and when OT curbs greed. The desire to personally have more than others is arguably one of nature's greatest hindrances to social rationality. Using the prisoner's dilemma game (where greed is one of the major motives to defect), Declerck, Boone, and Kiyonari (2014) showed that there is a three-way interaction between OT (versus placebo), a person's social value orientation, and social information (in the form of prior contact with the game partner). OT-exposed proselfs (who are by nature selfish) cooperated more in a prisoner's dilemma game when they had prior contact with their potential game partners, while they cooperated even less when their partners remained completely anonymous. Thus, when the partner is made salient through the combination of prior contact and OT, proselfs become more generous. The opposite situation, combining OT with an anonymous partner, exacerbates their self-interest motive. Such complex interaction between individual motivations and environmental conditions may tell us something about how OT could control affiliative bonding, not only between game partners, but also in real life.

Finally, throughout evolution men and women have fulfilled different biological and social roles and experienced different sexual selection pressures. Hence it could be argued that their perceptions of the social environment in which they live today (and in the past) also differ. Taken together with the knowledge that OT interacts with estrogen (see footnote 6), it should not be surprising that many sex differences in the effects of OT have been reported. For example, when judging moral dilemmas, men under the influence of OT display more self-interested moral judgments whereas women tend to respond more altruistically, taking into account the benefits to others (Scheele et al., 2014). Compared to a placebo, OT makes women (but not men) less disgusted by pathogen-infected scenes, while it causes men (but not women) to judge faces as less healthy (Declerck, Lambert, & Boone, 2014). At the neural level, administering OT to women (but not men) increased amygdala activation in response to threatening scenes. Another study found OT to increase activity in the striatum, basal forebrain, amygdala, and insula during cooperative decisions of men playing a prisoner's dilemma game, while it had no effect (or a negative effect) on these regions in cooperating women (Rilling et al., 2014). Considering that OT metabolism and its interactions with the sex hormones differ greatly between the sexes, these results could be due to dose-dependent effects as a result of differences in base-line levels of OT. More research and cross-comparisons with other species will be needed to sort out these sex-dependent responses, and to evaluate whether or not they may reflect evolved adaptations to optimize the nurturing of offspring and the protection of in-group members in a socially rational (yet sex-differentiated) way.

3.4 SUMMARY

The extent to which people engage in economic versus socially rational decision making is influenced by the relative proportions of neurotransmitters in the brain. While decision making is bound to involve an array of different interacting chemicals, we have limited the discussion in this chapter to three neurotransmitters—dopamine, serotonin, and oxytocin—that have clear ties with the ontogenetic and phylogenetic development of prosociality. DA by itself probably does not promote prosocial decision making, but rather sways people toward selfishness. However, DA could still be indirectly involved in generating the incentive motivation to act prosocially, if this act is anticipated to be rewarding. This would happen primarily through its interactions with 5-HT and OT, both of which appear to play a more important role in social cognition. 5-HT, especially, promotes economically rational prosocial decisions that, at the same time, serve the individual well, while OT facilitates a social rationality that gives the individual pleasure, yet biases decision to favor the group.

REFERENCES

Abu-Akel, A., Palgi, S., Klein, E., Decety, J., & Shamay-Tsoory, S. (2015). Oxytocin increases empathy to pain when adopting the other, but not the self-perspective. *Social Neuroscience*, *10*, 7–15.

Adolphs, R. (2010). What does the amygdala contribute to social cognition? *Annals of the New York Academy of Science (Year in Cognitive Neuroscience 2010)*, *1191*, 42–61.

Anacker, A. M. J., & Beery, A. K. (2013). Life in groups: The role of oxytocin in mammalian sociality. *Behavioral Neuroscience*, *7*, 1–10.

Andari, E., Duhamel, J. R., Zalla, T., Herbrecht, E., Leboyer, M., & Sirigu, A. (2010). Promoting social behavior with oxytocin in high functioning autism spectrum disorders. *Proceedings of the National Academy of Sciences*, *107*, 4389–4394.

Bakermans-Kranenburg, M. J., & van Ijzendoorn, M. H. (2008). Oxytocin receptor (OXTR) and serotonin transporter (5-HTT) genes associated with observed parenting. *Social Cognitive and Affective Neuroscience*, *3*, 128–134.

Bartz, J., Simeon, D., Hamilton, H., Kim, S., Crystal, S., Braun, A., ... Hollander, E. (2011b). Oxytocin can hinder trust and cooperation in borderline personality disorder. *Social Cognitive and Affective Neuroscience*, *6*, 556–563.

Bartz, J. A., Zaki, J., & Ochsner, K. N. (2011a). Social effects of oxytocin in humans: Context and person matter. *Trends in Cognitive Sciences*, *15*, 301–309.

Baumgartner, T., Heinrichs, M., Vonlanthen, A., Fischbacher, U., & Fehr, E. (2008). Oxytocin shapes the neural circuitry of trust and trust adaptation in humans. *Neuron*, *58*, 639–650.

Berridge, K. C. (2007). The debate over dopamine's role in reward: The case for incentive salience. *Psychopharmacology*, *191*, 391–431.

Berridge, K. C. (2012). From prediction error to incentive salience: Mesolimbic computation or reward motivation. *European Journal of Neuroscience*, *35*, 1124–1143.

Berridge, K. C., & O'Doherty, J. P. (2014). From experienced utility to decision utility. In P. Glimcher, & E. Fehr (Eds.), *Neuroeconomics: Decisions and the Brain* (second ed., pp. 335–345). London: Academic Press.

Berridge, K. C., Robinson, T. E., & Aldridge, J. W. (2009). Dissecting components of reward: 'liking', 'wanting', and learning. *Current Opinion in Pharmacology*, *9*, 65–73.

Bethlehem, R. A. I., van Honk, J., Auyeung, B., & Baron-Cohen, S. (2013). Oxytocin, brain physiology, and functional connectivity: A review of intranasal oxytocin fMRI studies. *Psychoneuroendocrinology*, *38*, 962–974.

Bos, P. A., Panksepp, J., Bluthé, R. M., & van Honk, J. (2012). Acute effects of steroid hormones and neuropeptides on human social-emotional behavior: A review of single administration studies. *Frontiers in Neuroendocrinology*, *33*, 17–35.

Bosch, O. J., Meddle, S. L., Beiderbeck, D. I., Douglas, A. J., & Neumann, I. D. (2005). Brain oxytocin correlates with maternal aggression: Link to anxiety. *Journal of Neuroscience*, *25*, 6806–6815.

Broad, K. D., Curley, J. P., & Keverne, E. B. (2006). Mother-infant bonding and the evolution of mammalian social relationships. *Philosophical Transactions of the Royal Society B*, *361*, 2199–2214.

Camerer, C. (2003). *Behavioral Game Theory: Experiments in Strategic Interaction*. Princeton, New Jersey: Princeton University Press.

Campbell, A. (2008). Aggression, attachment, and affiliation: The role of oxytocin in female social behaviour. *Biological Psychology*, *77*, 1–10.

Carmichael, M. S., Humbert, R., Dixen, J., Palmisano, G., Greenleaf, W., & Davidson, J. M. (1987). Plasma oxytocin increases in the human sexual response. *Journal of Clinical Endocrinology Metabolism*, *64*, 27–31.

Choleris, E., Pfaff, D. W., & Kavaliers, M. (2013). *Oxytocin, Vasopressin and Related Peptides in the Regulation of Behaviour*. Cambridge: Cambridge University Press.

Churchland, P. S., & Winkielman, P. (2012). Modulating social behavior with oxytocin: How does it work? What does it mean? *Hormones and Behavior*, *61*, 392–399.

Crockett, M. J. (2009). The neurochemistry of fairness. Clarifying the link between serotonin and prosocial behavior. Values, empathy, and fairness across social barriers. *Annals of the New York Academy of Science*, *1167*, 76–86.

Crockett, M. J., Clark, L., Tabibnia, G., Lieberman, M. D., & Robbins, T. W. (2008). Serotonin modulates behavioral reactions to unfairness. *Science*, *320*, 1739.

Cummings, J. L. (1995). Anatomic and behavioral aspects of frontal-subcortical circuits. *Annals of the New York Academy of Sciences*, *769*, 1–13.

Damsa, C., Bumb, A., Bianchi-Demicheli, F., Vidailhet, P., Sterck, R., Andreoli, A., & Beyenburg, S. (2004). Dopamine-dependent side effects of selective serotonin reuptake inhibitors: A clinical review. *Journal of Clincial Pscyhiatry*, *65*, 1064–1068.

Decety, J., Norman, G. J., Berntson, G. G., & Cacioppo, J. T. (2012). A neurobiobehavioral evolutionary perspective on the mechanisms inderlying empathy. *Progress in Neurobiology*, *98*, 38–48.

Declerck, C. H., Boone, C., & Kiyonari, T. (2010). Oxytocin and cooperation under conditions of uncertainty: The modulating role of incentives and social information. *Hormones and Behavior*, *57*, 368–374.

Declerck, C. H., Boone, C., & Kiyonari, T. (2014). The effect of oxytocin on cooperation in a prisoner's dilemma game depends on the social context and a person's social value orientation. *Social Cognitive and Affective Neuroscience*, *9*, 802–809.

Declerck, C. H., Lambert, B., & Boone, C. (2014). Sexual dimorphism in oxytocin responses to health perception and disgust, with implications for theories on pathogen detection. *Hormones and Behavior*, *65*, 521–526.

De Dreu, C. K. W. (2012). Oxytocin modulates cooperation within and competition between groups: An integrative review and research agenda. *Hormones and Behavior*, *61*, 419–428.

De Dreu, C. K. W., Greer, L. L., Handgraaf, M. J. J., Shalvi, S., Van Kleef, G. A., Baas, M., ... Feith, S. W. W. (2012b). Oxytocin modulates selection of allies in intergroup conflict. *Proceedings of the Royal B-Biological Science*, *279*, 1150–1154.

De Dreu, C. K. W., Greer, L. L., Handgraaf, M. J. J., Shalvi, S., Van Kleef, G. A., & Baas, M. (2010). The neuropeptide oxytocin regulates parochial altruism in intergroup conflict among humans. *Science*, *11*(328), 1408–1411.

De Dreu, C. K. W., Greer, L. L., Van Kleef, G. A., Shalvi, S., & Handgraaf, M. J. J. (2011). Oxytocin promotes human ethnocentrism. *Proceedings of the National Academy of Sciences*, *108*, 1262–1266.

De Dreu, C. K. W., Shalvi, S., Greer, L. L., Van Kleef, G. A., & Handgraaf, M. J. J. (2012a). Oxytocin motivates non-cooperation in inter-group conflict to protect vulnerable in-group members. *Plos One*, *7*, e46751.

Denk, F., Walton, M. E., Jennings, K. A., Sharp, T., Rushworth, M. F. S., & Bannerman, D. M. (2005). Differential involvement of serotonin and dopamine systems in cost-benefit decisions about delay or effort. *Psychopharmacology*, *179*, 587–596.

Depue, R. A., & Collins, P. F. (1999). Neurobiology of the structure of personality: Dopamine, facilitation of incentive motivation, and extraversion. *Behavioral and Brain Science*, *22*, 491–569.

Depue, R. A., & Morrone-Strupinsky, J. V. (2005). A neurobehavioral model of affiliative bonding: Implications for conceptualizing a human trait of affiliation. *Behavioral and Brain Sciences*, *28*, 313–395.

D'Esposito, M., & Grossman, M. (1996). The physiological basis of executive function and working memory. *Neuroscientist*, *2*, 345–352.

Diamond, A. (1996). Evidence for the importance of dopamine for prefrontal cortex functions early in life. *Philosophical Transactions of the Royal Society of London, Series B, Biological Sciences*, *351*, 1483–1493.

Di Simplicio, M., Massey-Chase, R., Cowen, P. J., & Harmer, C. J. (2009). Oxytocin enhances processing of positive versus negative emotional information in healthy male volunteers. *Journal of Psychopharmacology*, *23*, 241–248.

Dolen, G., Darvishzaden, A., Huang, K. W., & Malenka, R. C. (2013). Social reward requires coordinated activity of nucleus accumbens oxytocin and serotonin. *Nature*, *501*, 179.

Domes, G., Heinrichs, M., Berger, C., Glaescher, J., Buchel, C., Braus, D. F., et al. (2007a). Oxytocin attenuates amygdala responses to emotional faces regardless of valence. *Biological Psychiatry*, *62*, 1187–1190.

Domes, G., Heinrichs, M., Michel, A., Berger, C., & Herpertz, S. C. (2007b). Oxytocin improves mind-reading in humans. *Biological Psychiatry*, *61*, 731–733.

Domes, G., Lischke, A., Berger, C., Grossmann, A., Hauenstein, K., Heinrichs, M., et al. (2010). Effects, of intranasal oxytocin on face processing in women. *Psychoneuroendocrinology*, *35*, 83–93.

Ebitz, R. B., & Platt, M. L. (2014). An evolutionary perspective on the behavioral consequences of exogenous oxytocin application. *Frontiers in Behavioral Neuroscience*, *7*. Article 225.

Feldman, R., Gordon, I., Schneiderman, I., Weisman, O., & Zagoory-Sharon, O. (2010). Natural variations in maternal and paternal care are associated with systematic changes in oxytocin following parent-infant contact. *Psychoneuroendocrinology*, *35*, 1133–1141.

Figner, B., Knoch, D., Johnson, E. J., Krosch, A. R., Lisanby, S. H., Fehr, E., et al. (2010). Lateral prefrontal cortex and self-control in intertemporal choice. *Nature Neuroscience*, *13*, 538–539.

Fischer-Shofty, M., Shamay-Tsoory, S. G., & Levkovitz, Y. (2013). Characterization of the effect of oxytocin on fear recognition in patients with schizophrenia and in healthy controls. *Frontiers in Neuroscience*, *7*. article number 127.

Gamer, M., Zurowski, B., & Buechel, C. (2010). Different amygdala subregions mediate valence-related and attentional effects in humans. *Proceedings of the National Academy of Sciences*, *107*, 9400–9405.

Gordon, I., Zagoory-Sharon, O., & Leckman, J. F. (2010). Oxytocin and the development of parenting in humans. *Biological Psychiatry*, *68*, 377–382.

Guastella, A. J., Mitchell, P. B., & Mathews, F. (2008). Oxytocin enhances the encoding of positive social memories in humans. *Biological Psychiatry*, *64*, 256–258.

Hare, T. A., Camerer, C. F., & Rangel, A. (2009). Self-control in decision-making involves modulation of the vmPFC valuation system. *Science*, *324*, 646–648.

Hecht, D. (2014). Cerebral lateralization of pro- and anti-social tendencies. *Experimental Neurobiology*, *23*, 1–27.

Heinrichs, M., Neumann, I., & Ehlert, U. (2002). Lactation and stress: Protective effects of breast-feeding in humans. *The International Journal on the Biology of Stress*, *5*, 195–203.

Hellige, J. B. (2001). *Hemispheric Asymmetry: What's Right and What's left?* Cambridge: Harvard University Press.

Huber, D., Veinante, P., & Stoop, R. (2005). Vasopressin and oxytocin excite distinct neuronal populations in the central amygdala. *Science*, *308*, 245–248.

Hurlemann, R., Patin, A., Onur, O. A., Cohen, M. X., Baumgartner, T., Metzler, S., ... Kendrick, K. M. (2010). Oxytocin enhances amygdala-dependent, socially reinforces learning and emotional empathy in humans. *Journal of Neuroscience*, *30*, 4999–5007.

Hysek, C. M., Schmid, Y., Simmier, L. D., Domes, G., Heinrichs, M., Eisenegger, C., ... Liecht, M. E. (2014). MDMA enhances emotional empathy and prosocial behavior. *Social Cognitive, and Affective Behavior*, *9*, 1645–1652.

Israel, S., Lerer, E., Shalev, I., Uzefovsky, F., Riebold, M., Laiba, E., ... Ebstein, R. P. (2009). The oxytocin receptor (OXTR) contributes to prosocial fund allocations in the dictator game and the social value orientations task. *Plos One*, *4*, 1–9.

Jones, G. H., Hernandez, T. D., Kendall, D. A., Marsden, C. A., & Robbins, T. W. (1992). Dopaminergic and serotonergic function following isolation in rats: Study of behavioural responses and post mortem and in vivo neurochemistry. *Pharmacology, Biochemistry and Behavior*, *43*, 17–53.

Kemp, A. H., & Guastella, A. J. (2011). The role of oxytocin in human affect: A novel hypothesis. *Current Directions in Psychological Science*, *20*, 222–231.

Kirsch, P., Esslinger, C., Chen, Q., Mier, D., Lis, S., Siddhanti, S., ... Meyer-Lindenberg, A. (2005). Oxytocin modulates neural circuitry for social cognition and fear in humans. *The Journal of Neuroscience*, *25*, 11489–11493.

Koob, G. F., Riley, S. J., Smith, S. C., & Robbins, T. W. (1978). Effects of 6-hydroxydopamine lesions of the nucleus accumbens septi and olfactory tubercle on feeding, locomotor activity, and amphetamine anorexia in the rat. *Journal of Comparative Physiological Psychology*, *92*, 917–927.

Kosfeld, M., Heinrichs, M., Zak, P. J., Fischbacher, U., & Fehr, E. (2005). Oxytocin increases trust in humans. *Nature*, *435*, 673–676.

Kramer, P. D. (1993). *Listening to Prozac*. London: Fourth Estate.

Krueger, F., Parasuraman, R., Moody, L., Twieg, P., de Visser, E., McCabe, K., ... Lee, M. R. (2013). Oxytocin selectively increases perceptions of harm for victims, but not the desire to punish offenders of criminal offenses. *Social, Cognitive, and Affective Neuroscience*, *8*, 494–498.

Labuschagne, I., Phan, K. L., Wood, A., Angstadt, M., Chua, P., Heinrichs, M., ... Nathan, P. J. (2010). Oxytocin attenuates amygdala reactivity to fear in generalized social anxiety disorder. *Neuropsychopharmacology*, *35*, 2403–2413.

Lambert, B., Declerck, C. H., & Boone, C. (2014). Oxytocin does not make a face appear more trustworthy, but improves the accuracy of trustworthiness judgments. *Psychoneuroendocrinology*, *40*, 60–68.

Lamm, C., Batson, C. D., & Decety, J. (2007). The neural substrate of human empathy: Effects of perspective taking and cognitive appraisal. *Journal of Cognitive Neuroscience*, *19*, 42–58.

Le Moal, M., & Simon, H. (1991). Mesolimbic dopaminergic network: Functional and regulatory roles. *Physiological Reviews*, *71*, 155–234.

Lim, M. M., Wang, Z., Olazabal, X. R., Terwilliger, E. F., & Young, L. J. (2004). Enhanced partner preference in a promiscuous species by manipulating the expression of a single gene. *Nature*, *429*, 754–757.

Lischke, A., Gamer, M., Berger, C., Grossmann, A., Hauenstein, K., Heinrichs, M., et al. (2012). Oxytocin increases amygdala reactivity to threatening scenes in females. *Psychoneuroendocrinology*, *37*, 1431–1438.

Luminet, O., Grynberg, D., Ruzette, N., & Mikolajczak, M. (2011). Personality-dependent effects of oxytocin: Greater social benefits for high alexithymia scorers. *Biological Psychology*, *87*, 401–406.

McClure, S. M., Laibson, D. I., Loewenstein, G., & Cohen, J. D. (2004). Separate neural systems value immediate and delayed monetary rewards. *Science*, *306*, 503–507.

McGilchrist, I. (2009). *The Master and His Emissary: The Divided Brain and the Making of the Western World*. New Haven and London: Yale University Press.

Mesulam, M. M. (1998). From sensation to cognition. *Brain*, *121*, 1013–1052.

Meyer-Lindenberg, A., Domes, G., Kirsch, P., & Heinrichs, M. (2011). Oxytocin and vasopressin in the human brain: Social neuropeptides for translational medicine. *Nature Reviews Neuroscience*, *12*, 524–538.

Mikolajczak, M., Gross, J. J., Lane, A., Corneille, O., de Timary, P., & Luminet, O. (2010). Oxytocin makes people trusting, not gullible. *Psychological Science*, *21*, 1072–1074.

Modahl, C., Green, L., Fein, D., Morris, M., Waterhouse, L., Feinstein, C., & Levin, H. (1998). Plasma oxytocin levels in autistic children. *Biological Psychiatry*, *43*, 270–277.

Morhenn, V., Beavin, L. E., & Zak, P. J. (2012). Massage increases oxytocin and reduces adrenocorticotropin hormone in humans. *Alternative Therapies in Health and Medicine*, *18*, 11–18.

Morhenn, V. B., Park, J. W., Piper, E., & Zak, P. J. (2008). Monetary sacrifice among strangers is mediated by endogenous oxytocin after physical contact. *Evolution and Human Behavior*, *29*, 375–383.

Moskowitz, D. S., Pinard, G., Zuroff, D. C., Annable, L., & Young, S. N. (2001). The effect of tryptophan on social interaction in everyday life: A placebo controlled experiment. *Neuropsychopharmacology*, *25*, 277–289.

Nelson, E., & Panksepp, E. (1998). Brain substrates of infant-mother attachment: Contributions of opioids, oxytocin, and norepinephrine. *Neuroscience and Biobehavioral Reviews*, *22*, 437–452.

Niv, Y., Daw, N. D., Joel, D., & Dyan, P. (2007). Tonic dopamine: Opportunity costs and the control of response vigor. *Psychopharmacology*, *191*, 551–562.

O'Doherty, J., Dayan, P., Schultz, J., Deichmann, R., Friston, K., & Dolan, R. J. (2004). Dissociable roles of ventral and dorsal striatum in instrumental conditioning. *Science*, *304*, 452–454.

Olff, M., Frijling, J. L., Kubzansky, L. D., Bradley, B., Ellenbogen, M. A., Cardoso, C., ... van Zuiden, M. (2013). The role of oxytocin in social bonding, stress regulation and mental health: An update on the moderating effects of context and inter-individual differences. *Psychoneuroendocrinology*, *38*, 1883–1894.

Panksepp, J. (2006). Emotional endophenotypes in evolutionary psychology. *Progress in Neuro-Psychopharmacology & Biological Psychiatry*, *30*, 774–784.

Park, S. B., Coull, J. T., McShane, R. H., Young, A. H., Sahakian, B. J., Robbins, T. W., & Cowen, P. J. (1994). Tryptophan depletion in normal volunteers produces selective impairments in learning and memory. *Neuropharmacology*, *33*, 575–588.

Parker, K. J., Henna, H. A., Zeitzer, J. M., Keller, J., Blasey, C. M., Amico, J. A., & Schatzberg, A. F. (2010). Preliminary evidence that plasma oxytocin levels are elevated in major depression. *Psychiatry Research*, *178*, 359–362.

Pedroni, A., Eisenegger, C., Hartmann, M. N., Fischbacher, U., & Knoch, D. (2014). Dopaminergic stimulation increases selfish behavior in the absence of punishment threat. *Psychopharmacology*, *231*, 135–141.

Petrovic, P., Kalisch, R., Singer, T., & Dolan, R. J. (2008). Oxytocin attenuates affective evluations of conditioned faces and amygdala activity. *The Journal of Neuroscience*, *28*, 6007–6615.

Pillutla, M. M., & Murnighan, J. K. (1996). Unfairness, anger, and spite: Emotional rejections of ultimatum offers. *Organizational Behavior and Human Decision Processes*, *68*, 208–224.

Previc, F. H. (1998). The neuropsychology of 3-D space. *Psychological Bulletin*, *124*, 123–164.

Previc, F. H. (1999). Dopamine and the origins of human intelligence. *Brain and Cognition*, *41*, 299–350.

Previc, F. H. (2006). The role of extrapersonal brain systems in religious activity. *Consciousness and Cognition*, *15*, 500–539.

Previc, F. H. (2007). Prenatal influences on dopamine and their relevance to the rising incidence of autism. *Medical Hypotheses*, *68*, 46–60.

Previc, F. H. (2009). *The dopaminergic mind in human evolution and history*. Cambridge: Cambridge University Press.

Previc, F. H., Declerck, C. H., & De Brabander, B. (2005). Why "your head is in the clouds" during thinking: The relationship between cognition and upper space. *Acta Psychologica*, *118*, 7–24.

Puumala, T., & Sirvio, J. (1998). Changes in activities of dopamine and serotonin systems in the frontal cortex underlie poor choice accuracy and impulsivity of rats in an attention task. *Neuroscience*, *83*, 489–499.

Qi, J., Yang, J. Y., Song, M., Li, Y., Wang, F., & Wu, C. F. (2008). Inhibition by oxytocin of metamphetamine-induced hyperactivity related to dopamine turnover in the mesolimbic region in mice. *Naunyn Schmiedebergs Archives of Pharmacology*, *376*, 441–448.

Raleigh, M. J., Brammer, G. L., McGuire, M. T., & Yuwiller, A. (1985). Dominant social status facilitates the behavioral effects of serotonergic agonists. *Brain Research*, *348*, 274–282.

Raleigh, M. J., McGuire, M. T., Brammer, G. L., Pollack, D. B., & Yuwiller, A. (1991). Serotonergic mechanisms promote dominance acquisition in adult male vervet monkeys. *Brain Research*, *559*, 181–190.

Raleigh, M. J., Yuwiler, A., Brammer, G. L., Mcguire, M. T., Geller, E., & Flannery, J. W. (1981). Peripheral correlates of serotonergically influenced behaviors in vervet monkeys. *Pychopharmacology*, *72*, 241–246.

Riem, M. M. E., Pieper, S., Out, D., Bakermans-Kranenburg, M. J., & van Ijzendoorn, M. H. (2011). Oxytocin receptor gene and depressive symptoms associated with physiological reactivity to infant crying. *Social, Cognitive, and Affective Neuroscience*, *6*, 294–300.

Rilling, J. K., Demarco, A. C., Hackett, P. D., Chen, X., Gautam, P., Stair, S., ... Pagnoni, G. (2014). Sex differences in the neural and behavioral response to intranasal oxytocin and vasopressin during human social interaction. *Psychoneuroendocrinology*, *39*, 237–248.

Rilling, J. K., De Marco, A. C., Hackett, P. D., Thompson, R., Ditzen, B., Patel, R., & Pagnoni, G. (2012). Effects of intranasam oxytocin and vasopressin on cooperative behavior and associated brain activity in men. *Psychoneuroendocrinology*, *37*, 447–461.

Rilling, J. K., Gutman, D. A., Zeh, T. R., Pagnoni, G., Berns, G. S., & Kilts, C. D. (2002). A neural basis for social cooperation. *Neuron*, *35*, 395–405.

Robbins, T. W. (2000). Chemical neuromodulation of frontal-executive functions in humans and other animals. *Experimental Brain Research*, *133*, 130–138.

Robbins, T. W., & Everitt, B. J. (1996). Neurobehavioural mechanisms of reward and motivation. *Current Opinion in Neurobiology*, *6*, 228–236.

Rodrigues, S. M., Saslow, L. R., Garcia, N., Oliver, P. J., & Keltner, D. (2009). Oxytocin receptor genetic variation relates to empathy and stress reactivity in humans. *Proceedings of the National Academy of Sciences, 106*, 21437–21441.

Rolls, E. T. (2000). The orbitofrontal cortex and reward. *Cerebral Cortex, 10*, 284–294.

Ross, H. E., Freeman, S. M., Speigel, L. L., Ren, X., Terwilliger, E. F., & Young, L. Y. (2009). Variation in oxytocin receptor density in the nucleus accumbens has differential effects in affiliative behaviors in monogamous and polygamous voles. *The Journal of Neuroscience, 29*, 1312–1318.

Ross, H. E., & Young, L. J. (2009). Oxytocin and the neural mechanisms regulating social cognition and affiliative behavior. *Frontiers in Neuroendocrinology, 30*, 534–547.

Sasaki-Adams, D. M., & Kelley, A. E. (2001). Serotonin-dopamine interactions in the control of conditioned reinforcement and motor behavior. *Neuropsychopharmacology, 25*, 440–452.

Scheele, D., Striepens, N., Güntürkün, O., Deutschländer, S., Maier, W., Kendrick, K. M., & Hurlemann, R. (2014). Opposing effects of oxytocin on moral judgment in males and females. *Human Brain Mapping, 35*, 6067–6076.

Schultz, W. (2002). Getting formal with dopamine and reward. *Neuron, 36*, 241–263.

Shalvi, S., & De Dreu, C. K. W. (2014). Oxytocin promotes group-serving dishonesty. *Proceedings of the National Academy of Sciences, 111*, 5503–5507.

Shamay-Tsoory, S. G., Fischer, M., Dvash, J., Harari, H., Perach-Bloon, N., & Levkobitz, Y. (2009). Intranasal administration of oxytocin increases envy and shadenfreude. *Biological Psychiatry, 66*, 864–870.

Shamay-Tsoory, S. G., Tomer, R., Goldsher, D., Berger, B. D., & Aharon-Peretz, J. (2004). Impairment in cognitive and affective empathy in patients with brain lesions: Anatomical and cognitive correlates. *Journal of Clinical and Experimental Neuropsychology, 26*, 1113–1127.

Sheldon, K. M. (1999). Learning the lessons of tit-for-tat: Even competitors can get the message. *Journal of Personality and Social Psychology, 77*, 1245–1253.

Singer, T., Snozzi, R., Bird, G., Petrovic, P., Silani, G., & Heinrichs, M. (2008). Effects of oxytocin and prosocial behavior on direct and vicariously experienced pain. *Emotion, 6*, 781–791.

Skuse, D. H., & Gallagher, L. (2008). Dopaminergic-neuropeptide interactions in the social brain. *Trends in Cognitive Sciences, 13*, 27–35.

Soubrie, P. (2010). Reconciling the role of central serotonin neurons in human and animal behavior. *Behavioral and Brain Sciences, 9*, 319–335.

Spitzer, M., Fischbacher, U., Herrnberger, B., Gron, G., & Fehr, E. (2007). The neural signature of social norm compliance. *Neuron, 56*, 185–196.

Strathearn, L., Fonagy, P., Amico, J., & Montague, P. R. (2009). Adult attachment predicts maternal brain and oxytocin response to infant cues. *Neuropsychopharmacology, 34*, 2655–2666.

Striepens, N., Scheele, D., Kendrick, K. M., Becker, B., Schäfer, L., Schwalba, K., ... Hurlemann, R. (2012). Oxytocin facilitates protective responses to aversive social stimuli in males. *Proceedings of the National Academy of Sciences, 109*, 18144–18149.

Tabibnia, G., Satpute, A. B., & Lieberman, M. D. (2008). The sunny side of fairness—Preference for fairness activates reward circuitry (and disregarding unfairness activates self-control circuitry). *Psychological Science, 19*, 339–347.

Tekin, S., & Cummings, J. L. (2002). Frontal-subcortical neuronal circuits and clinical neuropsychiatry. An update. *Journal of Psychosomatic Research, 53*, 647–654.

Thaler, R. H. (1988). Anomalies—the Ultimatum Game. *Journal of Economic Perspectives, 2*, 195–206.

Tost, H., Kolachana, B., Hakimi, S., Lemaitre, H., Verchinski, B. A., Mattay, V. S., ... Meyer-Lindenberg, A. (2010). A common allele in the oxytocin receptor gene (OXTR) impacts prosocial temperament and human hypothalamic-limbic structure and function. *Proceedings of the National Academy of Science*, *107*, 13936–13941.

Tse, W. S., & Bond, A. J. (2002a). Serotonergic intervention affects both social dominance and affiliative behavior. *Psychopharmacology*, *161*, 324–330.

Tse, W. S., & Bond, A. J. (2002b). Difference in serotonergic and noradrenergic regulation of human social behaviours. *Psychopharmacology*, *159*, 216–221.

Tse, W. S., & Bond, A. J. (2003). Reboxetine promotes social bonding in healthy volunteers. *Journal of Psychopharmacology*, *17*, 189–195.

Tse, W. S., & Bond, A. J. (2006). Noradrenaline moght enhance assertive human social behaviours: An investigation in a flatmate relationship. *Pharmacopsychiatry*, *39*, 175–179.

Tucker, D. M., & Williamson, P. A. (1984). Asymmetric neural control systems in human self-regulation. *Psychological Review*, *91*, 185–215.

Van't Wout, M., Kahn, R. S., Sanfey, A. G., & Aleman, A. (2006). Affective state and decision-making in the ultimatum game. *Experimental Brain Research*, *169*, 564–568.

Volkmar, F. R. (2001). Pharmacological interventions in autism: Theoretical and practival issues. *Journal of Clinical Child Psychology*, *30*, 80–87.

Waegeman, A., Declerck, C. H., Boone, C., Van Hecke, W., & Parizel, P. M. (2014). Individual differences in a time discounting task. A fMRI study. *Journal of Neuroscience, Psychology, and Economics*, *7*, 65–79.

Welsh, M. C. (1996). A prefrontal dysfunction model of early-treated phenylketonuria. *European Journal of Pediatrics*, *155*(Suppl. 1), S87–S89.

Williams, S. M., & Goldman-Rakic, P. S. (1998). Widespread origin of the primate mesofrontal dopamine system. *Cerebral Cortex*, *8*, 321–345.

Wood, R. M., Rilling, J. K., Sanfey, A. G., Bhagwagar, Z., & Rogers, R. D. (2006). Effects of tryptophan depletion on the performance of an iterated prisoner's dilemma game in healthy adults. *Neuropsychopharmacology*, *31*, 1075–1084.

Xiao, E., & Houser, D. (2005). Emotion expression in human punishment behavior. *Proceedings of the National Academy of Sciences*, *102*, 7389–7401.

Yao, S., Zhao, W., Cheng, R., Geng, Y., Luo, L., & Kendrick, K. M. (2014). Oxytcoin makes females, but not males, less forgiving following betrayal of trust. *International Journal of Neuropsychopharmacology*, *17*. 17865–1792.

Young, K. A., Liu, Y., Gobrogge, K. L., Wang, H., & Wang, Z. X. (2014). Oxytocin reverses amphetamine-induced deficits in social bonding: Evidence for an interaction with nucleus accumbens dopamine. *Journal of Neuroscience*, *34*, 8499–8506.

Young, L. J., Lim, M. M., Gingrich, B., & Insel, T. R. (2001). Cellular mechanism of social attachment. *Hormones & Behavior*, *40*, 133–138.

Zak, P. J., Kurzban, R., & Matzner, W. T. (2004). The neurobiology of trust. *Annual Reviews of the New York Academy of Sciences*, *1032*, 224–227.

Zink, C. F., & Meyer-Lindenberg, A. (2012). Human neuroimaging of oxytocin and vasopressin in social cognition. *Hormones and Behavior*, *61*, 400–409.

CHAPTER 4

Individual Differences in Prosocial Decision Making: Social Values as a Compass

Ultimately, every person is wired for economic and social rationality. Every person has a virtuous side, but the determination to "help thy neighbor" can easily lapse, as in the following incident: on the night of September 1, 2010, a fire broke out in the kitchen of a residential house situated in the Belgian town of Boom. Three teenaged boys happened to walk by and, noticing the smoke escaping from the windows, they promptly made the necessary emergency call, then entered the house, ventured across the flames to the upstairs bedrooms where they awakened two girls and their grandmother and successfully escorted them to safety. Next they attempted to enter the scorching living room to rescue the father. They were caught in a veil of smoke when the firefighters arrived, but were able to exit the house without harm. The remarkable courage of these three youngsters did not go unnoticed; they were lavishly complimented by the local authorities and the newspapers. For one of the boys, however, the bravery would become a legend of a different kind. A few days later, while the father-homeowner was still hospitalized with life-threatening burn wounds, he trespassed into the damaged house and robbed the unfortunate family of their laptop and belongings, an act that promptly earned him the status of a fallen hero.

For most of us, the economic, self-serving, and social, other-regarding aspects of our personalities do not surface concurrently in such obvious ways. To some extent we all waver between saint and strategist, but extreme behaviors—as in the boy who first saves and then robs a family—are more likely triggered by a combination of unusually strong contextual stimuli and some enduring personality traits. People vary systematically in their generalized tendency to be mostly self-centered, skillfully exploiting situations to their advantage, or in their genuine concern for others. People hold stable values that determine not only the extent to which they will engage in prosocial

Neuroeconomics of Prosocial Behavior. DOI: http://dx.doi.org/10.1016/B978-0-12-801303-8.00004-5

behaviors, but also their underlying motives for doing so. Entering a burning house to save someone else's child is undoubtedly a prosocial act that comes with an immediate danger to the self, but even here the motives do not have to be purely selfless, because, in the long run, heroism tends to enjoy a fine reputation with generous benefits! This thought, however, may never occur to someone who values another's life as his own and who is naturally willing to take risks to save someone from the blaze, merely for the emotional satisfaction that comes with it. Depending on what exactly is valued, there may be multiple rational routes to cooperation.

The intrinsic willingness to engage in prosocial behavior—purely for its own sake—is described by economists as having "other-regarding (as opposed to self-regarding) preferences," and by psychologists as having a high "moral identity" or a "prosocial (as opposed to an individualist or proself) social value orientation." In this chapter, we will argue that these preferences, identities, or social values are, to a large extent, stable traits that strongly influence the type of rationality one is most likely to use. Values enter the utility function and bias the decision frame to yield within-individual consistency in choices. For the utilitarian, self-regarding type abiding by an economic rationality, the default decision heuristic is to act selfishly *unless* there are extrinsic incentives that align self-interest and group interest. For the socially rational other-regarding type, cooperation will be the default choice, *unless* the partner is deemed untrustworthy. This difference in relying on either an economic versus a social rationality will furthermore dictate the type of environmental cues a self-regarding versus other-regarding person will be most responsive to. We will summarize the evidence that self-regarding types are more sensitive to the presence or absence of extrinsic incentives that lead them to rely more heavily on the computational powers of the brain's cognitive control. Individuals who are other-regarding, in contrast, need to be especially attuned to social information and trust signals processed by the social brain (Declerck, Boone, & Emonds, 2013).

Before elaborating on the baseline differences in the neural activation patterns associated with opposing social value orientations, we digress on their ontogenetic origins. This is important because, by understanding where values come from, we may gain insight into the underlying causes that determine which rationality (economic or social) will predominate decision making.

4.1 HOW SOCIAL VALUES BECOME PART AND PARCEL OF STABLE PERSONALITY TYPES

For sure, everyone has witnessed the considerable heterogeneity in social values among people and, consequently, the extent to which they are eager to participate in cooperative endeavors. How much people intrinsically value cooperativeness is captured by a number of personality traits. For example, agreeable and extraverted people tend to cooperate more (Kagel & McGee, 2014; Kurzban & Houser, 2001; Lu & Argyle, 1991), while people scoring high on Machiavellianism (combining selfishness and opportunism) tend to cooperate less (Wilson, Near, & Miller, 1998). The tendency to view oneself as fair, ethical, and friendly defines an individual's moral identity, which has been shown to be predictive of baseline levels of prosocial behaviors (Aquino & Reed, 2002). Finally, social psychologists have long paid attention to individual differences in so-called social value orientation (SVO), a stable trait that reflects how people evaluate outcomes for self and others (Bogaert, Boone, & Declerck, 2008; Messick & McClintock, 1968; Van Lange, 2000). People with a prosocial value orientation value fairness (Stouten, De Cremer, & Van Dijk, 2005) and, in social interactions, they tend to maximize joint outcomes. They are by default cooperative across many different types of situations. People with a proself inclination are either self-maximizing or competitive and will cooperate only in those situations where it pays off to do so. Their cooperative behavior is purely strategic (Van Lange, 1999, 2000).

These personality types translate themselves into stable strategies adopted in experimental social dilemmas (see Chapter 1). For example, in a finitely repeated prisoner's dilemma game, a one-standard-deviation increase in agreeableness changes the predicted probability of cooperation from 67.9% to 80.6% (Kagel & McGee, 2014). A study by Kurzban and Houser (2005) shows that at least three distinct and stable behavioral strategies can be distinguished among participants playing a public goods game, and that the types using these strategies persist in time across different games (i.e., participants tend to engage in the same strategy from game to game). In their study, 63% of the players were classified as conditional cooperators, 13% as altruists, and 20% as free riders. Similar proportions were reported by Fischbacher, Gächter, and Fehr (2001), namely 50% conditional cooperators and one third of free riders. Importantly, in the Kurzban and Houser study (2005) the types did not differ significantly in their accumulated earnings, substantiating that both cooperating and free riding are genuine adaptive strategies, rather than maladaptive dispositions, noise, or confusion. But knowing that there are stable individual difference among the strategies people use to solve social dilemmas does not explain how these dispositions arise during ontogeny. Put simply, why do some people become mostly selfish while others are consistently considerate? There is little doubt that "learning to cooperate" is both nature and nurture, and the result of both genetic and environmental processes—a topic we turn to next.

4.1.1 Environmental Influences on Prosocial Behavior

Examples of environmental influences that affect the emergence of prosociality during early childhood abound. Parents who are warm and supportive to their children's needs will cultivate in them more positive behaviors. Vice versa, authoritative and punitive parents are more likely to encourage antisocial or deviant behaviors (Eisenberg & Fabes, 1998). Also the number of siblings, the quality of friendship relationships, television shows, and teachers are known to greatly impact the development of self-regarding versus other-regarding values (reviewed in Knafo & Israel, 2009).

An extreme example of how the early social environment can have lasting effects on the biological factors underscoring prosocial behavior is revealed by the study by Wismer Fries, Ziegler, Kurian, Jacoris, and Pollack (2005). They had the opportunity to examine children who had experienced severe neglect in orphanages immediately after birth and who had then been transferred to adoptive homes where they resided for at least two years before testing. Compared to a control group of children who had been raised by their biological parents, the orphans showed significant deviations in neuropeptide systems associated with establishing social bonds: they had lower baseline levels of vasopressin and failed to show an increase in peripheral oxytocin after physical contact with their adoptive mothers (see also Chapter 3). This poor oxytocin response may provide a convincing explanation for why depriving young (orphaned) children of adequate care leads to enduring changes in their socioemotional development (Wismer Fries et al., 2005).

Not only caretaking, but also social institutions and the society at large may shape values. For example, in a study by Herrmann, Thöni, and Gächter (2008), public goods experiments were conducted in 16 different countries. Not only did these researchers find sizable differences in the average cooperation rates of these countries, they also found that some countries had a surprisingly high proportion of spiteful individuals who punished the cooperators after contributions were revealed in the experiment. Further analyses show that this antisocial punishment is harsher in societies with weak norms of civic cooperation and a weak "rule of law" indicator. The latter measures "the extent to which agents have confidence in and abide by the rules of society, and in particular the quality of contract enforcement, the police, and the courts, as well as the likelihood of crime and violence" (Herrmann et al., 2008, p. 1366) Thus, at least values such as spite and vengeance appear to be influenced by an individual's societal background.

4.1.2 Genetic Influences on Prosocial Behavior

Two methods are commonly used to assess the contribution of genes to personality or complex behavior such as prosociality: (1) indirectly inferring the heritability of a trait via family studies and, especially, twin studies, and (2) DNA analyses to identify polymorphic loci that correspond to individual differences in behavior. The first method relies on the simple fact that closely related individuals (e.g., parent and offspring or first siblings) will share more genes compared to more distantly related (cousins and nephews) or unrelated individuals. Questionnaire data comparing the resemblance of traits in monozygotic twins (who share 100% of their genes and many of the same environmental influences) versus dizygotic twins (who only share 50% of their genes but experience roughly the same environment) have so far revealed significant heritability[1] for empathy, compassion, helping behaviors, and altruism (Ando et al., 2004; Knafo & Plomin, 2006; Rushton, Fulker, Neale, Nias, & Eysenck, 1986). Twin studies have also compared siblings' *actual behavior* displayed during economic games, revealing a significant heritability for trustworthiness. In a sample of Swedish and American participants playing a "trust game," monozygotic twins were more similar when it came to reciprocating the monetary investments they had been entrusted with (Cesarini, Dawes, Johannesson, Lichtenstein, & Wallace, 2009).

[1]Heritability is a population measure and can be defined as the fraction of the phenotypic variation in a population that can be attributed to the genetic variation of that population.

Based on genotype sequencing, the second method commonly used to establish a genetic basis for personality, associations between allelic variation, and behavior has been reported for most of the genes that code for the neurotransmitter systems discussed in Chapter 3, namely dopamine, serotonin, and oxytocin (reviewed in Knafo & Israel, 2009). These systems were acknowledged to play a role in (social) decision making. Dopaminergic genes, however, have more often been associated with nonsocial behaviors, such as reward dependence and sensation seeking, leading to addiction or social-conduct disorders. But the variants of these genes may serve as a protective function against impulsiveness and might therefore still enable rational decision making, especially when cognitive control capacities are needed. With respect to serotonin, several of the examined genes have been associated with individual differences in cooperativeness, but the variance they account for tends to be small (<5%). This should not be too surprising considering that it is unlikely that a single gene would exert a strong influence on the phenotypic variation observed in a behavioral trait. Genes are more likely to influence behavior through small, additive, or interactive effects on a number of cognitive and affective components, especially those that contribute to an individual's social and executive skills.

So far, the most convincing evidence relating genes to prosocial behavior has emerged from studies on the oxytocin receptor (OTR) polymorphism, not only in humans, but also in several other mammalian species (see references in Chapter 3). In humans, a number of single-nucleotide polymorphisms (SNPs) have been associated with a prosocial temperament and empathic concern (Park et al., 2010; Rodrigues, Saslow, Garcia, John, & Keltner, 2009; Tost et al., 2010; Wu, Li, & Su, 2012). Individuals who are homozygous for one of the variants of a particular polymorphism are reported to show risks of social dysfunctions, including impairments in maternal sensitivity (Bakermans-Kranenburg & Van Ijzendoorn, 2010) and attachment (Costa et al., 2009), and they have a higher likelihood of autism diagnosis (Wu et al., 2005). Also the personality trait social value orientation has been characterized by a specific haplotype of the OTR gene: at least three SNPs and one four-locus haplotype appear to be significant predictors of the prosocial–proself dichotomy (Israel et al., 2009). Importantly, the expression of certain OTR gene variants may be influenced by the social environment. For example, genotype does predict who will seek social support in stressful situations, but this relation applies only to cultures where giving socioemotional support to someone in need is a common cultural norm (Kim et al., 2010).

4.1.3 Gene Environment Interactive Effects on Prosocial Behavior

Because parents usually provide both the child's genotype and home environment, the effect of genes and childhood environment are often passively correlated (Plomin, Defries, & Loehlin, 1977; Scarr & McCartney, 1983; Dick et al., 2013). But genes and environment can also interact more actively to affect the child's emergent behaviors when, for example, a child selects (in as much as possible) environments that match her own temperament. A timid child may consistently avoid loud and flamboyant peer groups, in which case the genes underlying the temperamental trait of shyness are exerting an influence on the environmental exposure that will in time shape her behavioral tendencies. Arguably one of the more important influences on the development of prosocial values is what Plomin calls the *evocative* gene-environment interaction, which is the case when a child's genotype influences the *response* she receives from others. A cheerful and agreeable child will more likely evoke positive responses from her caregivers, fostering sympathy and kindness in return, while an ill-tempered or impulsive child will encounter more disapproval and reprimands, stimulating spirals of negativity. The point is that these environmental responses whereby a child is learning to internalize social values are, in fact, under some degree of genetic influence by means of his or her temperament.

Interestingly, heritability estimates of prosocial traits (i.e., the observed relative contribution of genetics to behavior in the entire population) tend to increase during early childhood (Knafo & Israel, 2009).[2] This is especially noticeable around the ages of three to four, when children are developing a self-image and starting to master executive functions. At this time, they also learn the difference between strategic and impulsive behavior. Could it be that, as children develop a sense of agency and become aware of the fact that

[2]After the age of 30, heritability measures of some traits may decrease again as the relative influence of environment pressures accompanying different lifestyles and experiences increases, and as people mature and make decisions that are more locally adaptive (Srivastava, John, Gosling, & Potter, 2003).

they can personally affect the outcome of a social interaction, the "evocative" influence of genes (the influence of genes trough early-environment interaction) becomes more prominent? This idea would fit the "two-step theory" of moral development described by Tomasello and Vaish (2013). Based on comparative child development studies, these authors maintain that very young children naturally display many forms of cooperative behavior. Children under two will voluntarily pick up an object that an adult accidentally dropped, open a door for someone who wants to exit, or point to the location of a toy to help someone locate it. Toddlers are able to take turns in coordination games, and they will actively try to reengage a partner who lost interest in a joint task, even if the task could be completed alone. They have a fundamental drive to collaborate with others to achieve shared goals. This contrasts sharply with the prosocial behavior of a chimpanzee who will use another chimp as a "tool" to achieve something personally and who will rarely engage in joint activity. While apes exhibit a kind of *attitudinal* reciprocity—helping those toward whom they have a positive attitude, in the hope of future reciprocity—the first step in the ontogeny of human prosociality is (according to the two-step theory) geared toward *helping another specific individual with whom they feel connected.*

Around the age of four, children make an ontogenetic switch to cooperating because of *a learned sense that it is the right thing to do.* They participate in the norms and cultural practices of their group, and they have internalized an agent-neutral morality that extends beyond a particular individual. They view every individual, including themselves, as members of the group that are expected to follow the same norms. This normative-based prosociality not only allows them to monitor their own behavior, but also to interfere with unjust behavior of third parties, thereby helping the group enforce the leading social norms. The switch to norm-based prosocial behavior is accomplished gradually over time because it depends to a large extent on social-cognitive maturation. As these sociocognitive skills often have a significant genetic component, it is no surprise that the heritability of prosocial behaviors also becomes more prominent at this age. The capacity to enforce norms would require in the first place the development of group-mindedness, which, in turn, depends on the child's propensity to form close affiliate bonds with others in the group. This capacity is likely associated with the oxytocin system and thus has a clear link with the genotype. Self-regulatory capacities are equally important to engage in abstract thinking and exert the necessary cognitive control to apply the norm to oneself. In Chapter 3 we summarized the evidence linking the role of self-regulatory capacities in abstract thinking to the dopaminergic system while using cognitive control to apply a norm to one-self involves the serotonergic system.

The development of agency and maturation of socioexecutive skills may influence the emergent prosociality in yet another way: as children are able to engage in second-order mental reasoning of the form of *I know that you know that I know that...*, they become able to anticipate, and even interfere with, the outcome of social interactions. At that time, children may start to experience with different strategies. They will come to realize that defection may be beneficial to themselves, but at the same time hurt others. Again, these experiential influences will interact with environment, because the strategies they are testing will be either positively or negatively reinforced, strengthening or weakening any genetic predisposition the child may have for preferring one strategy over another. A (sub)culture that rewards mutual cooperation and punishes defection will facilitate the internalization of a prosocial norm, while environments that do not encourage cooperation may interfere with the development of a norm-based morality and instead promote the use of executive functions to advance one's own position (sometimes even at a cost to others). Through reinforcement learning, both moral and selfish types will eventually have learned that cooperation pays off, but their focus on why this is so will be different: for the selfish type, the most rewarding value of cooperation will lie in accumulating material goods. They will have learned to cooperate especially, or only, when it is in their best interest, that is, when they can advance themselves in a loosely held group of individuals to whom they relate little. But to the intrinsically prosocial type, giving to and helping someone else can be equally rewarding. Their intrinsic motive to cooperate does not require additional benefits. In fact, as predicted by the overjustification effect, rewards have been found to sometimes undermine children's prosocial tendencies (Tomasello & Vaish, 2013). Children who have internalized prosocial norms have learned to base their self-image on idealized moral values such as serving the tightly knit group to which they feel very close and connected.

Norm internalization[3] continues to be reinforced by gene-environment interactions into adolescence. According to some theories, values, such as personality, are "set like plaster" by the age of 30 (Costa & McCrae, 1994). Other theories are more inclined to acknowledge the plasticity of behavioral traits in adulthood, emphasizing the role of culture and the numerous findings that people mature with age, making decisions that are incrementally more adaptive in their local environment. These theories additionally underscore that different traits are likely to follow different trajectories, depending on an individual's idiosyncratic experiences in the social environment. The trait "neuroticism," for example, tends to steadily decrease in strength in women after the age of 30, while scores on this same scale are lower to start with in men and remain stable throughout ontogeny (Srivastava et al., 2003). So it probably is with values: they can diverge in opposite directions because people differ, not only in their genetic endowment, but also in their life experiences and construal of the social environment.

4.2 SOCIAL VALUES DEFINE THE TYPE OF RATIONALITY THAT UNDERSCORES PROSOCIAL DECISION MAKING: A CONCEPTUAL MODEL

So far, we have argued that social values are not just "transitory motives" for cooperation, but that, through genetic influences and learning processes, they have become a stable part of personality that determine how prosocial decisions will be internally framed. A highly simplified schematic description of how individual differences in value orientations might lead to cooperative decisions is illustrated in Figure 4.1. This model, adapted from Declerck et al. (2013) and inspired by an extensive literature review by Bogaert et al. (2008), illustrates that there are two routes to cooperation depending on an individual's social preferences or value orientation. The essence of the model is that, on the one hand, individuals with self-regarding values are more sensitive to extrinsic incentives and will base their decision-making strategy on an

[3]Note that social norms are highly variable among different cultures; hence, how an individual, given his or her genetic endowment, will respond to a particular situation will depend on local socialization processes. For example, in cultures that promote face-saving values, ignoring the mishap of another person might be more appreciated than helping (which may put you at risk for demeaning the other). This could explain the finding that German and Israeli 5-year-old children display more prosocial behavior toward a distressed adult compared to Indonesian and Malaysian children—despite the fact that other studies report no cultural differences in the same response among 18-month-old children (Trommsdorff, Friedlmeier, & Mayer, 2007).

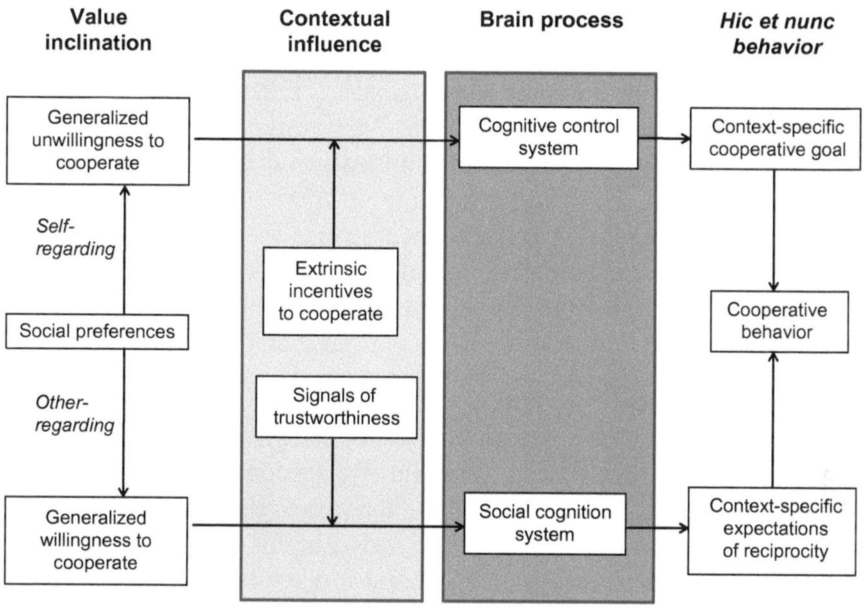

Figure 4.1 Two routes to cooperative behavior related to individual differences in value inclination. Adapted from Declerck et al. (2013), *Brain and Cognition*, and Bogaert et al. (2008), *British Journal of Social Psychology*.

economic rationality, thereby relying more intensively on the cognitive control system of the brain. On the other hand, individuals with other-regarding values are intrinsically motivated to cooperate but are also more focused on signals of trustworthiness. They will abide by a social rationality to make cooperative decisions and, accordingly, rely heavily on the social cognition system.

The processes highlighted by the arrows in the model (Figure 4.1) are compartmentalized in (1) value inclination, (2) contextual influences, (3) brain processes, and (4) *hic et nunc* context-specific behavior. In the following, we elaborate on behavioral and neuroeconomic experimental findings that corroborate the processes in each of these boxes.

4.2.1 Value Inclination

The first part of the model postulates that self-regarding and other-regarding individuals vary in their general willingness to cooperate, their generalized expectations of the cooperative behavior of others, and consequently, their aversion to betrayal. If these individual propensities arose through early gene-environment interactions and subsequent life-long (cultural) learning experiences (as described in Section 4.1), they would likely be associated with different neural activation patterns in subcortical brain regions that became sensitized in response to consistent differences in stimuli-outcome contingencies. Especially in the brain's reward system, these differences in "subjective expected utilities," (see Chapter 2) would be prominent and lead to different firing response patterns dependent on which outcome is most valued. If individual consistency in behavior is indeed underscored by idiosyncratic neural responses, this would comprise good evidence that, through genetic predisposition strengthened by learning processes, internalized social values have come to shape how utility is represented in the brain.

Evidence that social values do affect brain activity in responses in very basal regions come from two studies performed by Haruno and colleagues. In the first functional magnetic resonance imaging (fMRI) experiment (Haruno & Frith, 2010), the researchers compared brain activity of participants with either an individualist (self-regarding) or a prosocial (other-regarding) value orientation while they were evaluating different options of money allocations to themselves and others. The individualist orientation consistently preferred greater allocations to themselves than to others, while those with a prosocial orientation valued equal allocations the most. For the latter group, the degree to which each prosocial disliked inequity correlated with neural activity in the amygdala, a region that has been well studied in relation to aversive conditioning (Le Doux, 2003). The amygdala is known to play a role in judgment and decision making by enhancing the perceptual awareness of emotional events (Anderson & Phelps, 2001), which would be the case when prosocials experience or witness unfairness.

The second experiment (Haruno, Kimura, & Frith, 2014) shows a direct link between social value orientation and neural activity in the ventral striatum of the brain's reward system. Prosocial and proself participants were again scanned with fMRI while they were responding to offers in an ultimatum game. In this two-person game, a proposer (not under the scanner) can split a monetary endowment in any proportion between self and an anonymous other (the responder under the scanner). If the responder accepts the offer, the split is implemented and both parties receive the proposed share. If, however, the responder refuses, neither party receives anything. As expected, prosocial participants (who dislike unequal outcomes) rejected unfair offers more readily than individualists, and the behavioral difference between the two value orientations was tracked by a significant difference in activation in the ventral striatum. This suggests that the ventral striatum drives the decision to reject following the experience of betrayal. Furthermore, in both experiments, prosocials' increased neural activity in the amygdala and ventral striatum elicited by unequal outcomes was unaffected by cognitive load, suggesting that automatic emotional processes lie at the roots of their inequity aversion. In summary, prosocials seem to have internalized a prevailing prosocial norm, and this is reflected in how their brain responds to inequity, guiding a subsequent decision accordingly.

4.2.2 Contextual Influences

The second part of the model in Figure 4.1 suggests that extrinsic incentives and signals of trustworthiness are important contextual modulators of the relation between social values and cooperative behavior. Already at an early age, cues from the external environment influence the extent to which children will engage in prosocial behaviors. For example, already at age two, children are careful about who they interact with, and they will prefer to share toys with a familiar rather than an unfamiliar person, and are more likely to help a former collaborator compared to a stranger (Tomasello & Vaish, 2013). Presumably, previous cooperative acts are automatically interpreted to be predictive of future dependability. Three-year-old children are also less sympathetic (and show less prosocial behavior) to a person whom they perceive to be a crybaby, that is, a person who overreacts after being only mildly distressed. Thus, these very young children are already taking into account contextual cues when interpreting someone else's distress (Tomasello & Vaish, 2013).

In adulthood, people remain sensitive to cues that are indicative of traits such as honesty and trustworthiness and will, often unconsciously, adapt behavior accordingly. They will, for example, derive information from subtle cues such as a partner's pupil dilation or eye gaze. Cues that signal reputation opportunities are equally effective in inducing prosocial behavior, which may be a second factor explaining the higher rates of cooperation during face-to-face encounters compared to anonymous situations (e.g., Bohnet & Frey, 1999).

An important aspect of the model in Figure 4.1, however, is that stable social values dictate the type of cues people will be most responsive to. This reasoning follows a well-known tenet from social psychology, namely that humans strive to be internally consistent and that they will try to behave in accordance with their own social identity, which, as argued in the previous section, is to a certain extent dictated by personality and genetics. Thus, a person who scores high on, for example, the personality trait "agreeableness" is likely to have an other-regarding value orientation and will be intrinsically motivated to act in cooperative ways to portray his or her true "agreeable" identity as best as possible. This will be appreciated by other cooperative types, who will gladly return the honors, triggering a forward spiral of reciprocity. But also self-regarding people can benefit from the default cooperative nature of agreeable people, without giving anything in return. To avoid being taken advantage of, we predict that this vulnerability in the personality of agreeable people (or any other prosocial type) has to be accompanied by a superior attention to social cues, such as the trustworthiness signals emitted by others. Thus, their cooperative nature will be most apparent when they perceive themselves in a trustworthy environment. A good example of this is the report that prosocially oriented individuals in organizational settings perform better when they perceive a trustworthy manager (Grant & Sumanth, 2009).

In contrast, people who score low on agreeableness (or high on other personality types indicative of individualistic values) may fake a prosocial identity to elicit reciprocity. If they succeed, they often betray the trust that was extended to them, but this does not hurt their self-image as they are insensitive (or at least less sensitive) to the feelings of others. Their self-regarding values and their disinclination to cooperate may protect them from exploitation by others, but they do miss out on many of the opportunities for reciprocity that makes defection, in the long run, economically less interesting than mutual cooperation. This flaw in an "always defect" strategy can be bypassed if self-regarding types become very attuned to the different sorts of incentive structures that indicate that cooperation is lucrative.

Based on a comprehensive literature review, Bogaert et al. (2008) summarized the evidence that cooperative decisions can indeed be attained by two different psychological routes that correspond to individual differences in social value orientations: on the one hand, individuals with self-regarding values cooperate readily when there are extrinsic incentives (e.g., material compensation or reputation benefits) that align self-interest with the larger collective and thereby transform their general unwillingness to cooperate into a cooperative motivation. On the other hand, individuals with other-regarding values can be expected to willingly cooperate, as long as there is sufficient trust that their prosocial behavior will be reciprocated, given the particular decision-context they find themselves to be in at the moment. This model was then tested in a large-scale experiment (Boone, Declerck, & Kiyonari, 2010) that compared cooperative decisions of prosocials versus proselfs in one-shot social dilemma games while manipulating the presence of extrinsic incentives and trust.[4] As predicted, proselfs cooperated significantly more when cooperative incentives embedded in the game matrix of the social dilemma accentuated the win−win nature of the interaction, while these same incentives had less impact on prosocials. Conversely, generalized trust as well as induced trust signals were found to facilitate cooperative behavior in prosocials, but they had no impact on proselfs.

An interesting feature in the study of Boone et al. (2010) was that they manipulated incentives by altering the payoff structures of the social dilemma games: in the incentivized games (i.e., coordination or "assurance" games), the most could be earned by mutual cooperation, which contrasted sharply with the other condition where the payoff matrix offered mixed motives that pull the equilibrium toward noncooperation (i.e., prisoner's dilemma games). Another simple way to manipulate incentives to cooperate in social dilemmas is to vary the number of trials. This manipulation does not influence everybody alike. Stable individual differences in the behavioral tendency to strategically increase cooperative decisions when interactions become repeated, and decrease them in the last round, have been reported several times (Boone, De Brabander, & Van Witteloostuijn, 1999; Reuben & Suetens, 2009; Selten & Stoecker, 1986).

Evidence that reputation gains are primarily an incentive to cooperate for self-regarding individuals was nicely illustrated by the experiments conducted by Simpson and Willer (2008). They used a prisoner's dilemma

[4]The social value orientation was assessed using the triple-dominance personality test (Van Lange, 2000) whereby a person is asked nine times to choose between three options that divide a sum of money between the self and an anonymous other. One of the options is to split the money equally, which corresponds to a prosocial choice. The other two options, denoting the proself choices, are to choose for a split in favor of maximizing the money paid to oneself or to choose for a split that maximizes the difference between the outcome for self and other. An individual is categorized as having a particular value orientation if he or she makes at least six consistent choices.

game to show that individuals classified *a priori* as self-regarding respond strategically to reputation incentives: they cooperated when the outcomes of the game were made public for future partners to see, and they stopped cooperating when the games were played anonymously. Participants classified *a priori* as other-regarding were less affected by the publicity of the games. Furthermore, the self-regarding participants were aware of their own strategic behavior, and they tended to discount other's prosocial behavior when it was made public. Hence they realized that others were using the publicity for strategic self-enhancement.

4.2.3 Brain Processes and Behavior

The third and fourth compartments in the model in Figure 4.1 propose that specific brain regions are associated with processing the contextual cues that links the individual's *hic et nunc* decision to cooperate (or not) to context-specific goals or expectations of reciprocity. For other-regarding individuals, who naturally have a cooperative goal, trustworthiness will be an important factor underlying the *social* rationality of their decision. To assess signals of trustworthiness and form expectations of others, they will rely heavily on regions of the social brain. In contrast, a self-regarding individual who figures out that there are lucrative extrinsic incentives will compromise his or her unwillingness to cooperate in favor of an *economically* rational cooperative goal. To formally compute what a cooperative decision is worth, brain regions implicated in cognitive control will be recruited. For both the other- and self-regarding types, the decision to cooperate (or not) will be rational, as their generalized personal goals and expectations have become aligned with the specific environmental context.

That cognitive control is more critical in the cooperative decision-making process of self-regarding individuals is also suggested by the following experimental findings: when self-control is inhibited by a cognitive depletion task, only individuals with a low moral identity were found to have a hard time inhibiting the tendency to cheat on an exam by falsely reporting their score. Other-regarding individuals (with a high moral identity), in contrast, were unaffected by cognitive depletion, suggesting that being honest is their default behavior (Gino, Schweitzer, Mead, & Ariely, 2011).

In Chapter 2 (Figure 2.2) we indicated that the regions of the brain's cognitive control system that are necessary to process extrinsic cooperative incentives include the dorsolateral prefrontal cortex (PFC), dorsal anterior cingulate cortex (ACC), and lateral orbitofrontal cortex. On the other hand, processing trust signals relies on social cognition, recruiting the dorsomedial PFC, temporoparietal junction (TPJ), and amygdala in the social brain. We next review the neuroeconomic studies that have addressed individual differences in the neural correlates of cooperative decisions and evaluate to what extent they confirm these hypothesized differences between self-regarding and other-regarding individuals (see also Declerck et al., 2013, for a similar review).

4.2.3.1 Direct Measures

A first and direct method to investigate if individual differences correlate with brain processes implicated in cognitive control versus social cognition is to divide the participants into "cooperating" versus "noncooperating" groups based on the decisions they make during an experiment, and then compare the brain activation patterns between these groups. This design was used in one of the first experiments in neuroeconomics, revealing at the same time the promise of the field (McCabe, Houser, Ryan, Smith, & Trouard, 2001). The researchers compared participants who consistently cooperated with participants who also defected in a repeated trust game. The game was played against a human and a computer partner. For the consistent cooperators (who decide to trust), the human partner (compared to the computer) elicited significantly more activation in the medial PFC. This difference was not found for the noncooperating individuals, which suggests that social cognition matters less to them in this game. Similarly, Krueger et al. (2007) also compared brain activity of participants who were using different strategies in a repeated trust game. Compared to defectors (i.e., players who were not trustworthy and who assumed a self-interested partner just as they were themselves), trustworthy players (who positively reciprocated the trust extended to them) showed more activation in the paracingulate cortex (located within the dorsomedial PFC) and the septal area (an area associated with encoding goodwill and enduring social relations; see Krueger et al., 2007). Both studies underlie that regions of the social brain are more intensely recruited in a trust game by those participants who value cooperativeness the most (as indicated by their trust and reciprocity).

Interestingly, there are reports of *structural* differences in the right TPJ associated with individual differences in altruistic tendencies, while *functional* TPJ activation may depend more on context and how an individual interprets the demands of the task (Morishima, Schunk, Bruhin, Ruff, & Fehr, 2012). In an fMRI experiment, participants who were experiencing "advantageous" or "disadvantageous" inequality (i.e., experiencing higher or lower initial payoffs than a partner) were asked to allocate money in dictator-like games. Volume-based morphometry analyses indicated that gray matter volume in the right TPJ correlated significantly with the extent individuals were likely to act altruistically and reduce inequality when they were in the advantageous position. TPJ functional activation, however, did not correspond linearly with altruistic tendencies, but was highest when the maximum cost an individual was willing to pay for altruism fell just below the actual cost. This makes sense considering the TPJ's role in perspective taking: when the actual cost to pay either vastly exceeds the altruistic tendency (i.e., when selfishness predominates), or when the individual is so generous that actual cost does not matter, TPJ activation will do little to steer decision making in either direction. But when the conflict between economic and social benefits peaks, TPJ activation tips choice behavior toward the social side. And this is furthermore reflected by larger gray matter TPJ volume in those individuals with the strongest altruistic tendencies.

The predominance of cognitive control over social cognition in noncooperative participants is demonstrated in an experiment by Bhatt and colleagues, comparing brain activity of "high strategizers" and "low strategizers." The former type was identified as those individuals who deceived others during a bargaining game, revealing their self-regarding values. At the time of deception, these "high strategizers" activated the dorsolateral PFC to a greater extent than the other behavioral types (Bhatt, Lohrenz, Camerer, & Montague, 2010). In another experiment, however, no increased activation of cognitive control (or decreased activation of social cognition) could be related to strategy. The researchers compared the brain patterns of participants who varied in so-called strategic IQ, a measure of the extent to which people are able to infer the higher-order beliefs people form during iterated coordination games. Inferring the choices of others in this experiment was necessary to maximize one's own gain and is therefore compatible with a self-regarding inclination.[5] Regressing brain activation on strategic IQ only showed a positive correlation in the caudate

[5]Although other-regarding individuals also infer others' beliefs before making decisions in an interdependent game, they use this information to avoid betrayal. To them, the actual payoff is less relevant, as long as it is fair (see also Stouten et al., 2005).

nucleus, a region critical in reinforcement learning. This probably means that highly strategic people reinforce their own decisions when they can derive the strategies of others with a high degree of certainty (and hence be relatively sure of obtaining the expected reward from cooperation). In addition, the authors reported a negative correlation between strategic IQ and insula activation, suggesting that emotions in general play a less prominent role in the decision-making scheme of high strategizers (Bhatt & Camerer, 2005).

4.2.3.2 Indirect Measures

An alternative and more telling method to identify the brain processes associated with making economically versus socially rational decisions is to correlate brain activity to individual differences in personality traits that have been determined *a priori* with questionnaires. The advantage is that the individual differences are assessed independent of the behavior exhibited during the experiment. A good example is the classic fMRI experiment conducted by Spitzer, Fischbacher, Herrnberger, Gron, and Fehr (2007) that illustrates how norm compliance is economically rational, activating the brain's cognitive control regions. Participants played two versions of a dictator game. In the "no punishment condition," player 1 (whose brain is being scanned) received a sum of money to be split in any proportion between himself and another player (outside the scanner). In the "punishment condition," player 2 could impose a monetary sanction if the allotment was perceived to be unfair. On average, the presence of the punishment threat doubled the level of generosity. Brain contrasts between the two conditions indicated that the threat of punishment (which serves as a negative incentive to abide by the norm) is associated with increased activity in the dorsolateral PFC, the ventrolateral PFC, and the lateral orbitofrontal cortex. The last region is especially important in evaluating punishment threats (Kringelbach & Rolls, 2004). Interestingly, the activity in the lateral orbitofrontal cortex in the punishment condition correlated positively with high scores on the Machiavellianism scale. This shows that self-regarding values (inherent to Machiavellianism) interact with context (the presence or absence of a negative incentive) to enhance an economic rationality, which is facilitated by activation of a lateral part of the brain.

The experiment conducted by Emonds, Declerck, Boone, Vandervliet, and Parizel (2011) corroborates that cognitive control by the dorsolateral

PFC appears more activated during decision making of self-regarding compared to other-regarding individuals. Participants with either a prosocial or individualistic social value orientation were scanned with fMRI while they played a series of social dilemma games in which they could either cooperate or defect. In this experiment, prisoner's dilemma games and assurance games were juxtaposed, causing participants to mentally switch from a decision context where there is a strong temptation to defect (the prisoner's dilemma game) to a context that offers a strong incentive to cooperate (the assurance game). This made it possible to logically compute the gains from cooperation, leading the individualist participants to defect in the prisoner's dilemma game (where mutual defection is the only Nash equilibrium) and to cooperate in the assurance game (where mutual cooperation is the payoff-dominant Nash equilibrium). The prosocial participants, in contrast, did not show this strategic switch between games. As expected, individualists activated the dorsolateral PFC to a greater extent than the prosocials. This is consistent with the behavioral data indicating that, for each decision, they computed what the best response would be, and adapted their decision accordingly. In contrast, the prosocials used the same strategy throughout the games, and did not appear to discern between the different incentive structures (Emonds et al., 2011).

The corollary, that regions of the social brain would be more intensely recruited by prosocials, was not as straightforward as expected in the experiment by Emonds et al. (2011). Instead, the social brain was involved during decision making of both prosocials and individualists, but the pattern of activation was differentiated between the two types. With respect to the TPJ, the posterior part of the superior temporal sulcus (pSTS) was more activated in the individualists, and the anterior part more in the prosocials. This finding is consistent with more fine-grained anatomical distinctions of the STS. Its posterior part has been reported as more involved in first-time thought-provoking (cognitive) evaluative judgments, while the anterior part would take over in routine moral judgments (Borg, Hynes, Van Horn, Grafton, & Sinnott-Armstrong, 2006). That the latter would be more activated in prosocials makes sense considering their propensity for automatic processing and internalizing norms (Haruno & Frith, 2010; Haruno et al., 2014).

With follow-up studies, an interesting interaction between social value orientation (prosocials versus individualists) and the decision context emerged in yet another social brain region known as the precuneus

(Emonds et al., 2011; Emonds, Declerck, Boone, Seurinck, & Achten, 2014). The precuneus is involved in self-referencing and expectation matching, and is typically activated by tasks that rely on mentalizing, enabling comparison of outcomes for self and others (Cavanna & Trimble, 2006). When, in the first experiments, the decision context comprised both assurance and prisoner's dilemma games, increased activation in the precuneus was observed for those with an individualistic social value orientation. The researchers inferred that the precuneus activation helps individualists to compute the most self-serving option based on comparing the outcomes for self and others in the two different games (which is to compete in the prisoner's dilemma and to cooperate in the assurance game, see Emonds et al., 2011). But when (in a second experiment) only prisoner's dilemma games were played, the decision context became one that spurred the dominant response of defecting. With no cooperative incentives, the individualists will consistently favor the selfish response of defecting, which makes self-referencing and precuneus activation superfluous. In fact, in the prisoner's dilemma games, the precuneus was found to be more active in cooperating prosocials, whose decisions are based on comparing their own cooperative norm with what they expect from others (Emonds et al., 2014). Taking the findings of both of Emonds' experiments together, it appears that the precuneus may take part in decision making by computing the anticipated self–other outcome that is mostly valued. If the anticipated outcome yields equality and thereby matches one's own prosocial norm, the decision will be socially rational; if the outcome leads to the best outcome for the self, economic rationality is realized.

Finally, a recent experiment by Yoder and Decety (2014) corroborates that there is increased involvement of the social brain during evaluative judgments of individuals who have a high justice sensitivity (i.e., who react intensely to experiences of injustice and unfairness) compared to those with a low justice sensitivity. These authors showed that activity in the dorsomedial PFC and the right TPJ correlated positively with the task of evaluating the morality behind a number of everyday scenarios affecting others. The TPJ also showed a greater functional coupling with regions in the lateral and medial frontal cortex, suggesting that social information (e.g., regarding moral behavior) becomes integrated with conscious decision making, especially in people who are very sensitive to fairness (see also Buckholz & Marois, 2012).

To conclude, individual differences in the brain activation patterns of people are consistent with their social values and the environmental information they are most sensitive to. Cognitive control regions tend to show enhanced activation in self-regarding individuals during decision making, which is consistent with their over-reliance on processing incentives that tell them whether or not cooperation is economically rational. The evidence for the differential recruitment of the social brain is less clear-cut, as several of these regions are recruited in both self-regarding and other-regarding individuals. The patterns of activation tend to depend not only on the social values of the individual, but also on the specific nature of the task. The TPJ and the precuneus in the social brain especially may play a role in achieving ecologically rational decisions by integrating an individual's goals or expectations with the demands of the task (see Emonds et al., 2011, 2014; Morishima et al., 2012). These regions become engaged when the expected outcomes are close to a match with one's own values or norms.

4.3 COSTLY PUNISHMENT AND STRONG RECIPROCATORS

Social and economic rationality are theoretical constructs that may be difficult to distinguish in real life because both can generate the same behavior (e.g., cooperation). We have argued at length that values determine which rationality will predominate in a given person. Even extremely selfish individuals may still be cooperative when it is economically rational to do so, which may have led to Michael Ghiselin's famous saying "scratch an altruist and watch a hypocrite bleed" (Ghiselin, 1974, p. 247) Just from observing cooperative behavior it is impossible to infer whether or not the decision maker was incentivized by economics or acting on the intrinsic belief that this was collectively the right thing to do.

Some researchers (e.g., Gintis, Bowles, Boyd, & Fehr, 2003) in experimental economics have argued that the motives for socially rational behavior, generating collective benefits, are more apparent in the willingness to punish norm violators. The logic is based on the interpretation that punishment forms a "second-order" dilemma, whereby the entire group benefits from the punishing behavior of a few punishers only. In principle, everybody would like a norm-violator to be punished, but it is in one's own self-interest to let someone else do the job. But who?

After reviewing the anthropological evidence of sanctioning behaviors cross-culturally, Guala (2012) concludes that, in fact, no-one is really willing to pay individually to punish. Instead, people in all societies eagerly engage in symbolic punishment that does not cost anything (i.e., gossip, bad-mouthing, and ostracism), and, since the beginning of states, justice systems and law-enforcing agencies have become institutionalized to maintain large-scale peace and order. By doing so, the second-order dilemma is removed and sanctioning becomes a collective responsibility that does not single out anyone. Thus, the ubiquity of costly punishing behavior in laboratory games may well be an experimental artifact that cannot be translated to the field. The finding that some game players spend part of their endowment to punish other, unfair game players is possibly the result of a windfall effect, that is, the fact that the money was given to them instead of earned, which makes it easier to spend. Francesco Guala (2012) does not discount the importance of strong reciprocity and the laboratory research it has inspired, but advocates using this concept as an effective way to represent people's primary prosocial motives. Because it is unambiguously not in one's self-interest to punish, assessing whether or not someone is willing to punish in an experimental game is a useful tool to evaluate social preferences or values.

Individuals who do punish have been called *strong reciprocators* in behavioral economics, and we devote this last section of the chapter to investigating the individual differences in the drive to punish. What makes a strong reciprocator tick? To bypass the strategic considerations that punishment is costly and therefore not economically rational, a heuristic, driven by emotions and/or internalized prosocial norms, could trigger sanctioning behavior in the same way that heuristics trigger cooperative behavior because the anticipated outcome is to feel good. We explore in this section to what extent such a decision heuristic is a plausible stable trait, triggered by the same brain regions implicated in socially rational behavior.

4.3.1 Laboratory Experiments Showing Strong Reciprocity

Strong reciprocity is defined by Gintis et al. (2003) as "a propensity to cooperate with others and to punish those who violate the norm of cooperation, even when it is impossible to expect that costs will be repaid either by others or at a later date" (p. 154). Most of the evidence that *at least some* people are willing to bear the cost of punishment *some of the time* comes from behavioral experiments involving economic games. In the ultimatum game, for example, rejecting any positive offer is not economically rational and can therefore be considered the receiver's way of punishing a proposer who is perceived to be unfair (Camerer & Thaler, 1995). Cross-cultural research with the ultimatum game reveals that this deviation from the canonical model of self-interest is universal, but with considerable variability across societies. The modal rejection rates furthermore seem to parallel the structure of daily life. For example, the high rejection rates among the Hadza and the Ache reflect the fact that these small-scale foragers engage in high levels of conflict and attempt to hide meat that normatively ought to be shared. The Machiguenga and Tsimane, in contrast, hardly reject offers, which is consistent with their tight family units and their insensitivity to public opinion (Gintis et al., 2003; Henrich et al., 2005). Finally, the minimal accepted offer in the ultimatum game appears to covary with the extent to which a society exhibits cooperative norms (Henrich et al., 2006), suggesting that the unwillingness to accept unfairness is strengthened by the social environment and that punishment is encouraged by the community.

Public goods games, too, offer the opportunity to investigate the occurrence of strong reciprocity. It is perhaps no surprise that adding punishment opportunities to a series of games prevents the typical decline in cooperation rates, because the knowledge that selfishness will be sanctioned deters free riding (Fehr & Gächter, 2002). When, after a round of the game, participants are offered a new endowment that they can either keep to themselves or use to punish noncontributors to the public good, a significant proportion will personally pay the fee to impose the sanction (e.g., Kiyonari & Barclay, 2008; Yamagishi, 1986). More impressively, even third-party observers, who do not directly participate in the public goods games, are willing to use their allotment to fine an unfair player (Fehr & Fischbacher, 2004).

The strong reciprocity definition predicts that especially cooperators who endorse social rationality (those initiating cooperation unconditionally without being prompted by extrinsic incentives) will engage in punishing (Gintis et al., 2003). Consistently, in the experiment by Fehr and Gächter (2002), 75% of the punishment acts were executed by above-average contributors in public goods games. A field study comparing the success of forest management commons in Ethiopia corroborates that those individuals identified as cooperators in public goods games spent more time on monitoring others, and that this positively impacted the productivity of the commons (Rustagi, Engel, & Kosfeld, 2010). That sanctioning and monitoring are causally related to socially rational cooperation follows furthermore from findings that intentionality matters. While especially the cooperators in experimental games may be motivated to punish because they care about the outcome of the game (which would be economically rational), a significant proportion of them also take the intentions of the wrongdoers into account, which cannot be explained by economic rationality alone. Experimental designs that differentiate between intentional and unintentional defection reveal an increase in punishment when selfish intentions are clear (Falk, Fehr, & Fischbacher, 2008; Kiyonari, Declerck, Boone, & Pollet, 2012). Caring about intentions indicates a moral differentiation between acts of omission and commission, where only the latter would be deemed morally wrong. Arguably, this concern is more compatible with a social rather than an economic rationality, and thus is more typical of individuals holding other-regarding values.

4.3.2 Neural Correlates of Punishment

Can neuroeconomic research corroborate that punishing acts are driven by social rather than economic rationality involving more social and emotional brain regions to implement a norm-based heuristic, and requiring little cognitive control, which would indicate that people punish because of an incentive to do so? The evidence so far seems to sketch a more complicated picture. Both cognitive control *and* emotion-regulation regions appear to be consistently activated by punishing decisions, while social cognition (recruiting the dorsomedial PFC, temporoparietal junction, and amygdala) remains notoriously uninvolved.[6]

There is little doubt that punishing decisions are driven by emotion-regulation mechanisms, such as the kind we would expect from a heuristic that bypasses economic cost–benefit analyses. Negative affect resulting from, for example, dealing with injustice typically interferes with normal self-regulation processes and instigates a priority shift: when sufficiently distressed, brain resources become first and foremost

[6]The mentalizing network in the social brain may actually be involved in downregulating punishment decisions associated with parochial altruism. In Chapter 5 we will describe the results of an experiment indicating that bilateral TPJ and the dorsomedial PFC become activated to reduce the punishment of ingroup members compared to outgroup members who committed the same violation (Baumgartner, Gotte, & Gugler, 2012).

dedicated to reestablishing emotional homeostasis (Tice, Baumeister, & Zang, 2004). One of the first pieces of evidence substantiating that negative emotions lead to punishing decisions comes from the classical skin conductance experiment by Van't Wout, Kahn, Sanfey, and Aleman (2006). In an ultimatum game, skin conductance (a physiological proxy for emotional arousal) rises in response to an unfair offer, the magnitude of which being predictive of rejection.

In fact, justified revenge after being treated poorly may even feel rewarding and "taste sweet," and it has been inferred to serve as a homeostatic mechanism to restore positive affect. Using positron emission tomography (PET), de Quervain et al. (2004) tested the hypothesis that people derive satisfaction from punishing when someone intentionally abuses their trust. They compared three conditions: (1) punishment is effective but does not cost the punisher anything, (2) punishment is effective and costly, and (3) punishment is symbolic. Questionnaire data confirmed that players who felt betrayed experienced a strong desire to punish. When punishment was free, all participants punished maximally. Contrasting brain activity of punishing decisions in the effective conditions (free and costly) versus symbolic punishing decisions showed increased activity in the caudate nucleus within the dorsal striatum (a part of the reward system of the brain, see Chapter 2). Players who showed more dorsal striatum activation in the free condition also punished more when punishing became costly. Given that there are no individual differences in punishing behavior in the free condition, these findings suggest that dorsal striatum activation is related to individual differences in the felt need to punish, and hence in the anticipation that punishing would make them feel better.

Other emotion-regulation brain regions that have been reported to be necessary for enforcing punishment are the ventromedial PFC and the anterior insula, while the ventrolateral PFC may be required to inhibit punishing decisions. The role of the ventromedial PFC is evidenced by the fact that patients with these lesions tend to not punish in an ultimatum game and accept abnormally low unfair offers (Koenigs & Tranel, 2007). The ventromedial PFC is a part of the core of the brain's reward system and integrates affective information with the decision-making process (see Chapter 2). Apparently, ventromedial PFC patients are not bothered by negative affect from being treated unfairly; they tend to respond very rationally.

The insula, a key structure involved in generating awareness of visceral stimuli, is typically activated when experiencing disgust, as when exposed to an obnoxious smell (Phillips et al., 1997), and could serve as a "homeostatic alert" with enhanced activation indicating that some physical or emotional state is out of balance. In line with this, an fMRI study of the ultimatum game showed increased bilateral anterior insula activation in response to unfair offers (Sanfey, Rilling, Aronson, Nystrom, & Cohen, 2003). Furthermore, its activation was relative to the actual degree of unfairness and was predictive of rejection rates. The positive relation between activation of the anterior insula and rejection of unfair offers in an ultimatum game was later replicated by Tabibnia, Satpute, and Lieberman (2008). These latter authors also report that rejections were inversely correlated with ventrolateral PFC activation. Players who accepted a higher proportion of offers that they perceived to be unfair showed stronger correlations between accepting and ventrolateral PFC activation, which makes sense when one considers that this region has previously been linked to economically rational decision making in economic games that require players to maximize their expected outcome (De Martino, Kumaran, Seymour, & Dolan, 2006), and that it is generally associated with down-regulation of activity in regions supporting negative affect (e.g., Eisenberger, Lieberman, & Williams, 2003; Hariri, Mattay, Tessitore, Fera, & Weinberger, 2003).

But emotion regulation cannot be the entire story accounting for punishing decisions, because a number of studies have convincingly shown that an intact dorsolateral PFC is required to implement punishing decisions (hence its role would presumably be opposite to that of the role of the ventrolateral PFC). First, Knoch, Pascual-Leone, Meyer, Treyer, and Fehr (2006) used transcranial magnetic stimulation (TMS) to knock out the dorsolateral PFC of participants just prior to playing an ultimatum game. Compared to an untreated control group, the right-dorsolateral PFC-deficient participants accepted more unfair offers. The authors interpret this to mean that knocking out this region causes players to give in to their selfish impulse and accept any positive offer rather than implementing the culturally adaptive norm of rejecting. Second, in a follow-up study, Knoch, Gianotti, Baumgartner, and Fehr (2010) used electroencephalography to show that individuals with baseline hypoactivation of the lateral PFC accept a greater proportion of unfair offers, meaning again that, in the ultimatum game, the lateral PFC is needed to implement a punishing decision. People who are deficient in self-regulatory skills associated with the lateral PFC would, according to these results, be less likely to engage in socially appropriate punishing behavior, a proposition that fits current psychopathological reports of aberrant social conduct in patients with deficient self-control. Third, Baumgartner, Knoch, Hotz, Eisenegger, and Fehr (2011) showed that, when fairness and economic interest conflict, also the *connectivity* between the dorsolateral PFC and the ventromedial PFC facilitate an individual's willingness to incur the cost of punishment and reject unfair offers.

These results are puzzling because they point to the fact that the brain mechanisms supporting punishing decisions and strong reciprocity are not simple extensions of socially rational cooperative decisions. Earlier in this chapter, we associated activation of the dorsolateral PFC with cognitive control and economically rational decision making. Certainly a *Homo economicus* would prefer the less costly option of accepting in an ultimatum game than the more costly rejection! This interpretation seems to be consistent with the fMRI results of the experiment by Sanfey et al. (2003): they report that the decision to accept or reject is dependent on the relative activation of dorsolateral PFC versus insula activation. When insula activation is greater than dorsolateral PFC activation an unfair offer will be rejected. When dorsolateral PFC activation exceeds that of the insula, an unfair offer will be accepted. Thus, taking into account the results of both fMRI and TMS studies, it appears that the lateral PFC is involved in the economically rational cost–benefit analysis of the outcome (using self control to inhibit a punishing decision), as well as in providing the necessary self-control to implement a socially rational norm (allowing punishing).

4.3.3 Can this Paradox be Resolved by Gaining Insight into Individual Differences?

These inconsistent reports in the literature regarding the role of the lateral PFC in costly punishment in the ultimatum game (e.g., Sanfey et al., 2003 vs. Knoch et al., 2006) may not be so problematic when one considers individual differences in social values. Unfair offers are more difficult to respond to compared to fair offers and may therefore place higher cognitive demands on everyone. Consistently, both studies report that the dorsolateral PFC is necessarily involved in dealing with unfair offers. The difference is that, in the Sanfey study, increased activation of the dorsolateral PFC following unfair offers occurs regardless of the decision to punish, while in the Knoch study, its activation is especially needed for punishing. Could both findings be sample specific and reflect a difference in how cognitive control is used among people with heterogeneous social values? Only for the other-regarding types, for whom punishing is consistent with the values they believe in, is self-control necessary to overcome the economic cost of punishing and abide by the collectively beneficial norm. The self-regarding type, in contrast, needs self-control to suppress anger and resist punishing out of vengeance. This proposition, that self-control differentially leads to punishing decisions depending on values, implies that the decision to punish should be individually stable, just as values are a stable part of personality (see the discussion at the beginning of this chapter). Indeed, there is evidence that the behavioral inclination to either punish or accept in an ultimatum game may have a genetic component with a heritability of up to 40% (Wallace, Cesarini, Lichtenstein, & Johanesson, 2007).

Perhaps the best piece of evidence so far that values drive punishing decisions in an ultimatum game comes from a recent fMRI study investigating the neural differences between individuals that differ in social value orientations (see also Section 4.2.1). Prosocial individuals punished unfair offers more readily than individualists, and this was accompanied with a significant difference in the activation level of the nucleus accumbens (ventral striatum) and, to a lesser extent, in the amygdala. The nucleus accumbens lies at the core of the brain's valuation system, suggesting that "punishing" in this case was indeed the preferred outcome for prosocials. No difference was found in the insula and the dorsolateral PFC. As in other punishing experiments, these regions were also found to be activated, but not differentially so, between individuals with opposing value types (Haruno et al., 2014).

To conclude, injustice triggers a number of neural reactions that are universal, but how the neural activation translates into behavior may be value-dependent. Across all individuals, being treated unfairly elicits negative affect, which calls for emotion regulation, activating the ventromedial PFC and the anterior insula. In addition, the lateral PFC is activated (in all individuals) to solve the conflict between not paying the cost of personally punishing the offender (the economically rational response) and the pressure to conform to the socially acceptable norm of punishing (the socially rational response). Self-regarding individuals are more likely to resolve the conflict in favor of economic rationality and rely on the lateral PFC to overcome the emotional impulse of punishing. They keep the money and leave the punishing to someone else. Other-regarding people resolve the conflict by relying on the lateral PFC to resist the selfish impulse of not punishing. Consistent with social rationality, they will bear the cost of punishment out of deontological considerations that it is collectively the right thing to do.

4.4 SUMMARY

People vary in the social values they hold, and hence in the extent to which they adhere to economically versus socially rational motives to cooperate. Such individual differences do influence the neural correlates of decision making, which are apparent in the firing patterns of subcortical brain regions (the amygdala and the ventral striatum) as well as in regions implicated in cognitive control and social cognition. The former reflects the difference in utility that is ascribed to outcomes, while the latter is more likely the result of the self-regarding type's increased reliance on processing extrinsic incentives, while other-regarding types pay more attention to emanating social signals. Given that humans also differ in their propensity for experiencing social emotions and exerting cognitive control (e.g. Gray, 2004; Hamann & Canli, 2004), it is perhaps not surprising that differences in neural firing in regions such as the insula, amygdala, and lateral PFC appear to be associated with individual differences in social values.

The literature reviewed here suggests that the picture is complex and that there does not have to be a one-on-one relation between neural activation and behavior. Activating the lateral PFC, for example, can lead to punishing or tolerant decisions, depending on values and the type of impulses that one wants to control. For self-regarding individuals, activation of the lateral PFC can furthermore lead to cooperative or defect decisions, depending on the types of incentives that are offered. Values are the compass by which individuals navigate in the social world, and they will determine which kind of contextual information will become incorporated in the decision-making process.

The Lady Justice inside of us may not be so impartial after all. The blindfold she wears is tainted with her values, which will load her balance and weigh the events occurring in the outside world differentially. Her sword is swaying self-righteously, determined to defend her own, very personal way.

REFERENCES

Anderson, A. K., & Phelps, E. A. (2001). Lesions of the human amygdala impair enhanced perception of emotionally salient events. *Nature*, *411*, 305–309.

Ando, J., Suzuki, A., Yamagata, S., Kijima, N., Maekwa, H., Ono, Y., & Jang, K. L. (2004). Genetic and environmental structure of Cloninger's temperament and character dimensions. *Journal of Personality Disorders*, *18*, 379–393.

Aquino, K., & Reed, A., II (2002). The self-importance of moral identity. *Journal of Personality and Social Psychology*, *83*, 1423–1440.

Bakermans-Kranenburg, M. J., & Van Ijzendoorn, M. H. (2010). Oxytocin receptor (OXTR) and serotonin transporter (5-HTT) genes associated with observed parenting. *Social Cognitive and Affective Neuroscience*, *3*, 128–134.

Baumgartner, T. B., Gotte, L., & Gugler, L. (2012). The mentalizing network orchestrates the impact of parochial altruism on social norm enforcement. *Human Brain Mapping*, *33*, 1452–1469.

Baumgartner, T. B., Knoch, D., Hotz, P., Eisenegger, C., & Fehr, E. (2011). Dorsolateral and ventromedial cortex orchestrate normative choice. *Nature Neuroscience*, *14*, 1468–1477.

Bhatt, M. A., & Camerer, C. F. (2005). Self-referential thinking and equilibrium as states of mind in games: fMRI evidence. *Games and Economic Behavior*, *52*, 424–459.

Bhatt, M. A., Lohrenz, T., Camerer, C. F., & Montague, P. R. (2010). Neural signatures of strategic types in a two-person bargaining game. *Proceedings of the National Academy of Sciences*, *107*, 19720–19725.

Bogaert, S., Boone, C., & Declerck, C. H. (2008). Social value orientation and cooperation in social dilemmas: A review and conceptual model. *British Journal of Social Psychology*, *47*, 453–480.

Bohnet, I., & Frey, B. S. (1999). The sound of silence in prisoner's dilemma and dictator games. *Journal of Economic Behavior & Organization*, *38*, 43–57.

Boone, C., De Brabander, B., & Van Witteloostuijn, A. (1999). Locus of control and strategic behaviour in a prisoner's dilemma game. *Personality and Individual Differences*, *20*, 695–706.

Boone, C., Declerck, C. H., & Kiyonari, T. (2010). Inducing cooperative behavior among proselfs versus prosocials: The moderating role of incentives and trust. *Journal of Conflict Resolution*, *54*, 799–824.

Borg, J. S., Hynes, C., Van Horn, J., Grafton, S., & Sinnott-Armstrong, W. (2006). Consequences, action, and intention as factors in moral judgments: An fMRI investigation. *Journal of Cognitive Neuroscience*, *18*, 803–817.

Buckholz, J. W., & Marois, R. (2012). The roots of modern justice: Cognitive and neural foundations of social norms and their enforcement. *Nature Neuroscience*, *15*, 655–661.

Camerer, C., & Thaler, R. H. (1995). Ultimatums, dictators, and manners. *Journal of Economic Perspectives*, *2*, 209–219.

Cavanna, A. E., & Trimble, M. R. (2006). The precuneus: A review of its functional anatomy and behavioral correlates. *Brain*, *129*, 564–583.

Cesarini, D., Dawes, C. T., Johannesson, M., Lichtenstein, P., & Wallace, B. (2009). Experimental game theory and behavior genetics. Values, empathy, and fairness across social barriers. *Annals of the New York Academy of Science*, *1167*, 66–75.

Costa, B., Pini, S., Gabelloni, P., Abelli, M., Lari, L., Cardini, A., ... Galderisi, S. (2009). Oxytocin receptor polymorphism and adult attachment style in patients with depression. *Psychoneuroendocrinology*, *34*, 1506–1514.

Costa, P. T., Jr., & McCrae, R. R. (1994). Set like plaster: Evidence for the stability of adult personality. In T. F. Heatherton, & J. L. Weinberger (Eds.), *Can Personality Change?* (pp. 21–40). Washington, D.C: American Psychological Association.

De Martino, B., Kumaran, D., Seymour, B., & Dolan, R. J. (2006). Frames, biases, and rational decision-making in the human brain. *Science*, *313*, 684–687.

de Quervain, D. J. F., Fischbacher, U., Treyer, V., Schelthammer, M., Schnyder, U., Buck, A., et al. (2004). The neural basis of altruistic punishment. *Science*, *305*, 1254–1258.

Declerck, C. H., Boone, C., & Emonds, G. (2013). When do people cooperate? The neuroeconomics of prosocial decision-making. *Brain & Cognition*, *81*, 95–117.

Dick, D. M., Aliev, F., Latendresse, S., Porjesz, B., Schuckit, M., Rangaswamy, M., … Agrawal, A. (2013). How phenotype and developmental stage affect the gens we find: GABRA2 and impulsivity. *Twin Research and Human Genetics*, *16*, 661–669.

Eisenberg, N., & Fabes, R. (1998). Prosocial development. In W. Damon, & N. Eisenberg (Eds.), *Handbook of Child Psychology (Volume 3), Social, Emotional, and Personality Development* (pp. 701–778). New York: Wiley.

Eisenberger, N. I., Lieberman, M. D., & Williams, K. D. (2003). Does rejection hurt? An fMRI study of social exclusion. *Science*, *302*, 290–292.

Emonds, G., Declerck, C. H., Boone, C., Seurinck, R., & Achten, R. (2014). Establishing cooperation in a mixed motive social dilemma. An fMRI study investigating the role of social value orientation and dispositional trust. *Social Neurosciences*, *9*, 10–22.

Emonds, G., Declerck, C. H., Boone, C., Vandervliet, E., & Parizel, P. (2011). Comparing the neural basis of strategic decision-making in people with different social preferences, a fMRI study. *Journal of Neuroscience, Psychology, and Economics*, *4*, 11–24.

Falk, A., Fehr, E., & Fischbacher, U. (2008). Testing theories of fairness—intentions matter. *Games and Economic Behavior*, *62*, 287–303.

Fehr, E., & Fischbacher, U. (2004). Third-party punishment and social norms. *Evolution and Human Behavior*, *25*, 63–87.

Fehr, E., & Gächter, S. (2002). Altruistic punishment in humans. *Nature*, *415*, 137–140.

Fischbacher, U., Gächter, S., & Fehr, E. (2001). Are people conditionally cooperative? Evidence from a public goods experiment. *Economic Letters*, *71*, 397–404.

Ghiselin, M. T. (1974). *The Economy of Nature and the Evolution of Sex*. Berkeley, CA: University of California Press.

Gino, F., Schweitzer, M. E., Mead, N. L., & Ariely, D. (2011). Unable to resist temptation: How self-control depletion promotes unethical behavior. *Organizational Behavior and Human Decision Processes*, *115*, 191–203.

Gintis, H., Bowles, S., Boyd, R., & Fehr, E. (2003). Explaining altruistic behavior in humans. *Evolution and Human Behavior*, *24*, 153–172.

Grant, A. M., & Sumanth, J. J. (2009). Mission possible? The performance of prosocially motivated employees depend on manager trustworthiness. *Journal of Applied Psychology*, *94*, 927–944.

Gray, J. R. (2004). Integration of emotion and cognitive control. *Current Directions in Psychological Science*, *13*, 46–48.

Guala, F. (2012). Reciprocity: Weak or strong? What punishment experiments do (and do not) demonstrate. *Behavioral and Brain Sciences*, *35*, 1–59.

Hamann, S., & Canli, T. (2004). Individual differences in emotion processing. *Current Opinion in Neurobiology*, *14*, 233–238.

Hariri, A. R., Mattay, V. S., Tessitore, A., Fera, F., & Weinberger, D. R. (2003). Neocortical modulation of the amygdala response to fearful stimuli. *Biological Psychiatry*, *53*, 494–501.

Haruno, M., & Frith, C. D. (2010). Activity in the amygdala elicited by unfair divisions predicts social value orientation. *Nature Neuroscience*, *13*, 160–161.

Haruno, M., Kimura, M., & Frith, C. D. (2014). Activity in the nucleus accumbens and amygdala underlies individual differences in prosocial and individualistic economic choices. *Journal of Cognitive Neuroscience*, *26*, 1861–1870.

Henrich, J., Boyd, R., Bowles, S., Gintis, H., Fehr, E., Camerer, C., ... Tracer, D. (2005). "Economic man" in cross-cultural perspective: Behavioral experiments in 15 small-scale societies. *Behavioral and Brain Sciences*, *28*, 795–855.

Henrich, J., McElreath, R., Barr, A., Ensimger, J., Barrett, C., Bolyanatz, A., ... Ziker, J. (2006). Costly punishment across human societies. *Science*, *312*, 1767–1770.

Herrmann, B., Thöni, C., & Gächter, S. (2008). Antisocial punishment across societies. *Science*, *319*, 1362–1367.

Israel, S., Lerer, E., Shalev, I., Uzefovsky, F., Riebold, M., Laiba, E., & Ebstein, R. P. (2009). The oxytocin receptor (OXTR) contributes to prosocial fund allocations in the dictator game and the social value orientations task. *PLoS One*, *4*, e5535.

Kagel, J., & McGee, P. (2014). Personality and cooperation in finitely repeated prisoner's dilemma games. *Economics Letters*, *124*, 274–277.

Kim, H. S., Sherman, D. K., Sasaki, J. Y., Xu, J., Chu, T. Q., Ryu, C., ... Taylor, S. E. (2010). Culture, distress, and oxytocin receptor polymorphism (OXTR) interact to influence emotional support seeking. *Proceedings of the National Academy of Sciences*, *107*, 15717–15721.

Kiyonari, T., & Barclay, P. (2008). Cooperation in social dilemmas: Free-riding may be thwarted by second-order reward rather than punishment. *Journal of Personality and Social Psychology*, *95*, 826–842.

Kiyonari, T., Declerck, C.H., Boone, C., & Pollet, T. (2012). Costly punishment and group cooperation: the role of behavioral heterogeneity and apparent free-riding intentions. Unpublished Manuscript, University of Antwerp.

Knafo, A., & Israel, S. (2009). Genetic and environmental influences of prosocial behavior. In M. Mikulincer, & P. R. Shaver (Eds.), *Prosocial Motives, Emotions and Behavior, the Better Angels of Our Nature* (pp. 149–167). Washington DC: American Psychological Association Publications.

Knafo, A., & Plomin, R. (2006). Prosocial behavior from early to middle childhood: Genetic and environmental influences on stability and change. *Developmental Psychology*, *42*, 771–786.

Knoch, D., Gianotti, L. R. R., Baumgartner, T., & Fehr, E. (2010). A neural marker of costly punishment behavior. *Psychological Science*, *21*, 337–342.

Knoch, D., Pascual-Leone, A., Meyer, K., Treyer, V., & Fehr, E. (2006). Diminishing reciprocal fairness by disrupting the right prefrontal cortex. *Science*, *314*, 829–832.

Koenigs, M., & Tranel, D. (2007). Irrational economic decision-making after ventromedial prefrontal damage: Evidence from the ultimatum game. *Journal of Neuroscience*, *27*, 951–956.

Kringelbach, M. L., & Rolls, E. T. (2004). The functional neuroanatomy of the human orbitofrontal cortex: Evidence from neuroimaging and neuropsychology. *Progress in Neurobiology*, *72*, 341–372.

Krueger, F., McCabe, K., Moll, J., Kriegeskorte, N., Zahn, R., Strenziok, M., ... Grafman, J. (2007). Neural correlates of trust. *Proceedings of the National Academy of Sciences*, *104*, 20084–20089.

Kurzban, R., & Houser, D. (2001). Individual differences in cooperation in a circular public goods game. *European Journal of Personality*, *15*, S37–S52.

Kurzban, R., & Houser, D. (2005). Experiments investigating cooperative types in humans: A complement to evolutionary theory and simulations. *Proceedings of the National Academy of Sciences*, *102*, 1803–1807.

Le Doux, J. (2003). The emotional brain, fear, and the amygdala. *Cellular and Molecular Neurobiology*, *23*, 727–738.

Lu, L., & Argyle, M. (1991). Happiness and cooperation. *Personality and Individual Differences*, *12*, 1019–1030.

McCabe, K., Houser, D., Ryan, L., Smith, V., & Trouard, T. (2001). A functional imaging study of cooperation in two-person reciprocal exchange. *Proceedings of the National Academy of Sciences*, *98*, 11832–11835.

Messick, D. M., & McClintock, C. G. (1968). Motivational bases of choice in experimental games. *Journal of Experimental Social Psychology*, *4*, 1–25.

Morishima, Y., Schunk, D., Bruhin, A., Ruff, C. C., & Fehr, E. (2012). Linking brain structure and activation in temporoparietal junction to explain the neurobiology of human altruism. *Neuron*, *75*, 73–79.

Park, J., Willmott, M., Vetuz, G., Toye, C., Kirley, A., Hawi, Z., … Kent, L. (2010). Evidence that genetic variation in the oxytocin receptor (OXTR) gene influences social cognition in ADHD. *Progress in Neuro-Psychopharmacology & Biological Psychiatry*, *34*, 697–702.

Phillips, M. L., Young, A. W., Senior, C., Brammer, M., Andrew, C., Calder, A. J., … David, A. S. (1997). A specific neural substrate for perceiving facial expressions of disgust. *Nature*, *389*, 495–498.

Plomin, R., Defries, J. C., & Loehlin, J. C. (1977). Genotype-environment interactions and correlation in analysis of human behavior. *Psychological Bulletin*, *84*, 309–322.

Reuben, E., & Suetens, S. (2009). Revisiting strategic versus non-strategic cooperation. CentER working paper, No. 2009–22, Tilburg University.

Rodrigues, S. M., Saslow, L. R., Garcia, N., John, O., & Keltner, D. (2009). Oxytocin receptor genetic variation relates to empathy and stress reactivity in humans. *Proceedings of the National Academy of Sciences*, *106*, 21437–21441.

Rushton, J. P., Fulker, D. W., Neale, M. C., Nias, D. K. B., & Eysenck, H. J. (1986). Altruism and aggression: The heritability of individual differences. *Journal of Personality and Social Psychology*, *50*, 1192–1198.

Rustagi, D., Engel, S., & Kosfeld, M. (2010). Conditional cooperation and costly monitoring explain the success in forest commons management. *Science*, *330*, 961–965.

Sanfey, A. G., Rilling, J. K., Aronson, J. A., Nystrom, L. E., & Cohen, J. D. (2003). The neural basis of economic decision-making in the ultimatum game. *Science*, *300*, 1755–1758.

Scarr, S., & McCartney, K. (1983). How people make their own environments. A theory of genotype-environment effects. *Child Development*, *54*, 424–435.

Selten, R., & Stoecker, R. (1986). End behavior in sequence of finite prisoner's dilemma supergames. *Journal of Economic Behavior & Organization*, *3*, 47–70.

Simpson, B., & Willer, R. (2008). Altruism and indirect reciprocity: the interaction of person and situation in prosocial behavior. *Social Psychology Quarterly*, *71*, 37–52.

Spitzer, M., Fischbacher, U., Herrnberger, B., Gron, G., & Fehr, E. (2007). The neural signature of social norm compliance. *Neuron*, *56*, 185–196.

Srivastava, S., John, O. P., Gosling, S. D., & Potter, J. (2003). Development of personality in early and middle adulthood: Set like plaster or persistent change? *Journal of Personality and Social Psychology*, *84*, 1041–1053.

Stouten, J., De Cremer, D., & Van Dijk, E. (2005). All is well that ends well, at least for proselfs: Emotional reactions to equality violation as a function of social value orientation. *European Journal of Social Psychology, 35*, 767–783.

Tabibnia, G., Satpute, A. B., & Lieberman, M. D. (2008). The sunny side of fairness—preference for fairness activates reward circuitry (and disregarding unfairness activates self-control circuitry). *Psychological Science, 19*, 339–347.

Tice, D., Baumeister, R. F., & Zang, L. (2004). *The Role of Emotion in Self Regulation: Differing Role of Positive and Negative Emotions*. Mahwah, New Jersey: Lawrence Erlbaum Associates.

Tomasello, M., & Vaish, A. (2013). Origins of human morality. *Annual Review of Psychology, 64*, 231–255.

Tost, H., Kolachana, B., Hakimi, S., Lemaitre, H., Verchinski, B. A., Mattay, V. S., ... Meyer-Lindenberg, A. (2010). A common allele in the oxytocin receptor gene (OXTR) impacts prosocial temperament and human hypothalamic-limbic structure and function. *Proceedings of the National Academy of Sciences, 107*, 13936–13941.

Trommsdorff, G., Friedlmeier, W., & Mayer, B. (2007). Sympathy, distress, and prosocial behavior of preschool children in four cultures. *International Journal of Behavioral Development, 31*, 284–293.

Van Lange, P. A. M. (1999). The pursuit of joint outcomes and equality in outcomes: an integrative model of social value orientation. *Journal of Personality and Social Psychology, 77*, 337–349.

Van Lange, P. A. M. (2000). Beyond self-interest: A set of propositions relevant to interpersonal orientations. In W. Stroebe, & M. Hewstone (Eds.), *European Review of Social Psychology* (Vol. 11, pp. 297–331). New York: Wiley.

Van't Wout, M., Kahn, R. S., Sanfey, A. G., & Aleman, A. (2006). Affective state and decision-making in the ultimatum game. *Experimental Brain Research, 169*, 564–568.

Wallace, B., Cesarini, D., Lichtenstein, P., & Johanesson, M. (2007). Heritability of ultimatum game responder behavior. *Proceedings of the national academy of sciences, 104*, 15631–15634.

Wilson, D. S., Near, D. C., & Miller, R. R. (1998). Individual differences in Machiavellianism as a mix of cooperative and exploitative strategies. *Evolution and Human Behavior, 19*, 203–212.

Wismer Fries, A. B., Ziegler, T. E., Kurian, J. R., Jacoris, S., & Pollack, S. D. (2005). Early experience in humans is associated with changes in neuropeptides critical for regulating social behavior. *Proceedings of the National Academy of Science, 102*, 17237–17240.

Wu, N., Li, Z., & Su, Y. J. (2012). The association between oxytocin receptor gene polymorphis (OXTR) and trait empathy. *Journal of Affective Disorders, 138*, 468–472.

Wu, S., Jia, M., Ruan, Y., Liu, J., Guo, Y., Shuang, M., ... Zhang, D. (2005). Positive association of the oxytocin receptor gene (OXTR) with autism in the Chinese Han population. *Biological Psychiatry, 58*, 74–77.

Yamagishi, T. (1986). The provision of a sanctioning system as a public good. *Journal of Personality and Social Psychology, 51*, 110–116.

Yoder, K. J., & Decety, J. (2014). The good, the bad, and the just: Sensitivity predicts neural responses during moral evaluation of actions performed by others. *The Journal of Neuroscience, 34*, 4161–4166.

CHAPTER 5

Beyond Parochialism: Cooperation Across the Globe

Ever since humans adopted coordinated group living, at least as long as 1.8 million years ago during the Pleistocene, our species has been solving social dilemmas. During that epoch cooperative breeding, hunting, and food sharing were likely in place and facilitated by the existence of social norms that encouraged reciprocity and group-beneficial behaviors (Bowles & Gintis, 2011, Burkart et al., 2014; Hrdy, 2009). However, the benefits of prosociality also raised the possibility of deceit. Along with rising prosperity that came with successful coordination and cooperation, setting the stage for modern economies, the tension to choose between self-interest and collective interest grew proportionally, continuously increasing the pressure for a flexible decision making scheme that takes into account both personal incentives and social information to avoid betrayal. The neural networks of cognitive control (giving us the ability to be calculative and to self-regulate behavior) and social cognition (allowing us to take the perspective of others) are today's reflection of a brain that has been solving social dilemmas for many generations.

The prevalence of social dilemmas today and throughout human evolution has given rise to heuristic solutions that are neither purely selfish nor purely altruistic, but moderated by context to become either economically or socially rational. The fact that the brain is wired for both economic and social rationality may go a long way to explain our paradoxical human nature. It means we possess the necessary faculties to put ourselves first, as well as to show compassion and affiliation with others. We can be both kind and mean, interested or indifferent, helpful or hindering. Paradoxical behavior is the price our species paid for learning to cope efficiently with social dilemmas.

In the previous chapters of this book we have summarized the evidence that we are imprinted with two alternative heuristics that effectively elicit cooperation when certain environmental conditions are

Neuroeconomics of Prosocial Behavior. DOI: http://dx.doi.org/10.1016/B978-0-12-801303-8.00005-7

met, at least in dyads or small groups with well-defined (often experimentally induced) boundaries. We proposed (Chapter 1 and 4) that these two heuristic solutions are products of social learning and individual experiences processed by a brain that was shaped by multilevel selection to serve two disparate human motives:

1. Self-interest drives people to cooperate only when it personally pays off, which is the case when incentives align self-interest and group interest. This leads to the economically rational heuristic: *I am selfish unless there are cooperative incentives.*
2. People value groups, want to see them succeed, and are reinforced by the social rewards they obtain from cooperating. But they also want to minimize the chance that their cooperative efforts will be compromised by selfish others. This leads to the socially rational heuristic: *I am cooperative unless my partner is not trustworthy.*

Heuristics, however, are fallible and may lead to flawed outcomes when overapplied or used outside the domain in which they were developed. The socially rational cooperation heuristic, especially, which functions well within the confines of a small, trusted group, may break down with increasing group size. This is not to say that large groups are maladaptive for the human species, but that their advantage is most likely dissociated from the advantages of using cooperation heuristics. Larger groups have proven to be more efficient at providing protection, obtaining resources and developing technology. Groups of individuals can accomplish things that loners can't (Baumeister, Ainsworth, & Vohs, 2015). As population size increases, so does the complex body of information (in the form of culture) that can accumulate.

Today, human societies are large and contain a substantial body of knowledge and sophisticated technological tools. But within these societies, smaller groups of interacting individuals have also become increasingly impersonal, and diffuse. With a global population extending well over 7 billion, we are nested in a hive of competing networks, and the rivalry between groups goes far beyond bands or states fighting over resources and territories. People are at odds with each other at many levels: they belong to competing firms, have diverse ideologies, and are born into different social classes, while their alliances to these groups have also become more transient. Once we move outside of our circle of friends, who is left to be trusted? In this new world, overapplying cooperation heuristics that work well in small groups may have undesirable side effects at other levels. They create ingroup favoritism and parochialism, setting the stage for outgroup discrimination, ethnocentrism, and escalating conflicts.

In this final chapter we examine cooperation heuristics in the setting of competing ingroups and outgroups, revealing a dark side of prosociality. First we sidetrack on the meaning of heuristics and ecological rationality. Next we summarize the (neuro)experimental evidence for ingroup favoritism, which emerges naturally within the confines of small, well-defined groups. We conclude by exploring how to overcome parochialism and solve social dilemmas on a more global scale.

5.1 HEURISTICS AND RATIONALITY

A common misconception in Western thinking is to associate emotional influences on decision making with irrationality, and to only consider cognitively deliberated decisions as rational. While neuroscience has corroborated that the neural networks sustaining cognition and emotion are to a certain extent dissociated (e.g., Goel & Dolan, 2003), they *both* are involved in *ecologically rational* decision making and it is difficult to fathom one without the other.[1] What makes the decision *ecologically rational* is how well its outcome matches the economic and social information that is provided in the environment and becomes integrated in the decision-making process. Processing economic and social information may therefore include elements of both cognition and affect.

We borrow the concept of ecological rationality from Gerd Gigerenzer, who conceptualizes the brain as an adaptive toolbox of fast and frugal heuristics, intending "to capture how real minds make decisions under constraints of limited time and knowledge," hence *fast* and *frugal* (see Gigerenzer & Todd, 1999, p. 5). Heuristics are considered ecologically rational inasmuch as the outcome they produce is adapted to the structure of the environment. By achieving this

[1]See also the involvement of both emotion and cognition in the neural differentiation between top-down versus bottom- up processing (Frith & Frith, 2006); and the reflective C-system versus reflexive X- system described by Lieberman (2003, 2007).

in a minimum of effort with easily computed decision rules, they represent "bounded rationality[2] in its purest form" (Gigerenzer & Todd, 1999, p. 14).

The metaphor of an "adaptive toolbox" (Gigerenzer & Todd, 1999) is based on a set of computationally bounded decision principles that are easy to execute and do not rely on a runaway cascade of information search. These decision principles specify the precise steps that are needed for acquiring just enough information, including when to start and stop an information search and how much to weigh one cue relative to another. These principles are the building blocks of fast and frugal heuristics. By combining or nesting simple heuristics, and matching them to a particular environmental structure, reasoning can become fast, frugal, *and* ecologically rational. We do not imply that these (meta)heuristics *take over* decision-making, they merely introduce a bias in the available sensory information to facilitate one decision route over another.

The success of fast and frugal heuristics lies in trading off generality versus specificity. That is, heuristics that work well in one domain might lose accuracy in another domain, so that different environments require different combinations of heuristics to make adaptive decisions. Emotions are a good example of building blocks in the adaptive toolbox. There is no "general purpose" or all-encompassing emotion; they are always specific to an emotion-eliciting stimulus.

Fast and frugal heuristics are therefore not watered-down versions of "optimal" strategies. Their main performance criterion lies in assessing if they can yield real-world, accurate decisions in a minimum of time and using a minimum of information. For example, people are able to solve complex reasoning tasks semiautomatically if they are phrased as a social exchange in which cheating (obtaining something for nothing) is possible. This has been illustrated numerous times with experiments using the Wason four-card selection task, a tool originally developed to investigate analytical reasoning skills (see Cosmides, 1989; Evans & Stanovich, 1998). In its abstract form, the task requires people to decide which cards need to be turned over (without being

[2]Initiated by Herbert Simon, the study of bounded rationality vehemently rejects that rational solutions are *optimized*, as in utility maximization problems, or that they can even be optimized under constraints. The constraints themselves would again impose an endless pursuit of information to know exactly whether or not the restrictions have been met (Simon, 1978). See also Chapter 1.

redundant) to verify that a conditional statement is true. For example, a rule might say: "*If a card has a vowel on one side, then it must have an even number on the other side.*"[3] Analytical reasoning skills are required to solve this problem, making it rather difficult, which explains why correct answers for this task are rather low (even among college students), and tend to correlate with high scores on aptitude tests (Stanovich & West, 2000). However, when the statement becomes: "*If a consumer in a bar drinks alcohol, he must be at least 18 years old,*" most people readily identify that a consumer who drinks beer or looks very young could potentially disprove the rule, and they do not bother checking older-looking customers or those consuming lemonade. Neuroimaging studies that compare how the brain responds to the Wason-selection task framed as a social exchange versus a non-social (hazardous) situation reveal that the former activates more theory of mind regions (middle, inferior, and superior temporal gyrus). Thus, social cognition is differentially engaged when confronted with identical algorithms that are framed differently (Ermer, Guerin, Cosmides, Tooby, & Miller, 2007).

The point of this example is that, when humans sense that they are in a situation that involves a social exchange, and hence where there is a potential for abuse, they suddenly become much more adept at "reasoning" in the social domain. Thanks to the right heuristic in the toolbox, that which is computationally difficult becomes simple, almost automatic. Not surprisingly, these heuristics are effective in domains that are highly economically and socially relevant (Cosmides, 1989). In social exchanges, a defector (or cheater) is not only detrimental to the immediate self, but jeopardizes the continuation of fruitful collaborations in the entire group. Detecting (and subsequently punishing) defectors by heuristic processes can therefore be considered adaptive, rational behavior.

A major advantage of the toolbox idea is that by combining simple heuristics in diverse ways, it becomes possible to explain higher order cognitive mechanisms that at first sight seem to require complex algorithms (Gigerenzer & Todd, 1999). Thus, a socially rational heuristic in the form of *always cooperate unless my partner seems untrustworthy*

[3]If, in the example given, the visible sides are A, D, 3, and 8, then the correct answer consists of turning over the card with the depicted A and the card with the depicted 3. These are the cards that could potentially disprove the rule. Most people, however, will turn over only A, or A and 8 (which is irrelevant given that the rule is in one direction only), and they forget to verify that there is no vowel behind the uneven number (3).

may need to involve very little in the way of conscious computation. Already, we know that automatic processing involving neural signal changes in the caudate nucleus (a part of the brain's valuation system responsible for updating information) informs a decision maker to stop making costly investments when they are not sufficiently reciprocated (Baumgartner, Heinrichs, Vonlanthen, Fischbacher, & Fehr, 2008). Similarly, the economically rational heuristic *always defect unless there are lucrative incentives to cooperate* can bypass time-consuming cost–benefit computations in familiar environments. For example, the caudate nucleus again becomes increasingly active when a decision maker perceives himself in an environment with repeat interactions and where long-term accrual of benefits is possible (King-Casas et al., 2005; Lambert, Declerck, Boone, & Emonds, 2015; Watanabe et al., 2014). In this case, the profitability of cooperation will be quickly assessed through (unconscious) operant conditioning processes.

The disadvantage of relying on heuristics, however, is that they are domain-specific. Thus, the shortcuts for decision making that people learn in their familiar social group may not be as useful in other, unfamiliar groups, and definitely not in transient groups. For example, the effectiveness of a "cheater detection" heuristic, or rules of thumb that specify when to cooperate in small groups, lose their salience when overapplied in larger and/or diffuse populations where anonymity reduces the discernibility of individuals' decisions. At that point cooperation heuristics may cease to provide rational solutions to recurrent problems.

5.2 GROUPS DEFINE THE BOUNDARIES OF PROSOCIAL BEHAVIOR

Cooperation heuristics are useful as crude approximations to complex decision making, and they apparently work well in Wason-selection-like tasks involving social exchanges, dyadic relationships, and small, isolated groups. In fact, as long as shared group membership is common knowledge, people will get the sense that they are in a situation of interdependency; they will infer that the entire group, just like themselves, will benefit from mutual cooperation, turning the group into an arena of *generalized exchange*. This triggers a cooperation heuristic that promotes cooperating with ingroup members (those who are admitted to the group as dues-paying members), but not with outgroup members (Kiyonari & Yamagishi, 2004; Yamagishi & Kiyonari, 2000).

When groups compete, social and economic rationality become blurred, because the effort each member expends toward the group increases the chance of winning the intergroup competition, with subsequent additional benefits to both the self and the group.[4] Laboratory experiments with public goods games corroborate that, indeed, ingroup cooperation increases when there is intergroup competition (Bornstein, 2003; Erev, Bornstein, & Galili, 1993) or when the group is nested within a larger, overarching collective and group belonging is highlighted (Polzer, 2004; Wit & Kerr, 2002). Because this corresponds to an increase in individual payoffs, voluntary contributions to the group's well-being in times of competition also translate into individual economic profits due to the group's superior performance. Thus, prosocial behaviors that motivate ingroup favoritism and improve the chance of outcompeting an outgroup are both economically and socially rational: they bias outcomes to benefit both the self and the ingroup, but they may hurt the outgroup.

The ease with which humans form social groups in real life points to the importance we attach to them. People spend much time and effort and are willing to bear costs on behalf of their fan club, church, chat group, or support group, revealing their underlying desire for group inclusion and fear of social rejection. Social psychology experiments, furthermore, reveal that people are very sensitive to group membership manipulations. According to the so-called minimal group paradigm, individuals quickly identify with a novel group based on seemingly trivial categories such as wearing the same colored bracelet or having the same artistic preferences for Klee versus Kandinsky (Tajfel, Billig, Bundy, & Flament, 1971). This superficial categorization proves to be sufficient to elicit ingroup favoritism: even though participants do not stand to gain from belonging to a minimal group, they still show preferential treatment for the ingroup members and reward them with more favorable monetary allocations. When they are given the option of rewarding *both* ingroup and outgroup members with either small or large sums of money, they will prefer the smaller allocations (and deprive both groups of the larger sum) if giving less to the outgroup members in absolute terms ensures the relative

[4]This is consistent with Social Psychology research on the interindividual intergroup discontinuity effect, which shows that in social dilemma settings groups tend to be much more competitive than individuals (Wildshut, Pinter, Vevea, Insko, & Schopler, 2003).

superiority of the ingroup.[5] This suggests that heuristics help us to decide quickly and efficiently (rather than logically) on the basis of group membership, and that group belonging in the absence of economic profits can also be a sufficient motive for favoring the ingroup.

In the previous examples, arbitrary markers are imposed on group members *exogenously*. More importantly, however, experiments have also shown that groups can form *endogenously*, as long as some symbolic markers covary with expectations and, consequently, behavior (i.e., the markers may seem arbitrary because they are not themselves related to payoff, but they are informative and thus cannot be trivial in this case). Because the markers are predictive of pay-offs, the emergence of cooperation in such groups is economically rational. But because the markers are also the basis by which group members recognize each other and form group ties, they can also lead to socially rational cooperation. When people learn freely the advantages of interacting with individuals sharing the same markers, cultural boundaries can form around these markers, creating a strong incentive for displaying ingroup favoritism. If groups can form endogenously around a few symbolic emblems, this would furthermore provide an evolutionary foundation for the coevolution of cultural groups and parochialism (Efferson, Lalive, & Fehr, 2008).

5.2.1 Group Utility

Groups are valued because, in addition to providing economic benefits in terms of safety and synergy, they fulfill basic psychological needs, such as belonging (Baumeister & Leary, 1995), uncertainty reduction (Hogg, 2000), and social approval (Baumeister et al., 2015). According to social identity theory (Tajfel & Turner, 1986), group membership has the capacity to boost feelings of self-worth: positive and negative outcomes that occur at the level of the group affect one's self-concept. By identifying with a certain group, people shift their self-concept from the individual "I" to the collective "us," and their personal sense of well-being becomes intertwined with that of the group. This is corroborated by neuroimaging studies: when social categorization tasks that make use of minimal group paradigms are performed under functional magnetic resonance imaging (fMRI), they activate largely overlapping neural substrates (e.g., the dorsomedial prefrontal cortex, or PFC) for

[5]For example, the allocation of five monetary units for ingroup and two units for outgroup would be preferred over six units for both groups.

both social and personal identity (Molenberghs, 2013; Molenberghs & Morrison, 2012; Volz, Kessler, & von Cramon, 2009).

Just like any other valued resource, group membership can be assigned utility, guiding subsequent within- and between-group decisions. Correll and Park (2005) modeled ingroup utility based on (1) how much one perceives the group to be worth, (2) how strongly one identifies with the group, and (3) its entitativity. The group's worth refers to its more distal (economically valued) qualities, such as status or reputation, from which a neutral observer could infer whether or not the group qualifies as a valuable resource. Identification with the group refers to the connection between belonging to the group and one's self-concept. And finally, groups with well-defined entitativity are easier to identify with because they evoke a sense of continuity and coherence among the amorphous collection of people. Thus, ingroup utility is influenced by economic as well as socioemotional factors. The subjective value ascribed to the ingroup will be especially high when the group is perceived to be respectable, with objectively speaking good qualities, when group identity is relevant to the self-concept, and when the group has a clear entitativity. Minimal groups (based on trivial characteristics) are not very relevant in this respect and most likely yield low utility. In contrast, strong-standing religious groups that offer protection and incentives such as eternal life, whose primary goal it is to mold members' self-concept to be congruent with their own identity, and who are clearly demarcated from other such groups by their rules and regulations, have the potential to be extraordinarily valued. We return to this point in the next section.

An individual's intrinsic inclination to have self-regarding versus other-regarding values will take part in determining ingroup utility and bias the decision frame toward one or the other type of rationality. A self-regarding individual is less likely to identify strongly with the group based on internalized group norms, but may still treat ingroup members favorably, knowing that this is likely to elicit reciprocity from which "I" benefit (economically rational). These proself individuals use the group to their own benefit without losing themselves in it.[6] They stop cooperating with group norms when they realize the group cannot offer them what they want. In contrast, an other-regarding individual

[6]This idea is central to the "goal transformation theory" which holds that group identification aligns personal- and collective interest (De Cremer & Van Vugt, 1999). This effect has been shown to be stronger for proselfs than prosocials (Bogaert, Boone, & van Witteloostuijn, 2011).

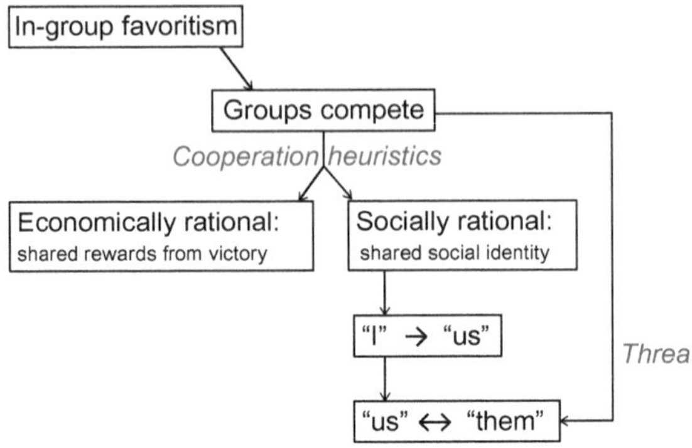

Figure 5.1 In small, isolated groups (in modern or pre-modern societies) parochialism may have its advantages. When these groups compete, ingroup cooperation and outgroup discrimination become helpful on two accounts: (1) economically, by reaping the benefits of the group's victory, and (2) socially, because shared group identity may boost feelings of self-worth. But when conflict escalates and the group is threatened, shared identity may turn into collective hate.

who strongly identifies with the group and conforms to its particular norms will treat ingroup members nicely because this enhances the well-being of the entire group from which "we" benefit (socially rational). For these prosocials, group membership helps them navigate through the social world. By doing what they are told, they develop deontological values that serve the group well, but at the cost of fluidity in behavior.

The greatest drawback of excessive prosociality toward ingroup members, however, is that it can create an "us versus them" mentality. As ingroup utility increases, so does the potential for outgroup derogation. Once the self-concept becomes intertwined with that of the group, threats to the ingroup also threaten one's identity. The course of events leading to potential out-group derogation ("us versus them") is summarized in Figure 5.1. In the next two subsections we elaborate on observations and experimental findings that prosociality in this case does not necessarily lead to virtuous decisions.

5.2.2 When Prosociality Becomes Parochial

While it is perfectly feasible that "ingroup love" exists without "outgroup derogation," we do not have to look far to find that motivations to protect "us" can, fair enough, also hurt "them." In this last century, over 200 million people were killed in intergroup conflicts, either in the form of war or genocides (Pinker, 2011). Outgroup hate surfaces, not surprisingly, when there is competition for a limited resource (Brewer, 2001), but also when the continued existence of the ingroup is threatened due to competing beliefs or ideologies (Correll & Park, 2005). For example, if a religious group senses that their purpose is challenged by nonbelievers, its members may resort to violence to defend their ideology. This may be a short depiction of what is recently occurring with the Islamic State (IS), an extremist, jihadist, group that, as of June 2014, proclaimed itself to govern parts of Iraq and Syria in the name of Mohammed. The group's aim is to expand the (nonrecognized) state into other territories and to bring all traditionally Muslim-inhabited regions of the world under its political control. Members and would-be IS fighters have been successfully recruited worldwide. Based on indoctrinated beliefs, IS disciples are not only willing to sacrifice their own lives, but they have engaged in terrorist acts, torture, executions, beheadings, sexual enslavement, and large-scale massacres. All this while their religious practices have been publically denounced, also by the larger Muslim community, and Amnesty International and the United Nations have accused them of ethnic cleansing on a historical scale.

What IS illustrates is how a prosocial motive (serving one's religious community as a devout believer in Mohammed) can drive decisions with a distressing aftermath. As we have explained earlier in this chapter, prosocial heuristics are built on socially adaptive building blocks, which can include emotions, parental love, and social or religious norms. But these heuristics have no intrinsic valence; they exist to improve the survival chances of a well-defined social group, and hence their prosocial connotation is also group dependent. Compassion becomes limited to the ingroup.

5.2.3 Neuroeconomic Studies on the Parochial Nature of Prosociality

Neuroimaging studies investigating the intergroup dynamics of empathy substantiate that ingroup love sometimes induces outgroup derogation as a side effect. The neural network underlying affective empathy comprises the anterior insula and dorsal anterior cingulate cortex (ACC; Lamm, Decety, & Singer, 2011), and these regions become more activated when viewing the suffering of ingroup members compared to outgroup members. For example, when Caucasian and Chinese participants were presented with video clips of a face being either pierced by a needle or touched lightly with a cotton-swab, the painful needle elicited more anterior insula and dorsal ACC activation, but only when the face was of the same race. The empathic response was absent for other-race faces (Xu, Zuo, Wang, & Han, 2009). Similar results were obtained when participants viewed a member of one's own sport team receive pain compared to a rival team (Hein, Silani, Preuschoff, Batson, & Singer, 2010).

Sport fans not only have less empathy for rival teams, they also typically display overt antipathy toward other-team fans, which today has become semiacceptable. An fMRI experiment conducted with baseball fans of the Boston Red Sox and New York Yankees replicated the diminished empathy response for the rival team, and in addition also revealed increased activity in ventral striatum when the rival team failed to score. Activity in the ventral striatum furthermore correlated with reports of increased pleasure (Cikara, Botvinick, & Fiske, 2011). Even more intriguing are the results of a series of experiments (reviewed in Cikara & Van Bavel, 2014) showing that soccer fans displayed increased activity in the ventral striatum when watching a rival team's supporter receive a painful electric shock. Again, the increase in ventral striatum activity was associated with a desire to harm this other-team fan.

While this research corroborates that group membership can induce both pro- and antisocial sentiments, not all outgroups are provocative in this negative sense. The reduced empathy response, for example, is moderated by how much the outgroup is despised. When the outgroup consisted of drug addicts, viewing them experiencing misfortunes reduced anterior insula activation (indicating a diminished empathic response). But when the outgroup consisted of old people in need, the empathic response was actually stronger and anterior insula activation increased (Cikara & Fiske, 2011).

Ingroup/outgroup manipulations also affect the neural correlates of punishment decisions. In Chapter 4 we described how punishing norm violators was associated with a neural network including (among others) increased activation in the lateral PFC (e.g., Knoch, Pascual-Leone, Meyer, Treyer, & Fehr, 2006; Sanfey, Rilling, Aronson, Nystrom, & Cohen, 2003) and the dorsal caudate (e.g., de Quervain et al., 2004). It now appears that punishment decisions are also modulated by the social cognition network, depending on whether the norm violator belongs to the ingroup or the outgroup (Baumgartner, Gotte, & Gugler, 2012). In this experiment, participants were military officers in training in the Swiss Army who had been randomly assigned to different platoons. In the first stage of the experiment, dyads (comprising person A and B) engaged in simultaneously played prisoner's dilemma games that involved transferring points. Next, a third-party observer (person C) was scanned with fMRI while deciding whether or not to spend a part of his or her endowment to punish unfair transfers of participant A. The results indicated that, when A belonged to a different platoon than C, punishing decisions were associated, as expected, with the hypothesized right lateral PFC and dorsal caudate. The stronger the connectivity in this network, the more outgroup members were punished. When, however, A belonged to the same platoon as C, punishment decisions were much reduced, and this was associated with increased activation in the dorsomedial PFC and bilateral temporoparietal junction (TPJ). Furthermore, the left TPJ also downregulated the effective connectivity between the dorsomedial PFC and the lateral PFC, which could have been responsible for the more lenient evaluation of ingroup defectors.

The parochial nature of prosocial behavior, or the tendency to favor one's own social group at the expense of nonmembers, is furthermore corroborated by neuroendocrine studies. Testosterone, for example, is known to regulate aggression, and fluctuating levels of testosterone can be moderated by the social distance of a competitor. In a rural community on the Caribbean island of Dominica, men showed increased levels of testosterone when they beat an outgroup member in a game of dominos, yet there was no such increase when men beat their friends (Flinn, Ponzi, & Muehlenbein, 2012).

Especially for the hormone oxytocin, there is accumulating evidence that it modulates within-group cooperation and between-group competition. In Chapter 3 we stated that oxytocin is probably crucial in establishing social rationality, and we elaborated on the neural mechanisms by which oxytocin enables the development of trust and facilitates cooperative behavior, namely by attenuating anxiety (reducing activity in the amygdala), linking prosocial activity with reward (increasing dopamine release in the nucleus accumbens) and enhancing the empathic response (increasing activity in the anterior insula). A host of recent empirical studies is now revealing that these oxytocin effects are group dependent, and that the same mechanisms that promote prosociality are apparently also responsible for parochialism, and perhaps even ethnocentric behaviors (summarized in De Dreu, 2012). The combination of increased trust and empathy that enable people to form close ties and help each other also create tendencies to take risks and protect others against threats from outside. By downregulating fear and motivating ingroup favoritism and noncooperation with a potentially threatening outgroup, De Dreu (2012) concludes that the oxytocin-induced goodwill is far from indiscriminate and contingent on perceived characteristics of the target. This supposes that oxytocin helps to categorize ingroup and outgroup members, for which there is also some evidence (De Dreu, Greer, Handgraaf, Shalvi, & Van Kleef, 2012; Lambert, Declerck, & Boone, 2014). Interestingly, the perception of the target can be dissociated from the social group through the process of individuation, allowing for affiliative emotions to develop toward a despised outgroup member that one has gotten to know personally. In a recent study, oxytocin administration to Jewish Israelis increased their empathic response to *individuated* Palestinians' pain (Shamay-Tsoory et al., 2013).

5.3 MOVING BEYOND PAROCHIALISM

A big challenge for humankind in the global world of today is to extend the boundaries of prosocial behavior and to curb individual greed, without compromising others' rights or resorting to intergroup violence. Already, there are many indications that we are moving in that direction, and that we are capable of "individuating" people far removed from us. Repeatedly, citizens of all nations have shown transoceanic empathy, for example when the legendary tsunami of 2004 washed away several coastal towns in the South Pacific, or when Typhoon Haiyan hit the Philippines in 2013. Similarly, Americans were able to count on the support of the entire world after the terrorist attack on New York's Twin Towers on September 11, 2001. Recently, in January 2015, more than 1.5 million people of all ages, races, religions, and political affiliations joined a solidarity march in Paris after the terrorist strike on the satirical newspaper *Charlie Hebdo*, killing several employees and two police officers. In unison they denounced violent extremism and called out for peace, freedom of speech, and religious tolerance.

According to Pinker (2011), violence has been steadily declining for more than 2000 years, so that we are now living in the most peaceful time in history. He attributes this decline to several coinciding historical forces that made way for some of our "inner motives" to surface, moving us closer toward cooperation and altruism instead of war and hostility. In the same vein, we devote these last pages of the book to proposing that (1) developing prosocial values, (2) individualizing through role differentiation, and (3) combining values with reasoning skills, would help to extend our altruistic efforts beyond our inner circle and sustain cooperation on a global scale.

5.3.1 Values Guide Heuristic Processing

Prosocial values are as much a product of socialization as the result of genetic developmental processes, and parents as well as social institutions devote much effort to canalizing the values of their society's youngsters to elicit normative and group-appropriate behavior (see also Fehr, 2003; Fehr, Bernhard, & Rockenbach, 2008). In Chapter 4 we argued that heuristic cooperative decision making reflects the extent to which an individual has internalized prosocial values as a result of social reinforcement. Recent neuroimaging findings, furthermore, corroborate that, when confronted with fairness-related issues, individual differences in prosocial values are tracked by a significant difference in neural activation in the amygdala and the nucleus accumbens, the latter lying at the core of the brain's valuation system and is thus representative of one's learned, intrinsic preferences (Haruno, Kimura, & Frith, 2014).

A behavioral study by Cornelissen, Dewitte, and Warlop (2011) provides additional evidence that only individuals with a prosocial value orientation cooperate intuitively (as a result of an internalized norm), and that this is not the case for individuals with proself values. In their experiment, participants played a dictator game with or without a cognitive load (i.e., an additional effortful task that prevents deliberating on the dictator task, which consisted of splitting a monetary allotment between the self and another, anonymous participant). As expected, under cognitive load (when the decision is presumably made heuristically), only prosocial participants became more generous with their donations, while proselfs stayed about as selfish in both conditions.[7]

[7]Similarly, in the set of experiments reviewed by Rand et al. (2014), there was significant heterogeneity in the extent to which individuals "intuitively" increase their cooperative decisions in one-shot public-goods games when time pressure was applied (which prevents deliberation and thus induces heuristic processing). However, while we would be inclined to attribute this heterogeneity to differences in internalized prosocial values, the authors explain it as a side effect of relying on online testing tools (e.g., Amazon Mechanical Turk), which has created a pool of returning participants that have become very adept at recognizing the economic pitfalls of cooperation in one-shot games. Compared to naïve participants, experienced participants remain selfish, even under time pressure. An alternative explanation (consistent with our proposition) is that the participant pool is prone to a selection bias, and that experienced participants are more likely to have a proself value orientation, especially when considering that economic games are economically incentivized.

What this experiment shows is that values can tip decision utility toward either type of rationality: for the prosocial type this is to cooperate heuristically even when there are no incentives to do so (i.e., donating money in a dictator game). Given the same task, the proself type will not donate money. We can think of values as the path people want to follow in life because it is the one that gives them the most satisfaction. The prosocial types experience more pleasure by donating, the proself types by keeping the economic resource. Values determine when and where someone will emphasize "I," or "us."

But, as we discussed earlier in this chapter, individuals with internalized prosocial values are especially prone to parochialism. In fact, there are reasons to believe that parochialism shares a common ontogenetic root with prosocial values (Fehr et al., 2008). At age three, children behave mostly selfishly in games that require allocating resources to the self and other. By the age of eight, however, they develop inequity aversion and show a clear preference for allocations that are equal, and this emerges together with the tendency to favor allocations that benefit one's own social group. Thus, intrinsic prosocial values that facilitate heuristic cooperation are, by themselves, not sufficient to avoid the pitfalls of parochialism.

5.3.2 Role Differentiation Reduces Greed and Enhances Moral Responsibility

Ever since Le Bon (1895) described the psychology of crowds and the mob violence that can result when individuals develop a "group mind," empirical research has documented how group submersion and uncritically following group norms can lead to simplistic thinking and a process called "deindividuation," amounting to a loss of self-awareness, personal responsibility, and evaluation apprehension. The problems that follow when situational norms encourage bad behavior also tend to increase with group size (Postmes & Spears, 1998). A forthcoming paper by Baumeister et al. (2015) proposes that antisocial behaviors and the aggressive tendencies that sometimes emerge in groups settings can be alleviated if individuals take on a differentiated role within the group. These authors develop a two-step model to explain how groups can become more than the sum of their members. In line with the thesis of this book, the first step is that groups form because individuals have a strong motivation to belong. A shared social identity at this stage is most important, serving as the glue that keeps group members loyal and motivated. In the second step, the enthusiasm for the group is combined with role differentiation. By "individuating" the self, each group member can gain approval based on his/her competence and ethical performance. Thus the group can engage in division of labor by which the contribution of each group member becomes critical to perform well. As Baumeister and colleagues (2015) write: "individual identification facilitates responsibility and accountability, putting moral pressure on individuals to behave well." (p. 12). The authors summarize the evidence of social psychology experiments that corroborate that the social dilemma problem becomes easier to solve (i.e., people put aside greed to favor the collectively beneficial outcome) when anonymity is reduced, record keeping is allowed, and accountability is heightened due to having a differentiated role. As societies grow larger and interactions with strangers become more common, the emotional ties generated by group identity weaken and become inadequate to ensure prosocial behavior. No wonder that large corporations, governments, and sports teams all rely on role differentiation to elicit peak performance! When it comes to getting the best out of group dynamics, identifying with the group and individualizing one-self do not have to be opposites.

5.3.3 Reasoning the Way Out of Parochialism

While cooperation facilitated by prosocial values and a shared social identity may proceed heuristically, we remain capable of conscious deliberation. This allows us to change perspective and reflect on the global and long-term implications of our decisions. Therefore, to not fall into the trap of parochialism or mob behavior, prosocial values need to be complemented with individual accountability and the capacity to reason one's way out of the negative consequences of value-loaded heuristic decisions. Ironically, the neural network of cognitive control, which in Chapter 2 we associated with self-interested, economically rational decision making, appears to also be the driver of reasoning. The neural tradeoff between reasoning and believing was shown in the classic fMRI study by Goel and Dolan (2003). They showed that a belief bias introduced during a reasoning task activates the ventromedial PFC (indicating value processing in the reward system), while arriving at the logically correct answer in the same reasoning task corresponds to activation in the lateral PFC (indicating cognitive control to resolve a conflict). Thus, if prosocial values are linked to ingroup favoritism, logical decision making may be compromised, only to be overridden by cognitive control of the lateral PFC.

Much evidence supports the proposition that caring for others involves reasoning and that, at the neural level, it activates the lateral PFC and the dorsal anterior cingulate gyrus (dACC), two cognitive control regions that are essential to suppress short-sighted impulses (McClure, Laibson, Loewenstein, & Cohen, 2004). To overcome the short-sightedness associated with parochialism, we need to rely on these cognitive control regions. In the following, we summarize some of the findings regarding their moderating role in social decision making.

First, cognitive control appears to be necessary to regulate socially undesirable responses, such as racial biases. These are apparent in fMRI experiments, revealing that implicit evaluation of other-race faces corresponds to increased activation in the amygdala (e.g., white people evaluating black faces that are presented for 30 ms, a time too short to process the stimulus consciously). When, however, these faces are presented for 525 ms, plenty of time for conscious reevaluation, no difference in amygdala activation between viewing black versus white faces is registered. Instead there is increased activity in the ventrolateral PFC, dorsolateral PFC, and ACC. Furthermore, the increase in cognitive control modulates the reduction in amygdala activation (Cunningham, Johnston, & Raye, 2004).

Second, Greene, Nystrom, Engell, Darley, and Cohen (2004) hypothesized that the "moral calculus" associated with consequentialism (i.e., deciding in favor of providing the greatest good for the greatest number of people) would involve more frontal lobe activity in comparison to deontological decisions (i.e., not breaking a categorical imperative). They scanned participants with fMRI while they evaluated a series of moral dilemmas. As expected, consequentialist judgments were indeed associated with more activity of the dorsolateral PFC, corroborating that cognitive control processes can override the emotional responses elicited by the dilemma. Cognitive control sways decisions to benefit a greater number of people when the benefit to these people outweighs the personal emotional cost of breaking a categorical rule (Greene et al., 2004).

Third, similar conclusions are reached when comparing the neural correlates between the moralities of justice versus care (Robertson et al., 2007).

Justice ethics refers to solving moral conflicts based on rules, rights, and regulations. In life they correspond to, for example, refraining from whistleblowing, or declining to provide classified information to a friend. In contrast, problem-solving with care ethics focuses on social issues and rests on the ideal of helping people in need. Examples are limiting the number of work hours to spend time with one's children, or volunteering to spend extra time on mentoring a new employee. An fMRI study shows that these two sets of ethical principles are also neurally dissociated: sensitivity to ethics of care showed increased activation in regions related to emotional processing (ventral posterior cingulate) and cognitive control (dorsolateral PFC), whereas ethics of justice was only associated with increased activation in the intraparietal sulcus, which has previously been shown to play a role in processing categorical representations (Robertson et al., 2007). Thus, from this study, it appears that socioemotional processing may not be sufficient to care for others, but that some cognitive control is also necessary.

Finally, in a recent essay, Frith (2014) theorizes that social responsibility (accepting responsibility for our actions that affect others) follows in part from imagining what would have happened if we had taken a different course of action. Regret is in essence an example of counterfactual thinking, and it involves neural activity in the frontopolar cortex and the PFC. When we realize we chose the wrong option, regret activates a neural network that gives us intentional control over choice behavior. Frith writes: "we are not automatons in a deterministic world. Through counterfactual thinking, we can create what might have been and what might be. We are not limited to reacting to the world. We can also change it." (p. 141).

Experiencing responsibility for our choices and actions might arguably be one of the most crucial elements in generating social cohesion on a large scale (Frith, 2014). By acting on our prosocial values with reason and control, we can provide long-term benefits to others without compromising our own basic needs, perpetuating trust, and in turn, relishing the fruits of mutual reciprocity on a larger scale.

5.4 SUMMARY AND EPILOG

The prevalence of social dilemmas that have confronted humans throughout their evolutionary history and continues to challenge us today has endowed us with a set of fast and frugal heuristics to arrive at ecologically rational cooperative decisions. Throughout this book we have argued that multiple rationalities can coexist, corresponding to decision outcomes that either benefit the self (economically rational) or a trusted group with whom one strongly identifies (socially rational). But prosocial heuristics that facilitate social exchanges are only crude decision making tools, useful to *approximate* solutions to the problem of cooperation in small, isolated groups. In the world of today, groups are becoming much more complex and they are often nested in many layers. Decisions that benefit one layer may be detrimental to other layers, especially when ideologies are in conflict, competition is tough, or resources are contested. Hence the same heuristics that in all likelihood contributed to the success of our species manifest themselves with parochialism, rivalry, and ethnocentrism. This is also what Elinor Ostrom was referring to in her presidential address to the American Political Science Association (Ostrom, 1998). In a passage where she explains the importance of sanctioning free riders to sustain cooperation, she warns about overapplying punishment as a prosocial norm: "If punishment consists of escalating retribution, then groups who overcome social dilemmas may be limited to very tight circles of kin and friends, who cooperate only with one another, embedded in a matrix of hostile relationships with outsiders. This pattern can intensify into feuds, raids, and overt warfare. Or tight circles of individuals who trust one another may discriminate against anyone of a different color, religion, or ethnicity."

With the growing world population estimated to reach 8 billion in 2024, the problem of overcoming social dilemmas will only intensify. In 1968, Garrett Hardin pointed out that we cannot reconcile personal wealth with the exponential population growth (Hardin, 1968). Already we are witnessing recurring "tragedies of the commons" as he predicted: rainforests, coral reefs, and polar ice are vanishing at a tremendous rate; fossil fuels are rapidly depleting; and global warming has brought the earth's biosustainability into question. Will we come up with rational solutions to reverse these trends?

In this chapter we have proposed three possible remedies. The first one is to cultivate prosocial values. Decisions are made in function of what we like, and what we like is what we value. Values are not purely acquired via biology or genetic inheritance. What we do inherit is the capacity to learn and to internalize certain values. Learned values have the capacity to steer rational decisions in the direction we desire, because they determine what types of information we will attend to, and hence the heuristics we are most likely to use. Or, to say it simply in Mahatma Gandhi's words, "Your habits become your values, and your values become your destiny."

The second and third remedy to solve today's dilemmas generated by exploding population growth is to increase personal accountability and cultivate cognitive control and economic rationality. Focusing on incentives is not necessarily selfish. Taking a global and long-term perspective is likely to affect the incentives we find desirable, and this may have liberating effects to compensate for the negative side effects of prosocial norms. Economic rationality can be the antidote for parochialism. Or, in plain words, norms and values that promote prosociality are best accompanied by a healthy dose of skilled reasoning!

Perhaps *Homo sapiens* could be an appropriate name after all when referring to ourselves, the big-brained, naked apes with highly developed cognitive control and social insight. This insight allows us to understand and trust others, while cognitive control gives us not only the capacity to be calculative, but also the power to overcome greed, suppress ingroup favoritism, and control hostile impulses. We can use these capacities to plan *how* we want to continue to live on a planet that is fast approaching its carrying capacity. This challenge will be the greatest social dilemma of them all. Only the future will tell if we planned it right, if we were truly wise.

REFERENCES

Baumeister, R. F., Ainsworth, S. E., & Vohs, K. D. (2015). Are groups more or less than the sum of their members? The moderating role of individual identification. *Behavioral and Brain Sciences* forthcoming.

Baumeister, R. F., & Leary, M. R. (1995). The need to belong: Desire for interpersonal attachments as a fundamental human motivation. *Psychological Bulletin*, *117*, 497–529.

Baumgartner, T., Gotte, L., & Gugler, L. (2012). The mentalizing network orchestrates the impact of parochial altruism on social norm enforcement. *Human Brain Mapping*, *33*, 1452–1469.

Baumgartner, T., Heinrichs, M., Vonlanthen, A., Fischbacher, U., & Fehr, E. (2008). Oxytocin shapes the neural circuitry of trust and trust adaptation in humans. *Neuron*, *58*, 639–650.

Bogaert, S., Boone, C., & van Witteloostuijn, A. (2011). Social value orientation and climate strength as moderators of the impact of work group cooperative climate on affective commitment. *Journal of Management Studies*, *49*, 918–944.

Bowles, S., & Gintis, H. (2011). *A Cooperative Species. Human Reciprocity and its Evolution.* Princeton, New Jersey: Princeton University Press.

Bornstein, G. (2003). Intergroup conflict: Individual, group, and collective interests. *Personality and Social Psychology Review*, *7*, 129–145.

Brewer, M. B. (2001). Ingroup identification and intergroup conflict: When does ingroup love become outgroup hate? In R. D. Gilbert, S. Fiske, & G. Lindzey (Eds.), *The Handbook of Social Psychology* (Vol. 2, pp. 554–594). Boston: McGraw Hill.

Burkart, J. M., Allon, O., Amici, F., Fichtel, C., Finkenwirth, C., Heschl, A., ... van Schaik, C. P. (2014). The evolutionary origin of human hyper-cooperation. *Nature Communication*, *27*(5), 4747.

Cikara, M., & Van Bavel, J. J. (2014). The neuroscience of intergroup relations: An integrative review. *Perspectives on Psychological Science*, *9*, 245–274.

Cikara, M., Botvinick, M. M., & Fiske, S. T. (2011). Us versus them: Social identity shapes neural responses to intergroup competition and harm. *Psychological Science*, *22*, 306–313.

Cikara, M., & Fiske, S. T. (2011). Bounded empathy: Neural responses to outgroup targets' (mis) fortunes. *Journal of Cognitive Neuroscience*, *23*, 3791–3803.

Cornelissen, G., Dewitte, S., & Warlop, L. (2011). Are social value orientations expressed automatically? Decision making in the dictator game. *Personality and Social Psychology Bulletin*, *37*, 1080–1090.

Correll, J., & Park, B. (2005). A model of the ingroup as a social resource. *Personality and Social Psychology Review*, *9*, 341–359.

Cosmides, L. (1989). The logic of social exchange: Has natural selection shaped how humans reason? Studies with the Wason selection task. *Cognition*, *31*, 187–276.

Cunningham, W. A., Johnston, M. K., & Raye, C. L. (2004). Separable neural components in the processing of black and white faces. *Psychological Science*, *15*, 806–813.

De Cremer, D., & Van Vugt, M. (1999). Social identification effects in social dilemmas: A transformation of goals. *European Journal of Social Psychology*, *29*, 871–893.

De Dreu, C. K. W. (2012). Oxytocin modulates cooperation within and competition between groups: An integrative review and research agenda. *Hormones and Behavior*, *61*, 419–428.

De Dreu, C. K. W., Greer, L. L., Handgraaf, M. J. J., Shalvi, S., & Van Kleef, G. A. (2012). Oxytocin modulates selection of allies in intergroup conflict. *Proceedings of the Royal B-Biological Science*, *279*, 1150–1154.

de Quervain, D. J. F., Fischbacher, U., Treyer, V., Schelthammer, M., Schnyder, U., Buck, A., & Fehr, E. (2004). The neural basis of altruistic punishment. *Science*, *305*, 1254–1258.

Efferson, C., Lalive, R., & Fehr, E. (2008). The coevolution of cultural groups and in-group favoritism. *Science*, *321*, 1844–1849.

Erev, I., Bornstein, G., & Galili, R. (1993). Constructive intergroup competition as a solution to the free rider problem: A field experiment. *Journal of Experimental Social Psychology*, *29*, 463–478.

Ermer, E., Guerin, S. A., Cosmides, L., Tooby, J., & Miller, M. B. (2007). Theory of mind broad and narrow: Reasoning about social exchange engages ToM areas, precautionary reasoning does not. *Social Neuroscience*, *1*, 196–219.

Fehr, E. (2003). The nature of human altruism. *Nature*, *425*, 785–791.

Fehr, E., Bernhard, H., & Rockenbach, B. (2008). Egalitarianism in young children. *Nature*, *454*, 1079–1083.

Flinn, M. V., Ponzi, D., & Muehlenbein, M. P. (2012). Hormonal mechanisms for regulation of aggression in human coalitions. *Human Nature*, *23*, 68–88.

Frith, C. D. (2014). Action, agency, and responsibility. *Neuropsychologia, 55*, 137–142.

Frith, C. D., & Frith, U. (2006). How we predict what other people are going to do. *Brain Research, 24*, 36–46.

Gigerenzer, G., & Todd, P. M. (1999). Fast and frugal heuristics. The adaptive toolbox ((chapter 3), 3–34). *Simple Heuristics That Make Us Smart*. New York: Oxford University Press.

Goel, V., & Dolan, R. J. (2003). Explaining modulation of reasoning by belief. *Cognition, 87*, B11–B22.

Greene, J. D., Nystrom, L. E., Engell, A. D., Darley, J. M., & Cohen, J. D. (2004). The neural basis of cognitive conflict and control in moral judgment. *Neuron, 44*, 389–400.

Hardin, G. (1968). The tragedy of the commons. *Science, 162*, 1243–1248.

Haruno, M., Kimura, M., & Frith, C. D. (2014). Activity in the nucleus accumbens and amygdala underlies individual differences in prosocial and individualistic economic choices. *Journal of Cognitive Neuroscience, 26*, 1861–1870.

Hein, G., Silani, G., Preuschoff, K., Batson, C. D., & Singer, T. (2010). Neural responses to ingroup and outgroup members' suffering predicts individual differences in costly helping. *Neuron, 66*, 149–160.

Hogg, M. A. (2000). Subjective uncertainty reduction through self-categorization: A motivational theory of social identity processes. *European Review of Social Psychology, 11*, 223–255.

Hrdy, S. B. (2009). *Mothers and Others. The Evolutionary Origins of Mutual Understanding*. Cambridge, MA: Harvard University Press.

King-Casas, B., Tomlin, D., Anen, C., Camerer, C. F., Quartz, S. R., & Montague, P. R. (2005). Getting to know you: Reputation and trust in a two-person economic exchange. *Science, 308*, 78–83.

Kiyonari, T., & Yamagishi, T. (2004). Ingroup cooperation and the social exchange heuristic. In R. Suleiman, D. V. Budescu, I. Fisher, & D. Messick (Eds.), *Contemporary Psychology Research on Social Dilemmas* (pp. 269–286). Cambridge, U.K.: Cambridge University Press.

Knoch, D., Pascual-Leone, A., Meyer, K., Treyer, V., & Fehr, E. (2006). Diminishing reciprocal fairness by disrupting the right prefrontal cortex. *Science, 314*, 829–832.

Lambert, B., Declerck, C. H., & Boone, C. (2014). Oxytocin does not make a face appear more trustworthy but improves the accuracy of trustworthiness judgments. *Psychoneuroendocrinology, 40*, 60–68.

Lambert, B., Declerck, C. H., Boone, C., & Emonds, G. (2015). Trust as a commodity, but only for proselfs: Individual differences in the neural substrates of learning to cooperate. Working paper, University of Antwerp.

Lamm, C., Decety, J., & Singer, T. (2011). Meta-analytic evidence for common and distinct neural networks associated with directly experienced pain and empathy for pain. *NeuroImage, 54*, 2492–2502.

Le Bon, G. (1895/1960). *The Mind of the Crowd*. New York: Viking.

Lieberman, M. D. (2003). Reflexive and reflective judgment processes. A social cognitive neuroscience approach. In J. P. Forgas, K. R. Williams, & W. von Hippel (Eds.), *Social Judgments: Implicit and Explicit Processes* (pp. 44–67). New York: Cambridge University Press.

Lieberman, M. D. (2007). Social cognitive neuroscience: A review of core processes. *Annual Review of Psychology, 58*, 259–289.

McClure, S. M., Laibson, D. I., Loewenstein, G., & Cohen, J. D. (2004). Separate neural systems value immediate and delayed monetary rewards. *Science, 306*, 503–507.

Molenberghs, P. (2013). The neuroscience of in-group bias. *Neuroscience and Biobehavioral Reviews, 37*, 1530–1536.

Molenberghs, P., & Morrison, S. (2012). The role of the medial prefrontal cortex in social categorization. *Social Cognitive and Affective Neuroscience*, *9*, 292–296.

Ostrom, E. (1998). A behavioral approach to the rational choice theory of collective action: Presidential address, American Political Science Association, 1997. *American Political Science Review*, *92*, 1–22.

Pinker, S. (2011). *The Better Angels of Our Nature: Why Violence Has Declined*. New York: Viking.

Polzer, J. T. (2004). How subgroup interests and reputations moderate the effect of organizational identification on cooperation. *Journal of Management*, *30*, 71–96.

Postmes, T., & Spears, R. (1998). Deindividuation and antinormative behaviour: A meta-analysis. *Psychological Bulletin*, *123*, 238–259.

Rand, D. G., Peysakhovich, A., Kraft-Todd, G. T., Newman, G. E., Wurzbacher, O., Nowak, M. A., & Kilts, C. (2014). Social heuristics shape intuitive cooperation. *Nature Communication*, *5*, 1–12.

Robertson, D., Snarey, J., Ousley, O., Harenski, K., Bowman, F. D., Gilkey, R., & Gilkey, R. (2007). The neural processing of moral sensitivity to issues of justice and care. *Neuropsychologia*, *45*, 755–766.

Sanfey, A. G., Rilling, J. K., Aronson, J. A., Nystrom, L. E., & Cohen, J. D. (2003). The neural basis of economic decision-making in the ultimatum game. *Science*, *300*, 1755–1758.

Shamay-Tsoory, S. G., Abu-Akel, A., Palgi, S., Sulieman, R., Fischer-Shofty, M., Levkovitz, Y., & Decety, J. (2013). Giving peace a chance: Oxytocin increases empathy to pain in the context of the Israeli-Palestinian conflict. *Psychoneuroendocrinology*, *38*, 3139–3144.

Simon, H. A. (1978). Rationality as process and product of thought. *American Economic Review*, *68*, 1–16.

Stanovich, K. E., & West, R. F. (2000). Individual differences in reasoning: Implications for the rationality debate. *Behavioral and Brain Sciences*, *23*, 645–726.

Tajfel, H., Billig, M. J., Bundy, R. P., & Flament, C. (1971). Social categorization and intergroup behavior. *European Journal of Social Psychology*, *1*, 149–177.

Tajfel, H., & Turner, J. C. (1986). The social identity theory of inter-group behavior. In S. Worchel, & L. W. Austin (Eds.), *Psychology of Intergroup Relations*. Chicago: Nelson-Hall.

Volz, K. G., Kessler, T., & von Cramon, D. Y. (2009). In-group as part of the self: In-group favoritism is mediated by medial prefrontal cortex activation. *Social Neuroscience*, *4*, 244–260.

Watanabe, T., Takezawa, M., Nakawake, Y., Kunimatsu, A., Yamasue, H., Nakamura, M., ... Masuda, N. (2014). Two distinct neural mechanisms underlying indirect reciprocity. *Proceedings of the National Academy of Sciences*, *111*, 3990–3995.

Wit, A. P., & Kerr, N. L. (2002). "Me versus just you versus us all" categorization in nested social dilemmas. *Journal of Personality and Social Psychology*, *83*, 616–637.

Xu, X. J., Zuo, X. Y., Wang, X. Y., & Han, S. H. (2009). Do you feel my pain? Racial group membership modulates empathic neural responses. *Journal of Neuroscience*, *29*, 8525–8529.

Yamagishi, T., & Kiyonari, T. (2000). The group as a container of generalized reciprocity. *Social Psychology Quarterly*, *63*, 116–132.

INDEX

S

T

V

W

FSC
www.fsc.org
MIX
Papier | Fördert gute Waldnutzung
FSC® C083411

Kolibri 360 GmbH
Ferdinand-Jühlke-Straße 7
99095 Erfurt, Deutschland
produktsicherheit@kolibri360.de